THE COMMUNITY INTERPRETER

*Professional Interpreter Training for
Bilingual Staff and Community Interpreters*

Fifth Edition

Marjory A. Bancroft, MA
Lourdes Rubio-Fitzpatrick, MA, LPC

Culture and Language Press

5th edition

© Marjory A. Bancroft and Lourdes Rubio-Fitzpatrick
2004, 2005, 2007, 2009, 2011

All rights reserved. No part of this publication may be reproduced or disseminated in any form or by any means, whether electronic or mechanical, including photocopying, recording or otherwise, without prior permission in writing from the authors.

ISBN: 978-0-9823166-2-7

CULTURE AND LANGUAGE PRESS

A division of

Cross-Cultural Communications
10015 Old Columbia Road, Suite B-215
Columbia, MD 21046
Voice: 410-312-5599
Fax: 410-750-0332
www.cultureandlanguage.net
ccc@cultureandlanguage.net

CONTENTS

Table of Contents

Acknowledgements 5
Preface 7
How to Use This Manual 9
About the Authors 15
Learning Objectives 17
Definitions 19

UNIT 1: ETHICS AND CONDUCT 23
1.1 The community interpreting profession 24
1.2 Ethics and standards of practice 66
REVIEW 98

UNIT 2: INTERPRETER SKILLS 105
2.1 The steps to execute a session 106
2.2 Basic interpreter skills 126
REVIEW 156

UNIT 3: CULTURE AND MEDIATION 163
3.1 Basic mediation skills 164
3.2 Cultural mediation 194
REVIEW 220

UNIT 4: COMMUNITY SERVICES 227
4.1 Legal interpreting 228
4.2 Community service systems 237
4.3 Terminology 281
REVIEW 290

CONTENTS

UNIT 5: STANDARDS OF PRACTICE ... 297
    5.1 Standards of practice ... 298
    5.2 Applying standards ... 336
    REVIEW ... 358

RESOURCES ... 365
    Sample Codes of Ethics ... 366
    Terminology ... 374
    Resources for Healthcare Interpreters ... 378
    Resources for Social Services Interpreters ... 382
    Resources for Educational Interpreters ... 383
    Resources for Legal Interpreters ... 386
    Videos ... 396
    Word Games ... 399
    Bibliography ... 400

Acknowledgements

There are not enough pages in this book to list all who have contributed to this program's growth and development. We are profoundly grateful to those who came before us and those who showed us the path ahead.

Over the last decade, the growth of community interpreting has astonished many. A profession once considered to be in its infancy has become a legacy for the future. This training manual builds on the vital work of others, including Cynthia Roat and Cross-Cultural Health Care Program (CCHCP), who created *Bridging the Gap: A Basic Training for Medical Interpreters*. This groundbreaking program inspired many medical and community interpreter training programs across the nation.

Pat Hatch has been a pillar of support for interpreters and has blazed a trail of advocacy across the mid-Atlantic. At the Maryland Office of Refugees and Asylees, she was instrumental in planning an interpreter training and management project that led, in part, to the creation of this program.

Thanks are also due to many others whose work or support contributed directly or indirectly to the many editions of this training manual and/or the professional development of the authors. First and foremost we thank Katharine Allen, who provided invaluable input for the note-taking and terminology resource sections of Units 2 and 4 and who, as the co-founder of InterpretAmerica with Barry Olsen, has helped shape a forum for the voices of those across North America who support quality interpreting. We are also grateful to the past and present Board and Committee members of the National Council on Interpreting in Health Care and many others who include Irfana Anwar, Zarita Araujo-Lane, Izabel Arocha, Shiva Bidar-Sielaff, Pamela Bohrer Brown, Jean Bruggeman, Rosa Carrillo, Olivia Carter-Pokras, Joy Connell, Eric Candle, Paul Cushing, Hank Dallman, Esther Diaz, Bruce Downing, Lois Feuerle, Julia Puebla Fortier, Isabel Framer, Emily Frelick, Marta Goldstein, Nora Goodfriend-Koven, Hermela Kebede, Nataly Kelly, Dr. Robert Like, Ellen Little, Priscilla Mendenhall, Holly Mikkelson, Laura Pfeifer, James Plunkett, Deborah Rosen, Susan London Russell, Barbara Rayes, Karin Ruschke, Kinza Schuyler, Ana Stover, Jorge Ungo, Amy Wilson-Stronks and Mara Youdelman.

Finally, our warmest thanks to the community interpreters whose work inspired us. We thank you for your experience, your passion and your hearts. The future of the profession belongs to you.

INTRODUCTION

Preface

Around the world, community interpreting is expanding at a breathtaking space. In many countries, there is an urgent need for trained community interpreters. In this age of increased migration, a growing number of immigrants and refugees need access to public services, and without community interpreters that access may be difficult or impossible. In some countries, including parts of Africa, the U.S. and Canada, those who speak indigenous languages also need interpreters.

Ten years ago, most countries in Asia and much of Europe, Africa and Latin America showed little concern for community interpreting and did not even consider it a profession. Conference interpreters were important in many countries, but almost anyone (including a friend, a family member, the receptionist, a cafeteria worker, or even someone in the waiting room) was expected to interpret for clients of community services. It did not appear to matter whether the "interpreter" was even fluently bilingual. Today, many of those same countries and regions now have professional interpreting services with qualified community interpreters.

The profession of interpreting in general is evolving swiftly around the world. For example:

- In December 2010, *U.S. News and World Report* listed Interpreter/Translator as one of its "50 Best Careers for 2011."[1] (Grant 2011).
- In 2010 a Canadian organization named Critical Link established itself as a key international nonprofit that works to support the profession of community interpreting worldwide.
- The International Organization for Standardization (ISO) is currently working with countries around the world to establish international standards for community interpreting.
- Common Sense Advisory, a leading market research firm for the language industry, estimates that the market for outsourced language services (primarily translation and interpreting) was worth more than $23 *billion* in 2009. The report also states the language services market is growing at a rate of 13.15% per year (Kelly & Stewart, 2010:2-3).

---

1 http://money.usnews.com/money/careers/articles/2010/12/06/the-50-best-careers-of-2011.html

INTRODUCTION

Here in the U.S., the Massachusetts Medical Interpreters Association, changed its name in 2007 to the International Medical Interpreters Association, and it now counts over 30 U.S. State Representatives in addition to international representatives in Beijing, Brazil, Canada, Hong Kong, India, Italy, Japan, Spain, South Africa and the UK. In 2009 and 2010, two national medical interpreter certification programs launched in the U.S. The number of federal, state and local government contracts for community interpreting and interpreter training is continually expanding.

Speaking two languages is no longer enough to become a community interpreter: it is increasingly recognized that any interpreter should be tested for language proficiency, attend professional training programs, and demonstrate the skills and qualifications to demonstrate that they can support professional ethics and standards of practice.

The profession of community interpreting is here to stay. There has never been a more exciting time to become a community interpreter.

INTRODUCTION

How To Use This Manual

This manual can be used:
- To support a 40- to 60-hour training program in general community interpreting.
- To support a 40- to 60- hour training program in medical, social services or educational interpreting.
- As a resource for self study continuing education.

The manual is divided into five units. Because it is long, participants have asked us to highlight sections of the manual that should be prioritized for study. While everything in the manual is important, we created many pages in the manual that are clearly labeled "Core Content." As a result, participants who have read the entire manual can study those particular pages as they prepare to take a final written evaluation that assesses their knowledge of the program.

In the often chaotic world of community services, informality may erode professional boundaries for bilingual employees and community interpreters alike. The common pressure on most community interpreters to function as de facto social workers makes it difficult for them to support the ethics and standards of professional interpreting. This manual and the program that it supports are intended help community interpreters apply professional interpreting ethics and standards to the challenges that face them in real life.

THE AUDIENCE FOR THIS MANUAL

This book is a training manual for:
1. Contract interpreters.
2. Staff interpreters.
3. Bilingual employees who interpret.
4. Volunteer interpreters.

It is designed for any community interpreter who wishes to develop his or her professional skills and knowledge. This manual supports community interpreters of spoken languages. It does not address sign language interpreting.

The core audience for this manual is any bilingual individual who interprets or seeks to interpret in the areas of health care, education and/or human and social services. It is not a manual for legal interpreters, although Unit 4 includes a brief introduction to the field of legal interpreting.

INTRODUCTION

The Community Interpreter is the only national training program in the U.S. that addresses all sectors of community interpreting and the special needs of bilingual staff who interpret. Licensed trainers and instructors across the U.S. use this manual to train interpreters for interpreter services; hospitals and other healthcare institutions; private nonprofit agencies and coalitions; social services agencies; refugee resettlement programs; and institutions of higher education, among other organizations.

Most training for community interpreters in the U.S. today consists of programs that target freelance interpreters or dedicated staff interpreters in health care. A growing number of these programs are at least 40 hours in length. In addition, a number of community colleges and universities now offer classes and certificate programs in medical interpreting. *The Community Interpreter* was developed to address two audiences that still remain widely neglected:

1. Community interpreters who interpret not only in health care but in social services, schools, and other community settings.
2. Bilingual employees who interpret as only one part of their job.

Community interpreting is considered to be interpreting that takes place in any community setting, with a particular focus on public and nonprofit community services. It is defined here as "a profession that facilitates access to community services for linguistically diverse clients who do not speak the language of service."

It is important to clarify what we mean when we say that community interpreting encompasses healthcare, education and human and social services. In this context healthcare, taken broadly, includes not only hospitals, clinics, community health centers and health departments but also mental health counseling, substance abuse services, school-based wellness programs, smoking cessation programs and flu and vaccine clinics, among many other services. Education refers primarily to K-12 schools but this program has been used to train interpreters from community colleges, Head Start programs, universities, private preschools and other educational organizations. Finally, human and social services is a broad category that can refer to almost any community service, including (but not limited to): crisis intervention, domestic violence, torture and trauma services, government social services, housing, transportation, senior centers, sexual assault services, sanitation departments, refugee resettlement and libraries. Participants for *The Community Interpreter* come from all these areas and many others.

INTRODUCTION

Bilingual employees

The authors have found that on a national level there is very little understanding about the needs of bilingual employees who interpret as one part of their job. Most bilingual employees do not find interpreting included in their job description, yet they are often expected to interpret. They may find it difficult to adhere to the formal demands of the interpreting profession, given the constraints and demands of their workplace. The most pressing concerns for bilingual employees who interpret usually relate to role boundaries.

Contract Interpreters

Freelance interpreters who work in a variety of community settings also face many challenges. The vast array of community services can seem intimidating because of the extensive terminology involved in so many different sectors of service, the different expectations and requirements in these services, their distinct professional cultures and the varying levels of formality involved (from the formal structure of a hospital to home visits for infants and toddlers programs). The complexity of working in so many different service systems, which are often new to the interpreter, can feel overwhelming at times. This manual is therefore intended to help contract interpreters navigate the often dizzying array of community services for which they may interpret.

INTRODUCTION

Overview of the Training

This manual is composed of five units and a sixth section that offers resources for professional development. Taken together, these units contain the basic "building blocks" of a 40-hour interpreter training that can be extended to 60 hours.

For those interpreters who wish to pursue healthcare interpreting, a companion one-day workshop entitled *Medical Terminology for Interpreters* with its own handbook is sometimes used in addition to or as part of *The Community Interpreter*. The program and this training manual are also accompanied by a workbook entitled *THE COMMUNITY INTERPRETER: Exercises and Role Plays*. Use and selection of the activities in the workbook by the instructor combined with scheduling opportunities and constraints will determine the length and duration of this program. A trainer's guide and train-the-trainers program are also available to support the delivery of *The Community Interpreter*. (For information about how to become a licensed trainer, please contact 410-312-5599 or send an email to ccc@cultureandlanguage.net. Information is also available at www.cultureandlanguage.net.)

Here, in essence, is the content of the program.

UNIT 1 looks at the foundation of the profession of community interpreting, including language proficiency, interpreter certification and language access laws. It then addresses codes of ethics and standards of practice for community interpreters.

UNIT 2 breaks down a typical interpreting assignment into its component parts so that participants can work on basic skills and practice each skill. This unit takes into account such fundamentals as modes of interpreting (consecutive, simultaneous and sight translation), use of first person, positioning, accuracy and professional introductions. It also considers message analysis and message conversion, memory skills and note-taking.

UNIT 3 addresses culture and mediation. It guides interpreters on how to intervene when a barrier to communication arises. It discusses interpreter roles, defines interpreter mediation and includes a series of straightforward, simple steps for successful mediation. It then introduces the topic of culture and cultural mediation (culture brokering) and shows why interpreters need to develop cultural competence.

UNIT 4 targets three important areas: health care; educational settings; and human and social services. If a particular group works only in one setting (such as K-12 schools or health care), Unit 4 can address that setting. Otherwise, all three areas may be addressed. This unit offers an overview of each field and considers some of its core issues or concerns. It includes a brief introduction to legal interpreting. The unit does not list terminology (an impossible task,

INTRODUCTION

considering the vast array of community services) but addresses how interpreters should develop their terminology in specific areas. Sessions of *The Community Interpreter* that focus solely on medical interpreting include exercises from *Medical Terminology for Interpreters* in this unit.

UNIT 5 returns to the standards of practice first introduced in Unit 1 and shows interpreters how to adapt ethics and standards to the complex realities of the field. It also addresses interpreter safety and self-care, advocacy and professional development.

INTRODUCTION

A Word About the Format of This Manual

Most community interpreters are not native English speakers. They come from cultures around the world. In an intensive 40-hour class, it takes time to read and absorb a training manual. For these reasons, the visual format of this manual is designed in such a way that the book:

- Gives basic information "at a glance."
- Accommodates different learning styles.
- Addresses how different cultures read and learn.
- Highlights what is important in the program.
- Includes a "core content" section in each unit to facilitate study.

The exercises in the accompanying workbook are intended _only as a guide_. Instructors will use the exercises that meet the needs of a particular group.

Good luck!

The authors frequently update this training program and manual based on feedback from participants, trainers, readers and, most of all, bilingual employees and community interpreters. Please do not hesitate to contact us with corrections, suggestions or ideas for future training.

> Marjory A. Bancroft, MA, Director
> Cross-Cultural Communications, LLC
> 10015 Old Columbia Road, Suite B-215
> Columbia, MD 21046-1865
> Voice: 410-312-5599 Fax: 410-750-0332
> Email: mbancroft@cultureandlanguage.net
> URL: www.cultureandlanguage.net
>
> Lourdes Rubio-Fitzpatrick, MA, LPC, DAPA
> 2413 Jackson Parkway
> Vienna, VA 22180
> 703-228-6814
> rubiofitz@gmail.com

INTRODUCTION

About the Authors

Marjory Bancroft

Marjory Bancroft is a national leader in the development of training programs for community interpreting, cultural competence and language access and has over 30 years in the field of language and education. She holds a BA and MA in French linguistics from Quebec City in addition to advanced language certificates from Spain, Germany, and Jordan. After an early career teaching translation, English and French for two universities, two immigrant schools in Montreal, continuing education and the Canadian Embassy in Washington DC, she spent several years interpreting, translating and directing an immigrant health program and a language bank of 200 interpreters and translators.

A past Board member of the National Council on Interpreting in Health Care, Marjory now sits on the Board of Advocates for Survivors of Torture and Trauma, the Advisory Committee for the NCIHC national healthcare interpreter training standards, the ISO subcommittee to establish international standards for community interpreting, and the interpreting subcommittee of ASTM International. She is also the Executive Director of THE VOICE OF LOVE, a national, all-volunteer project devoted to guiding those who interpret for survivors of torture, trauma and sexual violence. The author of numerous training manuals, facilitator guides and workbooks on community and medical interpreting and four train-the-trainer manuals for cultural competence, she speaks widely at conferences across the U.S.

INTRODUCTION

Lourdes Rubio-Fitzpatrick, MA, L.P.C., D.A.P.A.

Lourdes immigrated to the U.S. from Mexico City. A practicing interpreter and bilingual counselor with Arlington Public Schools in Virginia, she has more than 25 years of experience in the field of conference, community, legal, government and educational interpreting. Lourdes is fluent in Spanish, English, French, American Sign Language and Mexican Sign Language. She holds an MA in Special Education and an MA in Counseling from Gallaudet University. She is a lecturer on community and educational interpreting and translation for George Mason University. She is also an experienced trainer for medical, legal and community interpreters.

In addition to co-authoring *The Community Interpreter*, Lourdes authored another training manual, *An Introduction to Community Interpreting* (published by Northern Virginia Area Health Education Center). Lourdes' many translations include *A Basic Course in Sign Language*. In addition to developing several interpreting training curricula and programs for those who work with interpreters, she has contributed to the development of a computer program, *Mexican Sign Language/ American Sign Language Translator* (by the Institute for Disabilities Research and Training). Previously, Lourdes worked as a therapist and contributed to teen pregnancy and drug abuse prevention programs for Latinos in Washington, D.C. A licensed counselor, she supported the development of counseling services and parenting classes for Latino families in Virginia and helped to create the office of Hispanic Services at Gallaudet University. Lourdes is also one of the principal curriculum authors for THE VOICE OF LOVE, a national, nonprofit project devoted to guiding those who interpret for survivors of torture, trauma and sexual violence, and she is a member of their Board.

INTRODUCTION

LEARNING OBJECTIVES

UNIT 1   ETHICS AND CONDUCT (8 hours)

OBJECTIVE 1.1
Demonstrate knowledge about the profession of community interpreting.
1.1 (a) Discuss the history of community interpreting.
1.1 (b) List the qualifications and skills of community interpreters.
1.1 (c) Address the impact of language access laws on community interpreting.
1.1 (d) Develop awareness of self-monitoring and self-assessment for interpreters.

OBJECTIVE 1.2
Apply ethical principles for interpreters to simulated situations from real life.
1.2 (a) Describe the differences between ethics and standards of practice.
1.2 (b) Discuss ethics and standards for community interpreters.
1.2 (c) Develop strategies to apply ethical principles in real-life settings.

UNIT 2   INTERPRETER SKILLS (8 hours)

OBJECTIVE 2.1
Show the steps to execute an interpreted session.
2.1 (a) List the steps to execute an interpreted session.
2.1 (b) Discuss and select appropriate modes of interpreting.
2.1 (c) Practice interpreting in consecutive and simultaneous modes.
2.1 (d) Demonstrate basic sight translation skills.

OBJECTIVE 2.2
Analyze and practice basic interpreter skills.
2.2 (a) Demonstrate professional introductions, positioning and use of direct speech.
2.2 (b) Develop message analysis, note-taking and memory skills sufficient to interpret two to three sentences accurately without asking for repetition.
2.2 (c) Practice basic interpreting skills in simple role plays.

INTRODUCTION

UNIT 3 CULTURE AND MEDIATION (8 hours)

OBJECTIVE 3.1
Demonstrate basic mediation skills.
3.1 (a) List and practice the steps for mediation.
3.1 (b) Practice strategic mediation.
3.1 (c) Define and compare interpreter roles.

OBJECTIVE 3. 2
Develop and practice cultural mediation strategies.
3.2 (a) Define culture and cultural competence.
3.2 (b) Apply ethical decision-making to a communication barrier.
3.2 (c) Practice non-intrusive cultural mediation.
3.2 (d) Show awareness of stereotypes and bias.

UNIT 4 COMMUNITY SERVICES (4 hours)

Objective 4
Develop skills sets in particular sectors of community interpreting.
4.1 Contrast and compare legal and community interpreting.
4.2 Discuss service systems in health care, education and/or human and social services and their impact on interpreters.
4.3 Develop strategies to enhance competence in terminology

UNIT 5 STANDARDS OF PRACTICE (10 hours)

OBJECTIVE 5.1
Develop a working knowledge of standards of practice.
5.1 (a) Review the 32 NCIHC national standards of practice.
5.1 (b) Discuss strategies for promoting and practicing standards.
5.1 (c) Act out standards of practice ino challenging situations from real life.

OBJECTIVE 5.2
Apply national standards of practice to interpreting.
5.2 (a) Demonstrate the application of standards of practice in community service settings.
5.2 (b) Relate ethics and standards to professional development for interpreters.

DEFINITIONS

"A" language: The interpreter's primary or native language.

Adjunct interpreter (also known as **dual role**): A bilingual employee called upon to interpret on occasion or part-time as one of his or her professional duties.

Advocacy: Any action taken by an interpreter on behalf of a client when the client's safety, well being, dignity or equal access to a public service are compromised or at risk.

"B" language: The interpreter's second working language (i.e., his or her second-strongest language).

Certified interpreter: An **interpreter** who has passed a formal credentialing process administered by a professional organization or government entity *may* be **certified**. Certification is a credential awarded by a recognized certification body to interpreters who pass a rigorous, externally validated skills test with oral and written components that is based on national or international requirements for professional certification.[1]

Community interpreter: A professional interpreter, bilingual staff member or volunteer who interprets for community services such as health care, education and social services.

Community interpreting: A profession that facilitates access to community services for linguistically diverse clients who do not speak the language of service.

Consecutive mode: Rendering a message into another language when the speaker or signer pauses.

Cultural awareness: Recognition of the importance of cultural differences.

Cultural sensitivity: A willingness to accept and value cultural differences.

Cultural competence: The ability to provide services effectively across cultures.

Healthcare interpreting: Interpreting that takes place in any healthcare setting, including, but not limited to, hospitals, community health centers, doctor's offices, health departments, clinics and wellness services; also known as **Medical interpreting.**

---

[1] Interpreters who hold a training certificate or have taken a screening test administered by an employer are not considered certified interpreters according to professional interpreting standards-- even if their credentials are referred to as "certification."

DEFINITIONS

Interpreter: A person who accurately renders a message from a source into a target language.

Interpreting: The process of understanding and analyzing a spoken or signed message and re-expressing that message faithfully, accurately and objectively in another language, taking the cultural and social context into account. [American Society for Testing and Materials.] The purpose of interpreting is to facilitate communication between those who do not share a common language.

LEP: Limited English Proficiency: Individuals who do not speak English as their primary language and who have a limited ability to read, write, speak, or understand English may be limited English proficient, or "LEP," entitled to language assistance with respect to a particular type of service, benefit, or encounter. (***U.S. Department of Justice***)

Legal Interpreting: Interpreting related to legal processes and proceedings, including but not limited to lawyer-client representation, prosecutor-victim/witness interviews, and law enforcement communications.   Framer *et al* (2009:xi)

Mediation: Any act or utterance of the interpreter that goes beyond interpreting and is intended to address barriers to communication between parties who do not share a common language.

Medical interpreting: See **Healthcare interpreting.**

Pre-conference: A meeting between a service provider and an interpreter before the interpreted encounter to discuss issues related to the encounter. Also known as pre-session.

Post-conference: A debriefing between a provider and interpreter held after an interpreted encounter.

Register: Level of language. An individual's education, social status, age, culture, region of origin and/or other factors may influence register.

Sight translation: The oral or signed translation of a written document. (For example, an interpreter takes a patient education brochure and reads it aloud to the patient in another language.)

Simultaneous mode: Rendering a message into another language while a person is still speaking or signing the message.

DEFINITIONS

Source language: The language <u>from</u> which an interpreter interprets at any given moment.
Summarization: Rendering the gist of a message into another language.

Target language: The language <u>into</u> which an interpreter interprets at any given moment.

Translator: A person who professionally renders a written text into another language, in writing.

Transparency: Interpreting everything that is said or signed, including remarks addressed to the interpreter or any intervention by the interpreter.

Working languages: The languages into and from which one interprets.

UNIT 1
ETHICS AND CONDUCT

Unit 1 Objectives

OBJECTIVE 1.1
Demonstrate knowledge about the profession of community interpreting.
1.1 (a) Discuss the history of community interpreting.
1.1 (b) List the qualifications and skills of community interpreters.
1.1 (c) Address the impact of language access laws on community interpreting.
1.1 (d) Develop awareness of self-monitoring and self-assessment for interpreters.

OBJECTIVE 1.2
Apply ethical principles for interpreters to simulated situations from real life.
1.2 (a) Describe the differences between ethics and standards of practice.
1.2 (b) Discuss ethics and standards for community interpreting.
1.2 (c) Develop strategies to apply ethical principles in real-life settings.

OBJECTIVE 1.1

Demonstrate knowledge about the profession of community interpreting.

Introduction

Community interpreting has emerged as one of the fastest-growing employment sectors in the world. This growth is a recent trend: until a few years ago, most government and private agencies around the world did not consider community interpreting a profession at all. In most nations, community interpreting had no code of ethics or standards of practice, and there was little understanding about professional interpreting skills.

Until recently, few community agencies in almost any nations around the world had developed policies about whether or how to provide interpreters. Often, those agencies that

1.1 (a) Discuss the history of community interpreting.

1.1 (b) List the qualifications and skills of community interpreters.

1.1 (c) Address the impact of language access laws on community interpreting.

1.1 (d) Develop awareness of self-monitoring and self-assessment for interpreters.

UNIT 1

had developed such policies had no clear understanding about what the qualifications of a professional interpreter should be (if they considered the question of interpreter qualifications at all).

For decades, clients of community services who did not speak the language of service were usually expected, or even told, to bring their own interpreters. A family member or a friend had to interpret for them. Many immigrants still take their children out of school regularly to interpret for family members, but fortunately in many countries that situation is changing.

Today, professional associations and other organizations in many parts of the world are laying down standards, requirements and protocols for community interpreting. The field is rapidly emerging as a profession.

KEY QUESTIONS

What is interpreting?
Interpreting is the act of accurately rendering oral or signed communication between two or more parties who do not share a common language.

What is community interpreting?
Community interpreting is a profession that facilitates access to community services for linguistically diverse clients who do not speak the language of service.

Who is a community interpreter?
A community interpreter is a professional interpreter, bilingual staff member or volunteer who interprets for health care, education or other community services.

How is community interpreting delivered?
Community interpreting may be delivered in person, on the phone or by video.

UNIT 1

HISTORY OF THE PROFESSION

OBJECTIVE 1.1 (a) Discuss the history of community interpreting.

The First Interpreters

No one knows when the profession of interpreting began. It was practiced in ancient Egypt, where there may have been an interpreter guild. The ancient Greeks and Romans also used interpreters. Here, for example, is the earliest known image of an interpreter, which appears to date from 1,330 BC.

Horemhab was an exceptionally clever man who rose from the rank of commoner to become general of the Egyptian army, and eventually pharaoh. At the period depicted, he was already regent to the boy pharaoh Tutankhamen and was in charge of foreign affairs. He is shown conveying the pharaoh's reply to a delegation ... here we see the interpreter cleverly 'animated' by the device of a double figure facing both ways, as though turning alternately towards speaker and listener.

Harris (2010)

The Birth of a Profession

A slow evolution

Ever since ancient Egypt, interpreters around the world have worked for travelers, merchants, royalty, missionaries and diplomats. In addition, Christianity and Islam established empires and missions around the world that involved working with—and even training—interpreters. Perhaps the most famous interpreter during the age of exploration was a young woman of Mexican descent called Doña Marina who became famous under the name "la Malinche." She interpreted for the renowned explorer, Cortés. (Community interpreters who feel disrespected may take some consolation in knowing that while La Malinche was reviled and considered a traitor in her time at by many of her compatriots, today she is famous and revered.)

During the Middle Ages, there appear to have been no widespread interpreter guilds. It was not until the 20th century that interpreting came to be viewed, internationally, as a profession.

UNIT 1

The profession is established

The League of Nations began with two official languages, French and English, that required interpreters. Then in 1927, simultaneous interpreting was performed professionally in public in Geneva, Switzerland, at the International Labor Conference. However, simultaneous interpreting was too costly and complicated to perform regularly. Then Andre Kaminker invented the first simultaneous interpreting equipment, which debuted at the famous Nuremberg Trial for World War II war criminals. A profession was born.

After the Nuremberg events, conference interpreting was established in Europe and then around the world. It enjoys high prestige today. AIIC, the association of international conference interpreters, has members in more than 80 countries. Conference interpreting remains the most established interpreting profession in the world, performed in high-level government, diplomatic and corporate sectors.

Later in the 20th century, court interpreting became the second major sector of interpreting to establish itself in many nations. In 1978, a landmark law in the U.S., the Court Interpreters Act, established the requirements for court interpreting.

> **Spain, Standards of performance, 1548**
>
> Governor Mendoza: "Interpreters had to be duly sworn to perform their task 'well and faithfully,' expressing the matter before them 'clearly and frankly,' 'without hiding or adding anything,' 'without acting in favor of any of the parties,' and 'without deriving any profit from their task other than the pay due to them.'"
>
> Colonial legislation in the U.S. addressed 14 laws regulating the conduct of interpreters for indigenous populations in the Spanish colonies in America, including:
>
> - Interpreters for the Indian languages shall have the necessary capacities and qualities.
> - The interpreters shall not accept or ask for gifts.
> - The interpreters shall not hold private meetings with Indian clients.
> - The interpreters shall not act as advocates for the Indians.
>
> Pöchhacker, Franz (2004:13)

UNIT 1

The Early Years

Community interpreting was born in Australia, both as term and as a profession. This sector of interpreting began in the 1970s when an urgent need for interpreting in community services grew rapidly in Australia. National language access laws promoted the use of interpreters in public services. Up until that time, family, friends and volunteers had typically performed the role of interpreter, but the nation became aware that using untrained interpreters put everyone at risk. Australia developed a strong tradition of professional interpreting that helped to nurture and support the development of community interpreting worldwide. In the 1980s and 1990s, community interpreting spread to Europe, the U.S. and Canada. It was practiced informally there earlier, but not as a profession.

In 1995, the first international conference on community interpreting was held in Toronto, Canada and led to the establishment of Critical Link, now an international nonprofit organization that promotes community interpreting around the world. The profession itself has many other names today, but community interpreting remains the most common one. Increasingly, the profession has spread to parts of the world, including parts of Asia, Africa and Latin America, that until recently did not engage in community interpreting or even see a need for it.

NAMES FOR COMMUNITY INTERPRETING

Around the world, the profession of community interpreting is known by many different names. They include:

- Public services interpreting
- Dialogue interpreting
- Liaison interpreting
- Triangle interpreting
- Face-to-face interpreting
- Bidirectional interpreting
- Institutional interpreting
- Bilateral interpreting

Driving Forces

Three forces have helped to advance the community interpreting profession forward around the world. They are:

- Increased migration
- Language access laws
- Safety, liability and quality of care

Increased migration. The U.S. is one of many nations currently undergoing a large wave of immigration. Today, nearly 13 percent of the population is foreign born, and one child in four is an immigrant or an immigrant's child. Many nations around the world see similar trends. As a result, the need for trained, professional interpreters in community services is growing swiftly, yet many agencies have little funding to train interpreters or to pay for interpreting services. In countries like the U.S., the community interpreting profession has often developed with the support of associations and organizations that are concerned with the successful integration of immigrants into a nation's society.

Language access laws. In addition, many eligible families are denied benefits because children or other family members interpret information incorrectly. As a result, governments in the U.S., Australia, South Africa and many other countries have enacted laws to ensure that no individual is discriminated against on the basis of that person's country of origin. Such laws often address or establish the need for *qualified* community interpreters, helping to drive the professionalization of community interpreting. (The topic of language access laws is discussed in more detail later in this unit.)

Safety, liability and quality of care. In the research literature, anecdotal reports and hundreds of news stories, many tragic situations have been reported that show the consequences of working with no interpreters (or untrained interpreters). For example, some of the more famous cases in health care include that of a 13-year-old Latina girl who died in Arizona following a ruptured appendix; a Cambodian gentleman in California whose foot was amputated without his consent; a Haitian woman in New York who had an abortion without her knowledge or consent, and a Korean, also in New York, injured in the head by a soccer ball and who died despite the attempts of his wife to communicate his severe pain to the hospital. In addition, children have been inappropriately assigned to Special Education programs or suspended from school due to language barriers. A number of abused spouses who failed to get protection orders when they did not have interpreters to assist them were subsequently severely injured or killed. Many eligible families have lost, or been denied, food stamps, medical assistance and other vital benefits due to language barriers. A restaurant owner whose son interpreted for him during a health department inspection of his restaurant later beat his young son for "bad interpreting" because the health department closed his restaurant. Situations such as these have led to an increasing number of lawsuits caused by inaccurate interpreting and heightened awareness about the urgent need for trained, professional interpreters.

Current Trends

The profession of community interpreting is evolving rapidly across the U.S. and around the world. Organizations that provide community services increasingly hire bilingual employees for commonly spoken languages and ask them to interpret part time. (Unfortunately, these employees are often called "volunteer" interpreters, adding to the confusion that surrounds the question of who a "professional interpreter" might be.)

In addition, there is a worldwide trend to establish ethics and standards for community interpreters, to assess their language and interpreting skills, and to develop some common understanding of what qualifications are required to perform the work. For example, two critical organizations that develop international standards, the International Organization for Standardization (ISO) and American Society for Testing and Materials (ASTM), are both working on standards for interpreting. ISO Technical Group 37 is now developing international standards for community interpreting, and ASTM Committee F-43 is developing new standards for general interpreting, which includes community interpreting.

Today, many community service agencies have contracts with telephone and in-person interpreter services. Some agencies also have a "language bank," that is, a group of volunteer or low-cost interpreters listed by language. Language bank interpreters may interpret for one organization, such as a school system or health department, or for several agencies, such as a county network of nonprofit and government agencies. A growing number of healthcare organizations and schools systems engage full-time staff interpreters.

Today, there is a growing recognition that:

- Community interpreting is a profession, not a hobby.
- Interpreting involves complex professional skills.
- *All* interpreters should receive professional training.
- Community interpreters deserve fair compensation and respect.
- Family and friends of clients should not be expected to interpret, especially children.

Community interpreting is a profession with its own ethics, skills and standards. Many community interpreters strive for professional excellence. They care deeply about the important work they do, and a growing number of them ask how they can get certified. Increasing numbers of bilingual employees receive a pay differential if they interpret on the job.

Unit 1 of this training manual offers an overview of the current state of the community interpreting profession and puts a special focus on the foundation of the profession: *ethics* and *conduct*. This unit demonstrates that community interpreting is a vibrant, growing profession. Those who practice it have become a vital part of our community. They can and should take pride in the important work they do.

UNIT 1

Sectors of Interpreting

Today the "general" interpreting profession is comprised of different sectors with their own ethics, standards and professional cultures that do not always communicate well with each other. The main sectors include:

- Conference interpreting (e.g., diplomatic interpreting, high-level government interpreting).
- Legal interpreting.
- Business interpreting.
- Medical interpreting (although theoretically medical interpreting is part of community interpreting, it is increasingly seen as its own sector of interpreting).
- Community interpreting (interpreting for health care, education, human and social services and faith-based organizations).
- Remote interpreting (telephone and video).

Other sectors include:

- Diplomatic interpreting (for high-level government agencies).
- Escort interpreting (accompanying and interpreting for important figures).
- Media interpreting.
- Military interpreting.

Increasingly, the lines between these sectors are beginning to blur. In some countries, there is really only one profession of interpreting. In others, "professional" interpreting exists side by side with a shadow profession of community interpreting where family and friends and other ad hoc interpreters may be brought in instead of professional interpreters.

As time goes on, it seems likely that the lines between the sector will continue to blur until eventually we see the emergence of one, true general interpreting profession in some nations. In the U.S., for example, a dialogue is emerging between the sectors, in part under the aegis of a national forum for this dialogue called InterpretAmerica, established in 2010.

UNIT 1

Areas of Interpreting

Conference interpreting

History: The field of conference interpreting has been well established internationally since the 1950s. Worldwide, it is still the most professionalized sector of interpreting.

Certification: None in the U.S.

Code of Ethics: http://www.aiic.net/ViewPage.cfm/article24.htm

Standards of Practice: Also at http://www.aiic.net/ViewPage.cfm/article24.htm

Facts:
- Conference interpreters are the best paid and most highly respected interpreters.
- They often perform high-level government, corporate and diplomatic interpreting.
- Many are members of the International Association of Conference Interpreters (AIIC).
- Most have received training and education and/or professional guidance.
- Most work in teams and perform simultaneous interpreting.
- A growing number of community interpreters now perform conference interpreting at small, local conferences.

Legal Interpreting

Legal Interpreting

History: Established through the Court Interpreters Act of 1978.

Certification: Three programs: Federal court interpreter certification (Spanish); state court interpreter certification (up to 18 languages, through a consortium of 41 state members); and National Association for Judiciary Interpreters and Translators (NAJIT) certification (Spanish).

Code of Ethics: http://www.ncsconline.org/wc/publications/Res_CtInte_ModelGuideChapter9Pub.pdf or www.najit.org.

Standards of Practice: See http://www.ncsconline.org/wc/publications/Res_CtInte_ModelGuideChapter9Pub.pdf

Facts:
- NAJIT is an active professional association established in 1978 with about 1,200 members.
- In many countries, legal interpreting is considered part of community interpreting.
- Most court-certified interpreters receiver higher pay than non-certified interpreters.

UNIT 1

Business interpreting

History: Unregulated profession.

Certification: None in the U.S. Language services that offer interpreting may be certified through ISO or ASTM.

Ethics/standards: None, except for individual interpreter services or conference interpreting.

Facts:
- Most business interpreters are freelance.
- The pay varies, but it is generally higher than for community interpreters.
- Many are members of the American Translators Association (ATA) and/or state or local associations.
- ATA is the largest translator and interpreter association in the U.S.

Remote interpreting (telephone and video)

History: Well established in the U.S. and becoming more widespread around the world.

Code of Ethics and Standards of Practice: Published in *Telephone Interpreting: A Comprehensive Guide to the Profession* by Nataly Kelly (2008).

Facts:
- Many telephone interpreters work full time in call centers (especially for common languages); others work part-time on call, often from home. Pay varies.
- Many large companies offer this service 24-7, 365 days a year.
- All types of interpreting are performed.
- Increasingly, telephone/video interpreters are trained, tested and monitored for quality assurance. Many go through an internal credentialing process.

UNIT 1

Medical/Healthcare Interpreters (N.B. Medical interpreting is one sector of *community* interpreting)

History: In some countries, including the U.S., healthcare interpreting is more professionalized than other areas of community interpreting. The International Medical Interpreters Association is the largest medical interpreter association in the world. The U.S. National Council on Interpreting in Health Care is the national body that promotes the profession.

Certification: Two U.S. national medical interpreter certification programs are established: see www.certifiedmedicalinterpreters.org, and www.healthcareinterpretercertification.org . State certification for medical and social services interpreters currently exists only in Washington state..

Ethics and standards of practice: Available at www.imiaweb.org;www.ncihc.organd www.chiaonline.org.

Facts:
- Many full-time staff interpreters work and bilingual employees interpret in healthcare.
- The two national medical interpreter certification programs were established in 2009 and 2010.

Community interpreting

History: A young but growing profession established in Australia in the 1970s, and in the U.S. by the 1990s.

Certification: None.

Ethics and standards of practice: No national or international ethics and standards except medical interpreting. ISO is currently developing international standards for community interpreting.

Facts:
- Community interpreters are often the lowest-paid professionals in the field.
- They have high job satisfaction from helping people and changing lives for the better. Little training is available for community interpreting (except medical).

QUALIFICATIONS AND SKILLS

Objective 1.1 (b) List the qualifications and skills of community interpreters.

Basic Qualifications

Today, community interpreters are often asked to show proof of their qualifications and skills. Regardless of the level of experience and education, a consensus is beginning to emerge around the world regarding the minimum set of qualifications and skills that community interpreters should possess. Within the U.S., the profession increasingly recognizes that any community interpreter should demonstrate the following.

- Be 18 years or older.
- Hold a high school diploma or equivalent.
- Demonstrate bilingualism and literacy, preferably by showing proof of a validated language proficiency test.
- Hold a certificate for professional interpreter training, at least 40 hours.

There is still some disagreement about how much training an entry-level community interpreter should receive. However, a national de facto consensus has emerged that 40 hours is, in fact, the minimum length of training. To be eligible for either of the two national medical interpreter certification programs in the U.S., for example, candidates must hold a certificate for 40 hours of training or more in healthcare interpreting.

Basic Skills

In addition, community interpreters should:

- Adhere to relevant ethics and standards.
- Interpret 2-3 sentences without requesting repetition.
- Interpret with approximate accuracy.
- Interpret in first person.

National standards

There is no accepted national international standard for minimum qualifications and skills for community interpreters. However, in 2011 national standards for healthcare interpreter training were published by the National Council on Interpreting in Health Care (NCIHC) and are available at www.ncihc.org. Much of the information in this section derives from those standards, in addition to the requirements and prerequisites for interpreter certification programs

Types of Interpreters

Before considering more detailed information about the qualifications and skills that community interpreters should possess, it is important to know who performs community interpreting today. Broadly speaking, in most countries (including the U.S.), four types of individuals may be community interpreters:

Contract interpreters: These are the professional interpreters who make their living interpreting and may perform other freelance work, such as professional translation.

Staff interpreters: These professional interpreters hold a full-time job with one organization that carries the job title "Interpreter."

Bilingual staff: These adjunct interpreters hold one staff position and are asked to interpret occasionally or part-time as an extra duty.

Volunteers: Much of the work of community interpreting today is still performed by unpaid volunteers, most of whom are not trained or qualified to perform this work.

UNIT 1

Contract interpreters
1. Are paid by the hour.
2. Paid a minimum of 1-2 hours.
3. Work for one community service or several.
4. Often work in courts, schools, motor vehicle agencies, etc.
5. May or may not be trained to interpret.
6. Can earn from $10 to $100+ per hour.

Staff Interpreters
1. Work as full-time interpreters.
2. Have a job title as "interpreter" (or interpreter/translator).
3. May be trained and skilled.
4. Often work for larger organizations.
5. May work full time for interpreter services as "agency" interpreters.

Volunteer interpreters
1. May get an "orientation."
2. Work in a variety of settings.
3. Rarely get professional training to interpret.
4. Interpret part time/ occasionally.
5. May be part of a community language bank.

Bilingual staff
1. Are hired for any job position.
2. Usually interpret as only one part of the job.
3. May not see "interpreter" in the job description.
4. Are often not trained to interpret.
5. May not get extra time to interpret.
6. Some are part of an employee language bank

Critical Questions

QUESTION: Should all types of community interpreters, even volunteers, meet minimum standards for interpreting qualifications and skills?

ANSWER: Yes. Community interpreting is risky when performed by amateurs. Even volunteers should meet the minimum standards.

QUESTION: Are bilingual employees who interpret "professional" interpreters?

ANSWER: No one knows for certain. But if someone is paid to interpret as one part of the job, that person may be considered a professional interpreter.

Language Proficiency

Why is language proficiency so important?

Many interpreters (including a number of professional interpreters) *fail to realize that they lack adequate language skills to interpret accurately and that they should not interpret at all.* Interpreters who are not adequately fluent in their working language can make many errors that lead to problems such as:
- Misunderstandings
- Problems in service delivery
- Misdiagnoses and delayed diagnoses
- Unnecessary tests
- Lack of follow-up
- Loss of benefits
- Lawsuits
- Death

What is a language proficiency test?

A language proficiency test is an oral and/or written test that assesses to what degree you are fluent in a language. Simply believing you are bilingual does not make you so. Only a language proficiency test can determine if you meet the most fundamental requirement for interpreting: adequate fluency in all your working languages.

Types of language proficiency testing

Many types of tests are used to assess language proficiency. The most reliable tests are not sector-specific but designed to assess *general fluency* in a language.

In addition, some language tests are validated and reliable; other tests are not validated and should not be used.

Finally, some tests in the U.S. align with one of the two national scales, ACTFL and ILR (discussed below) and others do not. In Europe, the tests may align with a pan-European testing scale called CEFR (also discussed below). If a language test is not aligned or calibrated with one of these three scales, it is difficult to know what that language test really means for interpreters.

Who conducts validated tests for language proficiency in the U.S.?

- The U.S. government.
- Some state courts.
- Language Testing International.
- Certain language companies.

Language Proficiency Testing

Invalid tests
Many non-validated tests have been created by municipal agencies, school systems, health care organizations and training programs. *Non-validated tests should not be used to make formal assessments of interpreter language proficiency.* At best, such tests can be considered a screening tool to help decide whether a candidate should be tested for language proficiency.

What to test for
Ideally, interpreters should be tested in their oral skills (speaking and listening) and written comprehension in any and all languages for which they interpret, including their native language. If the cost of testing in both languages is too high, at a *minimum* test the candidate in oral skills in the *non-native language*.

Heritage speakers
Anyone who grew up as the child of a native speaker of another language and learned to speak that language at home is called a "heritage speaker." If you are a heritage speaker, you should (at a minimum) be tested in the language spoken at home.

> **True story**
>
> In Alaska, a patient of a community health center went into a diabetic coma because her interpreter was unable to read her English prescription correctly.

Exemptions
To reduce costs, some agencies exempt from a specific language test any interpreter who holds a degree from an accredited university where the language in question is the language of instruction. However, interpreters who hold a *degree* in a *foreign language* should still be tested for language proficiency. For example, someone with a BA in Spanish should not be exempted from a Spanish proficiency test if the interpreter's native language is English.

UNIT 1

Language Proficiency Scales

Most language proficiency test scales are subjective because they were not developed by psychometricians (experts in testing) and the raters who are the examiners or testers are not adequately trained. As a result, one rater might listen to one oral test and give the speaker a high score while a second rater might listen to the same recording and assign a lower score. Tests like these have no objective value.

A valid language proficiency test should be based on a recognized language proficiency scale and undergo a process of external validation overseen by professional psychometricians. The testing organization should have a process in place to train the raters who grade the test and a means of comparing raters' evaluations to ensure consistency (inter-rater reliability). Two validated proficiency scales, established for decades in the U.S., have attained national recognition and acceptance. They are explained in the box below.

Two U.S. National Language Proficiency Scales:
ACTFL and ILR
American Council on the Teaching of Foreign Languages (ACTFL) and Interagency Language Roundtable (ILR)

Types of tests: Oral/listening; written/reading.
Languages tested: ACTFL tests are available in 60+ languages. ILR tests in the languages needed by the U.S. government.
ACTFL Levels: Novice, Intermediate, Advanced, Superior, with three additional levels (high, mid, low) for each of the four descriptors. E.g., one candidate might score "Advanced High."
ILR Levels: 1 (elementary); 2 (working proficiency); 3 (professional proficiency); 4 (advanced professional proficiency); 5 (ideal native speaker in oral and written skills), with two additional levels (+ or -) for each of the five numeric descriptions. (e.g., 3+ in oral, 3 in reading). E.g., one candidate might score "3+." To apply results from the scales to interpreters in real life, one must decide a "cut-off" level above which the interpreter may safely interpret.

Examples of the Proficiency Levels That May Be Needed to Interpret

ACTFL: Superior strongly preferred. However, at a minimum, the "qualified" interpreter should score Advanced High on the ACTFL scale. A "trained" interpreter might score Advanced Mid or Advanced Low. For any lower score, the interpreter would ideally be considered (at most) a "hospitality interpreter."
ILR: Level 3 or higher strongly preferred. At a minimum, the "qualified" interpreter should score 2+ on the ILR scale. The "trained" interpreter would score 2 or 2-. For any lower score, the interpreter should be considered at most a "hospitality interpreter."

UNIT 1

ILR, ACTFL and CEFR
ILR and ACTFL Scales

ILR Scale	ACTFL Scale	Definition
5	Native	Able to speak like an educated native speaker
4+ 4	Distinguished	Able to speak with a great deal of fluency, grammatical accuracy, precision of vocabulary and idiomaticity
3+ 3	Superior	Able to speak the language with sufficient structural accuracy and vocabulary to participate effectively in most formal and informal conversations
2+	Advanced High	Able to satisfy most work requirements and show some ability to communicate on concrete topics
2	Advanced	Able to satisfy routine social demands and limited work requirements
1+	Intermediate - High	Able to satisfy most survival needs and limited social demands
1	Intermediate - Mid Intermediate - Low	Able to satisfy some survival needs and some limited social demands
0+	Novice - High	Able to satisfy immediate needs with learned utterances
0	Novice - Mid Novice - Low 0	Able to operate in only a very limited capacity Unable to function in the spoken language No ability whatsoever in the language

UNIT 1

CEFR

What is the CEFR?
CEFR is an acronym for the Common European Framework of Reference for Languages: Learning, Teaching, and Assessment (CEFR) has emerged as the dominant scale for language proficiency testing in the European Union. CEFR is similar in scope and concept to ACTFL and ILR scales.

CEFR was established by the Council of Europe and developed between 1989 and 1996 to create a method both for assessment and teaching of all languages in Europe. Then in 2001, a European Union Council Resolution mad an official recommendation to use CEFR to establish language ability (i.e. proficiency) validation. CEFR has three primary reference levels broken into six more specific levels.

CEFR Scale

A Basic Speaker

A1 *Breakthrough or beginner:* Can understand and use familiar everyday expressions and very basic phrases.
A2 *Waystage or elementary:* Can understand sentences and frequently used expressions.

B Independent Speaker

B1 *Threshold or pre-intermediate*: Can understand the main points of clear standard input on familiar matters regularly
B2 *Vantage or intermediate*: Can understand the main ideas of complex text on both concrete and abstract topics.

C Proficient Speaker

C1 *Effective Operational Proficiency or upper intermediate:* Can understand a wide range of demanding, longer texts, and recognize implicit meaning.
C2 *Mastery or advanced:* Can understand with ease virtually everything heard or read.

UNIT 1

ILR Interpretation Standards

No discussion of interpreter skills and qualifications is complete without an overview of the ILR interpretation standards (which should not be confused with ILR language proficiency standards). These federal U.S. standards are available at www.govtilr.org. The following excerpts include examples of descriptors in the standards.

Skill Level Descriptions

Level 5 (Master Professional Performance):
Able to excel consistently at interpreting in the mode (simultaneous, consecutive, and sight) required by the setting and provide accurate renditions of informal, formal, and highly formal discourse. Conveys the meaning of the speaker faithfully and accurately, including all details and nuances, reflecting the style, register, and cultural context of the source language, without omissions, additions or embellishments. Demonstrates superior command of the skills required for interpretation, including mastery of both working languages and their cultural context, and wide-ranging expertise in specialized fields. Outstanding delivery, with pleasant voice quality and without hesitations, unnecessary repetitions, and corrections. Exemplifies the highest standards of professional conduct and ethics.

Level 4 (Advanced Professional Performance):
Able to interpret in the mode (simultaneous, consecutive, and sight) required by the setting and provide almost completely accurate renditions of complex, colloquial, and idiomatic speech as well as formal and some highly formal discourse. Conveys the meaning of the speaker faithfully, including many details and nuances,. Demonstrates mastery of the skills required for interpretation, including command of both working languages and their cultural context, expertise in some specialized fields, and ability to prepare new specialized topics rapidly and routinely.

Level 3 (Professional Performance Level):
Able to interpret consistently in the mode (simultaneous, consecutive, and sight) required by the setting. Can convey many nuances, cultural allusions, and idioms, though expression may not always reflect target language conventions. Adequate delivery, with pleasant voice quality. Hesitations, repetitions or corrections may be noticeable but do not hinder successful communication of the message. Can handle some specialized subject matter with preparation. Performance reflects high standards of professional conduct and ethics.

Level 2 (Limited Working Performance Level):
Unable to transfer information reliably in most instances. May communicate some meaning when exchanges are short, involve subject matter that is routine or discourse that is repetitive or predictable, but may typically require repetition or clarification. Expression in the target language is frequently faulty.

Level 1 (Minimal Performance):
Unable to transfer more than isolated short phrases.

Level 0 (No Performance):
No functional ability to transfer information from one language to another.

Levels of Qualification

As discussed before, all community interpreters should meet certain minimal qualifications and skills:

Qualifications

- Be 18 years or older.
- Hold a high school diploma or equivalent.
- Demonstrate bilingualism and literacy, preferably by showing proof of a validated language proficiency test.
- Hold a certificate for professional interpreter training, at least 40 hours.

Skills

- In addition, community interpreters should:
- Adhere to relevant ethics and standards.
- Interpret 2-3 sentences without requesting repetition.
- Interpret with approximate accuracy.
- Interpret in first person.

However, additional expectations about qualifications and skills will vary according to the interpreter's level of experience and credentialing. For the sake of clarity, community interpreters can be divided into at least four categories that correspond to their levels of qualification, regardless of whether they are volunteers or paid interpreters:

- Hospitality interpreters
- Trained interpreters
- Qualified interpreters
- Certified interpreters

The level will depend in great part on the interpreter's language proficiency, training and credentialing, so it is important to look at each level, one by one.

Hospitality Interpreters

> *A hospitality interpreter may perform <u>basic</u> interpreting for meeting, greeting or directing clients, scheduling appointments, helping clients with forms and providing other basic interpreting services.*

Hospitality interpreters perform an important role in community interpreting. They should meet all the basic minimum qualifications and skills requirements discussed above for community interpreters in general, and in addition they should:

- Demonstrate basic bilingualism and literacy equivalent to the level of ILR 1 to 1+/ACTFL *Intermediate Mid* to *Intermediate High*.[1]
- Hold a certificate for basic interpreter training, e.g. an introductory workshop.

The role of hospitality interpreters is important. Hospitality interpreting involves interpreting for simple, basic encounters where no important decisions will be made that could affect a client's safety, well being, service outcomes or vital needs. Hospitality interpreters will ideally perform interpreting that involves simple tasks which facilitate access to the service. Yet clients need to obtain access to many services, and hospitality interpreters may make it possible for them to do so.

---

1 To understand these ILR/ACTFL notations, refer to the ILR-ACTFL table above.

Trained interpreters

Professionally trained interpreters who demonstrate a certain level of language proficiency may perform basic interpreting encounters such as a parent-teacher interview, standard discharge instructions, nutritional counseling with a dietician, a driver's license application at motor vehicles or a basic intake appointment at a job training center.

Qualifications

In addition to meeting the minimal requirements, professionally trained interpreters should:

- Demonstrate basic fluency equivalent to the level of ILR 2- to 2/ ACTFL Advanced Low or Advanced Mid.
- Hold a certificate for a professional training program of 40 hours or longer.[1]

Skills

Trained interpreters should know how to:

- Adhere to professional ethics and standards.
- Develop adequate memory skills to interpret 2-3 sentences without requesting repetition.
- Perform adequately in consecutive and sight translation modes.
- Perform professional introductions.
- Interpret as accurately and completely as possible.
- Observe first person as a default and know when to make exceptions.
- Demonstrate a minimal competency in (or familiarity with) simultaneous mode.[2]
- Adopt an unobtrusive position that facilitates direct client-provider communication.
- Manage the flow.
- Maintain register.
- Make decisions about dialect/regionalisms.
- Perform ethical decision-making.
- Assess cultural elements of language.

---

[1] NCIHC national standards for training do not specify a minimum program length. However, the two national medical interpreter certifications require a 40-hour training program as a prerequisite for certification, and 40 hours is widely considered the minimum basic standard in the field.

[2] The question of whether or not community interpreters should be expected to perform in simultaneous mode is a topic of some debate in the field. One concern is that the interpreter who has received inadequate training or lacks experience to perform it safely should not attempt to perform in simultaneous mode due to the high risk of errors.

- Address advocacy issues.
- Perform self-monitoring of their performance.
- Effectively address barriers to communication.
- Practice self care.
- Observe safety protocols.

Finally, trained interpreters are expected to render the spirit, tone and intent of the message and to interpret for meaning.

General knowledge

There is a growing consensus strongly reinforced by NCIHC national training standards (www.ncihc.org) that a professionally trained interpreter should know:

- Some background and history about the interpreting profession, including other fields of interpreting.
- Information about the types of interpreting careers.
- Modalities of interpreting (e.g. face-to-face, telephone, video).
- Cultural aspects of interpreting.
- What cultural competence is and how to promote it.
- How to develop skills in terminology.
- Where to find resources for professional development.

Qualified Interpreters

> Qualified interpreters may perform the more difficult and challenging assignments, e.g., a patient exam in hospital Emergency Room, a meeting in a school about a child's Special Education services, or a social services interview to learn why a customer was denied income assistance.

Qualifications and Skills

The "Qualified Interpreter" should meet all the qualifications and skills described for the Trained Interpreter. In addition, there is a growing (if not universal) consensus that to be considered qualified, the interpreter should also:

- Show proof of a validated language proficiency test[1] with a score of the leveo of ILR +2 or higher/ACTFL Advanced High or higher.
- Demonstrate sufficient fluency in the working languages to converse in a culturally appropriate fashion and convey the meaning of a message accurately and completely.
- Where possible and available, obtain a formal "qualified
- interpreter" credential for court interpreting or "Associate
- Healthcare Interpreter" or healthcare interpreting.
- Have had life experiences either in the countries and/or in cultural communities in which their working languages are
- spoken.
- For medical interpreting: have knowledge about health literacy
- and medical terminology.

Interpreters who cannot find a certification test in their language may become "qualified" in other ways. Currently, national healthcare certification is available only in Spanish, although a few other languages are in development. State court interpreter certification is available in up to 18 languages (depending on the state). If you cannot obtain certification in your language, try to become a "qualified" interpreter.

---

1 See the previous section in this unit on Language Proficiency Testing.

Certified Interpreters

> **Certified interpreter**: An **interpreter** who has passed a formal credentialing process administered by a professional organization or government entity may be **certified**. Certification is a credential awarded by a recognized certification entity to interpreters who pass a rigorous, externally validated skills test with oral and written components that is based on national or international requirements for professional certification.[1] *Certification represents the highest credential currently available for community interpreters.*

Qualifications

The qualifications required for certification will vary according to the specific certification program. In general, in addition to the basic qualifications listed above, the following are often or typically required for medical and/or legal interpreter certification:

- Show proof of a passing score from a recognized interpreter certification exam.
- Show proof of language proficiency testing (specific requirements vary).
- Demonstrate adequate skills in consecutive and sight translation modes.
- Demonstrate adequate or minimal skills in simultaneous interpreting (generally required for court interpreter certification and also required for one of the two national programs in medical interpreter certification).
- Show proof of interpreter training (medical interpreter certification).

Skills

The certified interpreter is typically expected to master the skills taught in basic interpreter training (listed above). Expected skills may include (depending on the certification program):

- Demonstrate a level of accuracy determined by the certification exam (e.g., 70 percent).
- Manage an interpreted encounter.
- Show knowledge of the healthcare or legal system (depending

---

[1] Interpreters who hold a training certificate or have taken a screening test administered by an employer *are not certified interpreters according to professional interpreting standards*-- even if their credentials are referred to as "certification."

THE COMMUNITY INTERPRETER

on the certification).
- Prepare for an interpreted encounter (medical only).
- Show cultural responsiveness (medical only).
- Interpret oral communication.
- Sight translate short documents.
- Translate short, simple documents.[1]

Knowledge

Certified interpreters may also be expected to demonstrate knowledge of:
- Medical or legal terminology
- Roles of the medical interpreter (medical only)
- Interpreter ethics and standards of practice
- Medical specialties (medical only)
- Relevant legislation and regulations

---

[1] This requirement of the CCHI healthcare certification examination is a disputed one, but it is based on the "KSA" (knowledge, skills, abilities) requirement of certification programs. In general, certification programs must base their exams not on what those practicing a profession *should* do but what they actually *do* perform each day in their jobs. CCHI determined through a detailed job analysis survey that, in fact, a majority of practicing healthcare interpreters translate short documents such as discharge instructions. For details visit the CCHI website, www.healthcareinterpretercertification.org.

Interpreter Certification

In general, for any profession, there are three basic types of certification:

1. Government certification (licensure)[1]
2. Professional certification
3. Program certificates (not authentic certification)

Government certification

Certain federal and state government agencies offer certification programs for general and/or specialized interpreters. In the U.S., certification for community interpreters (health care and social services) exists only in the state of Washington. Other states such as Oregon are working to establish similar programs in medical or community interpreting. Certification for court interpreters is offered through both federal and state courts.

Professional certification:

A professional certification exam is administered by an interpreter's association or a professional certification body. Such certification exists in many countries around the world. In the U.S., professional certification is available for sign language, legal and medical interpreters.

Program certificates:

Program certificates for interpreters for training or language assessment are often referred to as certification. They are not accepted by the interpreting profession as certification. Many school systems, municipal agencies, language companies and training agencies call their interpreters "certified." However, *a training or program certificate is not certification*. If you merely hold a certificate, *you are not a certified interpreter.*

---

[1] Licensure is not the same as certification, although the two are related. For clarification, please see Kelly (2007).

Question: If I complete a 40-hour interpreter training and receive a certificate, may I call myself a "certified interpreter"?

Answer: *No.* In most professional interpreting circles, "certified" refers to government or professional certification only. It is important (and ethical) to represent one's credentials accurately, for example, by stating "I am not certified, but I have obtained a 40-hour certificate for professional interpreter training."

Question: Are community interpreters certified in the U.S.?

Answer: Strictly speaking "community" interpreters cannot be certified except in the state of Washington, where interpreters are state-certified to interpret for publicly funded health and social services. However, interpreters may obtain medical or legal interpreter certification in the U.S. Interpreters who obtain certification for interpreting in federal and/or state courts are called court certified.

Accepted Certification Programs

Programs in the U.S. that the community interpreting professions accept as valid certification include:

- National Board for Certified Medical Interpreters
- Certification Commission for Healthcare Interpreters
- Federal court interpreter certification
- State court interpreter certification
- NAJIT certification for judiciary interpreters and translators
- Washington state certification for medical and social services interpreters
- RID certification for ASL (American Sign Language) interpreters

UNIT 1

Medical Interpreter Certification

> **Certification**: A process by which a governmental or professional organization attests to or certifies that an individual is qualified to provide a particular service. Certification calls for formal assessment, using an instrument that has been tested for validity and reliability, so that the certifying body can be confident that the individuals it certifies hold the qualifications needed to do the job. Sometimes called qualification.
> NCIHC (www.ncihc.org)

Certification for medical interpreters

There is no national certification program for community interpreters at this time in the U.S., although one such program may emerge soon in Canada. However, in the U.S and many other countries, a great deal of money is invested in assuring quality health care and patient safety. As a result, medical interpreting is the most professionalized sector of community interpreting in the U.S.

Is it true there are two medical interpreter certification programs in the U.S.?

Yes. In 2009 and 2010, two national medical interpreter certification programs were established. The history of these two certification programs began in the 1990s, when many groups across the country expressed a strong interest in developing medical interpreter certification. The Massachusetts Medical Interpreters Association (MMIA, which later became the International Medical Interpreters Association, IMIA) piloted some early testing in Massachusetts and California. Many specialists in the field, however, felt that a national organization should lead the program. It soon became clear that to preserve unity in the field, it would be necessary for a broad coalition to lead national certification, rather than a single group.

As a result, in 2008, a 15 organizations across the country came together to form the National Coalition on Health Care Interpreter Certification (NCC) with a view to developing a national certification program. NCC was supported by many in the field. However, there were some internal divisions.

One program splits off

In January 2009, IMIA and Language Line University separated from the NCC and jointly announced their own national medical interpreter certification program. Together, they founded the National Board of Certification for Medical Interpreters (NBCMI) as the legal certifying entity for this certification. IMIA, as the largest professional association in the world for medical interpreters, felt that they had a vested interest in spearheading the process.

UNIT 1

Two programs are born

Subsequently, NCC regrouped and founded the Certification Commission for Healthcare Interpreters (CCHI) to develop its own certification program. In late 2009, NBCMI announced the launch of their interpreter certification, followed a year later by the CCHI certification. At this time, there are therefore two national medical interpreter certification programs in the U.S. Both are actively certifying Spanish interpreters and both appear to be successful, although the two certification exams are somewhat different.

In addition, through a process of portfolio review and a written test, CCHI offers a second credential called "Associate Healthcare Interpreter" for languages for which no oral exam is available. (This title would be a "qualified interpreter" credential). The "Associate Healthcare Interpreter" title holds less weight than certification, but many interpreters have applied for and obtained it.

Currently, both certification examinations are available in Spanish, and both NBCMI and CCHI are developing tests in other languages.

Pros and cons

While some observers are concerned about the presence of two national medical interpreter certification programs in one country, other have taken the two programs in stride. They point to the differences between the two tests (for example, NCBMI emphasizes medical terminology while CCHI includes a component of simultaneous interpreting and an assessment of written translation). A number of observers feel that the profession as a whole is learning from the two programs and that competition between them may ultimately have enhanced both. It is to be hoped that progress in the area of healthcare interpreter certification "trickles down" to other, less developed areas of community interpreting.

Finally, by promoting national education about "real" certification, both programs have helped to clarify some of the confusion created when certain organizations conduct an internal assessment and then call their interpreters "certified," a problem that has caused tremendous confusion in the field and has devalued genuine certification programs.

THE COMMUNITY INTERPRETER

UNIT 1

Medical Interpreter Certification Timeline

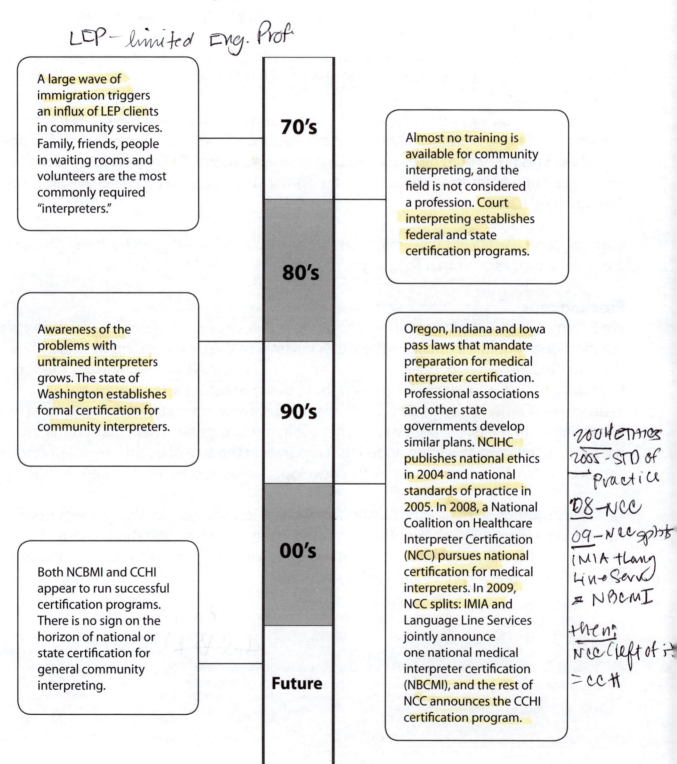

Language Access Laws

OBJECTIVE 1.1 (c) Address the impact of language access laws on community interpreting.

> No person in the United States shall, on ground of race, color, or national origin, be excluded from participation in, or be denied the benefits of, or be subjected to discrimination under any program or activity receiving Federal financial assistance.
>
> **-Title VI of the Civil Rights Act of 1964**

Title VI is the most influential language access law in the U.S. (Other countries, such as South Africa and Australia, have their own equally influential laws about language access.) Under Title VI, any agency that receives federal funding is required to take *reasonable steps* to provide equal access to public services for clients with Limited English Proficiency (LEP). Even if the agency receives only a little federal assistance for *one* program or service, it must support equal access to *all* its services and programs. Without Title VI, the profession of community interpreting might not exist in the U.S.

Question:
What is a language access law?

Answer:
It is a law that mandates the use of language assistance for persons who do not speak the national language(s) or the language of service provision. The intent of such laws is to prevent discrimination in public services by supporting equal access to funded services such as healthcare, social services, the justice system, housing, transportation and schools.

In the U.S., Title VI of the Civil Rights Act, a federal law, is the oldest and most important language access law. Many other countries around the world have similar laws.

Legal Requirements Under Title VI

What do agencies have to do under Title VI?
Under Title VI, any agency that receives federal funding may be expected to provide interpreters for LEP persons at its own expense in addition to providing other language assistance. Other "reasonable steps" may include the following:

- Provide notice to LEP persons about their rights to language assistance.
- Develop a written policy and procedures.
- Translate vital documents such as consent forms, descriptions of services and financial qualification forms.
- Provide staff training about how they are expected to serve LEP clients.

The Four-Factor Analysis
Title VI applies to all services, programs and agencies that receive federal funding, whether the money comes directly from the federal government or is filtered down through a state or local agency. This means that Title VI applies to most healthcare organizations, schools, courts and human and social service agencies. Each agency that receives federal funding is expected to make an assessment that balances four factors:

(1) The number or proportion of LEP persons eligible to be served or likely to be encountered.
(2) The frequency with which LEP individuals come in contact with the programs.
(3) The nature and importance of the programs, activities, or services.
(4) The resources available and costs.

The intent of the four-factor analysis is to help federally-funded organizations protect meaningful access to public services while not imposing an undue burden on smaller organizations.

For more information about Title VI, go to www.lep.gov.

UNIT 1

Other Language Laws

As a federal law, Title VI has made an impact on services provided by agencies that receive Federal Financial Assistance. A growing number states and cities have also enacted language access laws, including several cities in California, New York City, Philadelphia and Washington, D.C. There are now a large number of such laws. Here are just two examples of state and municipal language laws:

Maryland	Washington, D.C
In 2002, Maryland passed a law to protect immigrants and refugees who speak limited English. The law is Annotated Code of Maryland, state Government Article 10-1101-1104. Essentially, this law mirrors Title VI. It requires agencies that receive State funding to take reasonable steps to provide equal access to public services for individuals with limited English proficiency, including the following: * Provide interpreters for LEP clients at no cost to clients. * Provide translations of forms and documents ordinarily provided to the public into any language spoken by 3% or more of the population within that geographic jurisdiction.	On April 7, 2004, Washington D.C. passed a bill mandating language assistance at 22 city agencies. Each agency is required to designate a language-access coordinator to develop and implement the LEP plan. This law also requires the D.C. Office of Human Rights to monitor compliance with the law. D.C. agencies are expected to hire additional bilingual employees and translate official materials into several languages. Affected services include the Police Department, Department of Health, Department of Employment, D.C. Public School and Department of Motor Vehicles.

For more information on language access laws in the U.S., visit the following websites:

- www.lep.gov: A government website about language access policies. http://www.lep.gov.
- U.S. Department of Health and Human Services, Office of Civil Rights: http://www.hhs.gov/ocr
- National Health Law Program, Language Access Resources: A national nonprofit agency whose website provides many valuable documents about language access http://www.healthlaw.org
- For a "cheat sheet" from the New York Lawyers for the Public Interest: http://www.nylpi.org/images/FE/chain234siteType8/site203/client/Language Access Legal Cheat Sheet_Final - 9.9.09.pdf

UNIT 1

Other Language Access Laws and Standards

Many other laws, requirements and professional standards address language access in community services. Here are only a few examples.

Federal laws
- Department of Health and Human Services Regulations (45 C.F.R. §80.1, et. seq)
- Executive Order 13166: Improving Access to Services for Persons with Limited English Proficiency
- Medicare Regulations for Medicare Advantage Program (42 C.F.R. §§422.2264 & 422.112)
- Medicaid Managed Care Requirements (42 C.F.R. §438.10)

National, Industry and Accreditation Standards

National standards that promote language access were developed by the HHS Office of Minority Health (OMH). Entitled, "Culturally and Linguistically Appropriate Service (CLAS) Standards," they were first published in 2000. Available on the OMH website, these national standards are now undergoing revision.

[handwritten: OMH - off of Minority Health.]

Industry standards around the world and the U.S. were created to assure quality in language services, for example:
- ASTM F 2089-01: Standard Guide for Language Interpretation Services. The American Society for Testing and Materials (ASTM) international standard identifies the components of quality language interpretation services and establishes criteria for each component. ASTM, which is the largest U.S.-based international standards organization, is currently redeveloping its international standards for general interpreting (Committee F-43, Subcommittee 1).
- SO TC37/SC2/N527c, Project 13611. ISO, the international standards organization, is developing international standards for community interpreting.
- ANSI, the American National Standards Institute, is cooperating with ISO on the development of international standards for interpreting and translation.

Accreditation standards demonstrate that certain institutions, such as hospitals, meet accepted standards, e.g., for quality of care. They include:
- The Joint Commission, which accredits U.S. hospitals, has included strong language in its standards to address the needs of LEP patients.
- National Committee for Quality Assurance (NCQA) has developed draft standards addressing services to LEP patients.

Language Access Laws and Community Interpreting

→ publicly funded agencies

Community interpreters should be well informed about language laws in their own and other countries. In the U.S., language access laws are critical to the professionalization of community interpreting. Lawsuits and actions taken by federal enforcement agencies have greatly influenced the provision of interpreters in community services and thus helped to establish the profession of community interpreting. This is also true in several other countries.

To this day, however, many organizations in the U.S. and elsewhere that receive public funding are unfamiliar with language access laws. For example, an office manager might schedule Spanish interpreters but might inform clients who speak other languages, "Come back with an interpreter." (Requiring clients to bring interpreters may be a violation of federal and state or local language access laws.) Interpreters should be well informed about language access laws because:

- Sometimes the interpreter is the only person who understands the risks involved when agencies that are required to provide qualified interpreters fail to do so.
- By citing the law, the interpreter can inform the agency and protect the client from harm.
- By citing the law, the interpreter can help the agency to address major risk and liability.
- The interpreter can also help the agency to ensure the quality of service and quality of care.
- In doing all these things, the interpreter helps to promote the profession of community interpreting.

Interpreters should know Lang Access Laws:
1. *Interpreters would know when agencies fail to provide qualified Interp.*
2. *protect client from harm*
3. *can address agencies of major risks & liabilities*
4. *ensure quality of service*
5. *help promote the profession*

UNIT 1

Family and Friends Should Not Interpret

Most language access laws discourage working with unqualified interpreters in general, and family and friends in particular. In addition, many organizations have learned the hard way that family members and friends should not interpret because they are usually not qualified to do so and cannot be impartial.

The risk to clients and the legal liability for problematic outcomes is very high. Most family members and friends of clients:
- Lack interpreting skills.
- Are not adequately fluent in both languages.
- Have difficulty remaining objective or impartial.
- Usually add their own opinions or remarks.
- Do not know the terminology of community services.
- Sometimes hide key information because they are embarrassed or confused.
- Are often reluctant to share bad news or fatal diagnoses.

In many cases, family members who interpreted have covered up abuse.

In addition, many agencies today realize that it may be a violation of federal law, and in some cases of state or municipal law, to tell clients to bring their own interpreters to public services. However, family members are still often asked to interpret.

This state of affairs is unfortunate. Professionalizing the field of community interpreting will help everyone to understand that family members and friends should not be asked to interpret in community services.

UNIT 1

Let No Child Interpret

Many community interpreters in the U.S. have interpreted when they were children (sometimes very young children) for family and friends. If you interpreted as a child for your family or their friends, you may think this experience helped you to grow as a person, or you may feel it traumatized you. It is important to know that experts on interpreting strongly advise against asking children to interpret and a growing number of organizations explicitly prohibit it.

There are many reasons for this concern. The vast majority of children who interpret:
- Have not mastered language at an adult level.
- Lack technical vocabulary.
- Do not know how to mediate when a barrier to communication arises.
- Do not know how to explain culture.
- Are unfamiliar with cultures in an adult context (whether ethnic, regional, professional or personal).
- Are often traumatized by interpreting (e.g., when they announce a fatal diagnosis, a loss of social service benefits, etc.).
- Miss school because they are pulled out to interpret.
- Find they are causing an upheaval or reversal in family roles, which often confuses and disturbs the family.
- May not question authority (e.g., to request clarification when they do not understand).

Many children are pulled from school on a regular basis to interpret for their families. Some have been asked to inform their parents about a diagnosis of advanced cancer or a sexually transmitted disease (including HIV). One child was asked to tell a mother that her fetus dead in the womb. A boy of 11 was told to inform his mother about his own cancer diagnosis. Children at many parent-teacher interviews or meetings have had to tell their parents about their own poor grades or their truant behavior, their learning disability or their possible expulsion from school. In social services, child interpreters have informed their parents about denials of benefits, the loss of medical assistance, eviction notices and gas and electric cut-offs. Children have even interpreted for parents who are charged with abusing them and for police at the scene of domestic violence incidents. Children as young as three have been asked to interpret for family members!

It may be a violation of a client's civil rights to have a child interpret in a publicly-funded health or human service setting. As interpreters, be informed and educate your workplace and community. Protect children and families. Never ask a child to interpret.

Self Monitoring and Self Assessment

Objective 1.1 (d): Develop awareness of self-monitoring and self-assessment for interpreters.

Few interpreters receive regular monitoring or feedback. This lack of feedback puts a burden on you to monitor your own performance for accuracy and smooth delivery. Most people think interpreting is easy. It is not. Consider just some of the factors to consider about the quality of your own performance:

Linguistic Skills
- Demonstrate language proficiency.
- Observe nonverbal cues and body language.
- Listen to speech patterns.
- Apply semantic and contextual knowledge.
- Process meaning quickly.
- Distinguish accents (of the client or provider).
- Know regionalisms.

Communicative Skills
- Match meaning to words.
- Convey the meaning of non-equivalent concepts.
- Manage the flow.

Institutional Knowledge
- Know how service delivery systems work.
- Be familiar with policies, procedures and protocols.
- Observe organizational standards and requirements.

Socio-cultural Knowledge
- Be familiar with the cultures of the client and provider
- Observe the acculturation of clients and foreign-born providers (their degree of assimilation).
- Be aware of your own cultural background, cultural sensitivity and potential bias.
- Know the institutional culture of the service.

In the final analysis, perhaps only you, the interpreter, will know if you have mastered the skills and possess the knowledge you will need to perform accurate, effective interpreting.

Listening Skills

Active listening is a valuable skill in nearly every area of life. For interpreters, that skill is vital. Self-recording, for example, is an excellent exercise for interpreters, but the real value of the exercise comes when the interpreter learns to *listen* during the interpreted session. The ability to "tune out" external noise and focus entirely on the meaning of what is said by listening to and assessing the message holistically is an exercise so complex that few of those who engage the services of interpreters realize how complex it is. When you engage in active listening, the idea is not only to catch words but the whole message and its context. You must understand a message to render it accurately.

Listening to a recording of a session you have just interpreted, even for practice, is another form of listening that offers the following benefits:
- You are not paying attention to human beings, so you can focus on what you interpreted.
- You can pause the recording to note down comments or errors, or to listen again.
- You may listen to the recording as often as you wish.
- You can begin to make global assessments of your performance, because you are no longer interpreting and can "hear" yourself.
- You can distance yourself and try to be neutral and objective.
- You can consciously apply the lessons learned in training.

Things to look for include:
- What works: how is your performance overall? (Note that we learn, in general, more by building on our strengths more than by "battling" our flaws.)
- What is your greatest strength as an interpreter? What improvements are you seeing?
- What makes you sound like a "professional" interpreter?
- How is your delivery? Is it smooth, jarring, easy to understand, accented (because you were nervous), stop-and-start?
- What were your errors? Write them down: omissions, additions, changes, etc. Now categorize them. Were most of these errors omissions or additions, for example?
- What areas show the greatest need for improvement?

Only you can learn to monitor your own performance. It is a professional responsibility to do so, and also a rich and fascinating exercise that will carry you far in the profession.

OBJECTIVE 1.2

Apply ethical principles for interpreters to simulated situations from real life.

Introduction

Ethics are the bedrock of a profession. Knowledge about a profession is not enough. To become a practicing member of that profession, you must know, respect and adhere to its code of ethics.

Community interpreting in most countries lacks a formal code of ethics and standards of practice. That is one of the reasons why community interpreting is often not taken seriously as a profession. Fortunately, community interpreters can turn to other areas of interpreting to find relevant ethics and standards. In the U.S., for example, we have guidance for various types of interpreters.

1.2 (a) (a) Describe the differences between ethics and standards of practice.

1.2 (b) Discuss ethics and standards for community interpreting.

1.2 (c) Develop strategies to apply ethical principles in real-life settings.

- *General interpreters:* The American Translators Association (ATA), the largest professional association of translators and interpreters in the country and one of the largest in the world, publishes a basic code of ethics for both translators and interpreters. ATA members (currently about 13,000, of whom approximately one quarter are interpreters) are required to adhere to those ethics, which are available at www.atanet.org.

- *Legal interpreters:* Federal, state and professional ethics are available for legal interpreters.[1]

- *Healthcare interpreters:* in the U.S. there are national (NCIHC) ethics and standards of practice at www.ncihc.org in addition to international (IMIA) ethics and standards at www.imiaweb.org.

Because healthcare is a key sector of community interpreting, this unit will discuss healthcare interpreting ethics as the most appropriate ethics available in the U.S. to guide community interpreters.

---

[1] They are available at http://www.uscourts.gov/uscourts/FederalCourts/Interpreter/Standards_for_Performance.pdf, http://www.ncsconline.org/wc/publications/Res_CtInte_ModelGuideChapter9Pub.pdf, and www.najit.org.

Ethics and Standards

Objective 1.2 (a) Describe the differences between ethics and standards of practice.

What is a "code of ethics"?

A code of ethics is a set of rules that govern the conduct and behavior of members of a profession. Usually, codes of ethics are *binding*. One purpose of a code of ethics is to deter wrongdoing and promote ethical conduct.

> **Code of Ethics**
>
> The principles of right and wrong that are accepted by members of a profession in the exercise of their professional duties.
> National Council on Interpreting in Health Care

Who creates codes of ethics?

One purpose of a code of ethics is to deter wrongdoing and to promote ethical conduct.

Codes of Ethics for Interpreters

- **Legal Interpreting**: Federal courts, consortium of 41 state courts and NAJIT.
- **Community Interpreting**: No national code except for medical. Ohio has a code for community and court interpreters.
- **Medical Interpreting**: National code: NCIHC. International code: IMIA. Influential code: CHIA.
- **General interpreting**: American Translators Association and other interpreting organizations.
- **International interpreting**: Australia, New Zealand, Latin America, Europe, Canada, Africa.

THE COMMUNITY INTERPRETER

Standards of Practice

> **STANDARDS OF PRACTICE**
>
> A clear set of guidelines that delineate expectations for the interpreter's conduct and practice.
> National Council on Interpreting in Health Care

Standards of practice are formal guidelines that show those who practice a certain occupation how to perform their work well and conduct themselves in a professional manner.

A great deal of confusion prevails between ethics and standards of practice. Many interpreters (and those who employ them) do not know the difference between ethics and standards.

The difference is simple. Think of ethics as the rules, and standards as the guidelines. Ethics are the strictest rules of any profession, and standards help you put ethics into practice and perform well. If ethics are about "right and wrong," standards are about quality performance.

Standards of practice open our eyes. They help us to understand that while ethics may seem black and white, real life is often shades of gray. As a result, standards provide us with more detailed guidance to help us to make decisions that promote our professional competence and ethical behavior.

How Ethics and Standards Connect

What is the difference between ethics and standards?

- Ethics are the "rules" of a profession. Standards are the guidelines.
- Ethics show interpreters what you MUST do. Standards show you HOW to do it.
- Ethics are strict and rigid. Standards are more flexible.

Why do interpreters need to respect both ethics and standards?

Ethics and standards of practice show you how to:

- Perform at a professional level.
- Promote quality interpreting.
- Support beneficial outcomes.

Similarities and differences		
Codes of ethics or codes of conduct	Standards of practice	Both ethics and standards…
Are usually binding	Are not binding	Guide the interpreter's behavior
Are rules	Are recommendations	Promote quality interpreting
May be rigid	May be flexible	
May include serious consequences for violations	Have consequences for violations that may vary (e.g., a reprimand)	Lay down official policy and sound practice
Constitute the received wisdom of experts in the field	Also constitute the received wisdom of the field but are practical and may include details about tasks, skills and performance	Are important, because violations of either may lead to difficulties for all parties, including interpreters
Focus on right or wrong		Define what an interpreter should do
	Focus on what works (and is professionally sound)	Support complete, accurate interpreting

Standards of practice are often organized under the rubrics (headings) of codes of ethics. This structure makes ethics and standards easier to remember and reinforces the importance of ethics.

UNIT 1

Ethics and Standards Around the World

Around the globe, codes of ethics and standards of practice for community interpreters are emerging, most often in medical interpreting. Legal interpreters (who are considered community interpreters in many countries, if not the U.S.) also have a growing number of codes of ethics to regulate their professions. Here is information you should know about codes of ethics for community interpreters.

- The International Medical Interpreters Association (IMIA), the largest medical interpreters association in the world, has developed its own code of ethics and standards of practice, which are available at imiaweb.org. Community interpreters should become familiar with these documents, as they are arguably the most influential standards for any area of community interpreting in the world. The IMIA ethics and standards have been translated into a number of languages. IMIA's website (www.imiaweb.org) offers a listing of other relevant ethics and standards.

- Canada has developed what may be the most detailed national or international standards for community interpreting (including legal interpreting). This document, *The National Standard Guide for Community Interpreting Services*, specifically addresses medical, legal, educational and social services interpreting.

> **Legal Interpreting Ethics**
>
> In the U.S., unlike many other countries, legal interpreting does not fall under the umbrella of community interpreting. Community interpreters in the U.S. are typically expected to adhere to ethics and standards laid out for medical interpreting. However, these standards conflict in part with the ethics, standards, protocols, requirements and professional culture of legal interpreting. For more information about these differences, see Unit 4.

- Australia is historically the world leader in community interpreting. The ethics and standards of the Australian Institute of Interpreters and Translators (AUSIT), which are available at www.ausit.org, apply to both general and community interpreting

- Within the U.S., national ethics and standards of practice for healthcare interpreting were published by the National Council on Interpreting in Health Care (www.ncihc.org). They have influenced the development of all sectors of community interpreting. The ethics and standards of of the California Healthcare Interpreting Association (www.chiaonline.org) are also influential.

UNIT 1

Common Guidelines

Examples of Principles from Interpreter Codes of Ethics and Standards of Practice Around the World (Bancroft 2004)

Confidentiality	Accuracy	Impartiality
Maintain strict confidentiality.	Be complete/interpret everything.	Maintain impartiality/neutrality.
Disclose only with client agreement or by law.	Be accurate.	Give no advice/recommendations.
Waive confidentiality in public settings.	Make no additions or omissions.	Insert no opinions, even if asked.
Offer no identifying details.	Retain fidelity to message/meaning.	Do not show feelings in face, gestures.
Adhere to confidentiality indefinitely.	Convey spirit of message.	Allow no influence of personal beliefs.
Professional Competence	Promptly disclose and rectify errors.	Decline or withdraw from assignments affecting impartiality.
Use first person.	Maintain language register.	Exert no influence on parties.
Accept no assignments if unqualified.	Interpret vulgar language, gestures.	Do not engage in side conversations.
If discovered incompetent, withdraw.	Interpret disturbing messages.	Do not give parties personal contact info.
Accurately represent qualifications.	Favor meaning over literal interpreting.	Do not drive client anywhere.
Prepare for assignments.	Interpret nonverbal cues.	Refrain from interpreting for known parties.
Consult dictionary as needed.	Interpreter interprets untruths.	Be unobtrusive/maintain low profile.
Confirm arrangements in advance.	Interpret insults to client.	Engage in no discrimination or prejudice.
Ask for pauses to manage flow.	Ask for clarification as needed.	Avoid stereotyping.
Ask parties to slow speech as needed.	Interpret within cultural context.	Make no referrals to third parties.
Maintain transparency.	**Professionalism**	**Compensation**
Adopt appropriate positioning.	Maintain high performance standards.	No additional fees.
Pre-Session	Honor integrity of self and profession.	No gifts, gratuities, benefits.
Hold pre-session with client, provider.	Be punctual or early.	May share gifts of food with colleagues.
Clarify interpreter roles.	Respect laws/legal requirements.	Charge fair, reasonable fees (if contractor).
Ask parties to speak to each other.	Be accountable for decision-making.	Pro bono services sometimes acceptable.
Ask parties to pause if needed.	Do not cancel without good cause.	Accept no assignments from clients.
State everything will be interpreted.	If canceling/delayed, notify promptly.	**Professional development**
Provide clear introduction.	Be polite, courteous and discreet.	Pursue professional development.
Interpreter Roles	Keep cell phones/audible beepers off.	Maintain contact with the language.
Be flexible: adapt to situation.	Bring/send no third parties to work.	Support development of colleagues.
Maintain appropriate positioning.	Remain until dismissed.	Incorporate research into practice.
May perform some advocacy.	Dress in appropriate attire.	**Professional solidarity**
May provide information & referral.	**Interpreter rights and well being**	Engage in professional solidarity/support.
If in conflict over role, withdraw.	Protect safety of interpreter.	Make no malicious remarks re: colleagues.
Report any advocacy to supervisor.	Practice self care.	Assist and support beginners.
Check for understanding.	Take break if too tired to interpret well.	Express respect for colleagues.
Do not interfere with provider roles.	**Client rights**	Promote the dignity of the profession.
Refer client questions to provider.	Do not exploit client trust.	**Conflict of Interest**
Do not answer client questions.	Respect gender needs/roles.	Avoid/declare conflict of interest.
Let provider explain forms.	Promote client self determination.	Withdraw if conflict of interest presents.
Do not practice dual roles.	Promote patient self-sufficiency.	Inform parties of conflict.

Ethics and Standards For Community Interpreters

Objective 1.2 (b) Discuss ethics and standards for community interpreters.

Three seminal sets of ethics and standards for medical interpreters have helped to shape the profession of community interpreting in the U.S. In order of publication, they are the ethics and standards published by:

- IMIA (International Medical Interpreters Association, which was then the Massachusetts Medical Interpreters Association). Code of ethics: 1987/2006. Standards of practice: 1995.
- CHIA (California Healthcare Interpreting Association): 2002.
- NCIHC (National Council on Interpreting in Health Care): ethics: 2004. Standards: 2005.

Because NCIHC published a *national* code of ethics and *national* standards of practice, they are the particular focus of Unit 1. The *National Code of Ethics for Interpreters in Health Care* is a detailed document with full commentary. For reasons of length and copyright it cannot be included here, but every interpreter should refer to a complete copy of that document. Until a national code of ethics is established for community interpreters, the authors urge community interpreters in the U.S. to adhere to and respect the NCIHC code of ethics and standards of practice while also closely studying those of IMIA and CHIA. (International readers of this manual whose country has not adopted national ethics or standards may also wish to study the IMIA, NCIHC and CHIA ethics and standards.) A summary of all three codes of ethics follows.

BASIC PRINCIPLES FROM THE NCIHC

The complete code of ethics with full commentary by NCIHC, together with the NCIHC Standards of Practice for Interpreters in Health Care, can be found at www.ncihc.org.

NATIONAL CODE OF ETHICS FOR INTERPRETERS IN HEALTH CARE

1. Confidentiality
2. Accuracy
3. Impartiality
4. Role Boundaries
5. Cultural Awareness
6. Respect
7. Advocacy
8. Professional Development
9. Professionalism

IMIA Code of Ethics
(Established in 1987 and revised in 2006)

Established in 1987 and revised in 2006, this code is available at www.imiaweb.org.

> 1. Interpreters will maintain confidentiality of all assignment-related information.
> 2. Interpreters will select the language and mode of interpretation that most accurately conveys the content and spirit of the messages of their clients.
> 3. Interpreters will refrain from accepting assignments beyond their professional skills, language fluency, or level of training.
> 4. Interpreters will refrain from accepting an assignment when family or close personal relationships affect impartiality.
> 5. Interpreters will not interject personal opinions or counsel patients.
> 6. Interpreters will not engage in interpretations that relate to issues outside the provision of health care services unless qualified to do so.
> 7. Interpreters will engage in patient advocacy and in the intercultural mediation role of explaining cultural differences/practices to health care providers and patients only when appropriate and necessary for communication purposes, using professional judgment.
> 8. Interpreters will use skillful unobtrusive interventions so as not to interfere with the flow of communication in a triadic medical setting.
> 9. Interpreters will keep abreast of their evolving languages and medical terminology.
> 10. Interpreters will participate in continuing education programs as available.
> 11. Interpreters will seek to maintain ties with relevant professional organizations in order to be up-to-date with the latest professional standards and protocols.
> 12. Interpreters will refrain from using their position to gain favors from clients.
>
> The IMIA was the first organization to author an ethical code of conduct specifically for medical interpreters. IMIA members uphold high standards of professionalism and ethical conduct for interpreters. At the core of this code of conduct are the twelve tenets above. These tenets are to be viewed holistically and as a guide to professional behavior. Members who do not adhere to the standards of practice or the code of ethics can be terminated.

CHIA Ethical Principles

In 2002, CHIA published *California Standards for Healthcare Interpreters: Ethical Principles, Protocols and Guidance on Roles & Intervention*. The following summary of ethical principles is taken from that document, available at www.chiaonline.org.

1. Confidentiality
Interpreters treat all information learned during the interpreting as confidential.

2. Impartiality
Interpreters are aware of the need to identify any potential or actual conflicts of interest, as well as any personal judgments, values, beliefs or opinions that may lead to preferential behavior or bias affecting the quality and accuracy of the interpreting performance.

3. Respect for individuals and their communities
Interpreters strive to support mutually respectful relationships between all three parties in the interaction (patient, provider and interpreter), while supporting the health and well being of the patient as the highest priority of all healthcare professionals.

4. Professionalism and integrity
Interpreters conduct themselves in a manner consistent with the professional standards and ethical principles of the healthcare interpreting profession.

5. Accuracy and completeness
Interpreters transmit the content, spirit and cultural context of the original message into the target language, making it possible for patient and provider to communicate effectively.

6. Cultural responsiveness
Interpreters seek to understand how diversity and cultural similarities and differences have a fundamental impact on the healthcare encounter. Interpreters play a critical role in identifying cultural issues and considering how and when to move to a cultural clarifier role. Developing cultural sensitivity and cultural responsiveness is a life-long process that begins with an introspective look at oneself.

Commentary on the NCIHC National Code of Ethics

The commentary below is by the authors and reflects and integrates other codes of ethics and standards of practice for interpreters around the world (Bancroft 2004). In addition, this commentary is intended to support all community interpreters, not only those who work in healthcare.

Introduction

Currently, in the U.S. and most other countries, there is no national code of ethics for community interpreters. The authors therefore urge community interpreters to support the NCIHC, IMIA and CHIA codes of ethics (or those codes of ethics available in the interpreter's country). The NCIHC, IMIA and CHIA ethics and standards taken together support and complement each other. All three sets of ethics and standards are invaluable even for those interpreters who work in non-healthcare settings such as schools or social services.

The NCIHC code of ethics was the result of a long national process. During that process, focus groups across the country were consulted, 2,500 copies of a survey about the draft code were distributed (about 500 were returned), ethicists, researchers, policymakers, trainers, lawyers, interpreter service coordinators and others were consulted, and the voices and comments of hundreds of interpreters and their supporters were addressed in the final published document, which is possibly the most sophisticated code of ethics available for interpreters anywhere in the world. The depth and breadth of its approach to ethics merit careful study and reflection.

Thus, the nine principles below, two of which are controversial both within and outside the U.S., represent perhaps some of the highest-level thinking carried out in community interpreting anywhere in the world. All community interpreters should study the complete document, available at www.ncihc.org.

Confidentiality

The interpreter treats as confidential, within the treating team, all information learned in the performance of their professional duties, while observing relevant requirements regarding disclosures.

Importance of confidentiality. The ethical principle of confidentiality helps to ensure that no information revealed by the interpreter becomes public information that could identify the client or provider. By breaking confidentiality you may violate trust and could harm both your reputation and the organization's. Confidentiality is extended to any private matters concerning the organization. Confidentiality is to be respected indefinitely.

Breaking confidentiality. Always safeguard information shared in an interpreted session or during the course of the interpreter's professional duties that could identify the client without consent except under the following conditions:

- You may break confidentiality if required by law (e.g., if you receive a subpoena to testify in court, you *might* be required to testify but should contact a lawyer immediately to make the determination). Try always to consult with an attorney before testifying in court about an interpreted encounter.
- Depending on state reporting requirements, you may be required to report suspicion of child abuse or vulnerable adult abuse and imminent danger of suicide or homicide. You may consult a supervisor or call your state or municipal Department of Social Services to verify.
- In many cases, you may share information with other staff members who are also bound by confidentiality and who serve the same client if that information is (a) relevant to the service being provided and (b) to the client's benefit for the interpreter to share.
- If *all identifying details are removed*, you may share stories at professional in-services, trainings and other educational events for interpreters.

State-by-state requirements. In a number of states, interpreters are mandated to report child abuse or the suspicion of child abuse, even if it means breaking confidentiality. For a discussion of this issue and to learn in which states interpreters may be "mandated reporters," see information published by the National Health Law Program, "Interpreters: Are They Mandatory Reporters of Child Abuse?" available at www.healthlaw.org. Note that similar laws may apply to reporting elder abuse, harm to oneself or harm to others.

Accuracy

The interpreter strives to render the message accurately, conveying the content and spirit of the original message, taking into consideration the cultural context.

This principle requires you to:
- Transmit the tone of voice, expressivity and context of the message.
- Consider the intent behind the message.
- Where appropriate, assess the speaker's body language.
- Communicate cultural content.
- Interpret casual remarks.
- Interpret negative, rude or obscene comments or gestures.

Rude or obscene language. It may be extremely difficult for community interpreters to interpret everything that is said, and this is especially true if one party is angry or uses offensive language. However, interpreting the whole message, including its meaning and intent, is a strict requirement in virtually all areas of interpreting. Nothing in the message should be added, omitted or changed. If the language is rough, interpret it "as is." However, since literal equivalents are not commonly found for curse words and other offensive language, the interpreter will need to find equivalents that are equally rude or offensive.

If you don't know the "bad words" in both languages, here are a few suggestions:
- Ask other interpreters.
- Purchase a specialized dictionary. An increasing number of bilingual dictionaries and glossaries for slang and obscene language are available in many languages (and there are several such dictionaries for Spanish-English alone).
- An increasing number of bilingual glossaries for offensive language are also becoming available online
- Phone applications of all kinds of glossaries are increasingly available, so you may wish to try them as well.
- Build your own bilingual glossary of "bad words" and study them.

Exactness. Many interpreters feel that the interpreter should interpret "everything that is said, exactly as it is said." Technically that is not possible. However, you should make every effort to do so. The effort to be exact will increase the precision of your interpreting. Give it your best.

Rambling clients. Many untrained interpreters find it acceptable to cut off a client who rambles. Such interpreters often summarize a long answer. *Summarizing, however, is not acceptable*, except as a last resort. Otherwise, interpret everything that is said (no matter how irrelevant it may seem) and let the provider decide to cut short a conversation. Otherwise, you are put in the position of deciding which information is important for the other party to hear, and which information is not important. The interpreter is neither qualified nor authorized to make those decisions.

Summarizing: Exceptions to the rule. On rare occasions, as a last resort, you may have to summarize. Examples include:

- Emergency situations, such as a hospital emergency room, a 911 distress call, a fire or emergency work with the Red Cross.

- When too many people speak at once.

- When a client is incoherent (e.g., due to mental illness, dementia or inebriation).

- If a client speaks too quickly and refuses to be interrupted, and simultaneous mode is not fast enough to keep up.

There may be other extreme exceptions. Before resorting to summarization, however, first try switching to simultaneous mode. Consider summarizing an absolute last resort, and note that summarization is prohibited in legal interpreting (whether inside or outside the courtroom).

Interpreter errors: If you make an error, correct it as soon as you realize the mistake was made.

Impartiality

The interpreter strives to maintain impartiality and refrains from counseling, advising or projecting personal biases or beliefs.

Neutrality. Impartiality means that the interpreter will remain unprejudiced, fair and nonjudgmental in his or her behavior. You are a human being, however, and therefore you have feelings. You are biased. That said, impartiality in your behavior combined with the conscious decision to be non-judgmental helps to promote accurate interpreting and successful communication.

Striving for impartiality means that you should:

- Insert no personal opinions or advice, even if asked to do so.
- Accept that you have feelings and you are not neutral, but strive to keep personal feelings from influencing the emotional affect, content or tone of your interpreting.
- Reflect the emotions of the speaker in your voice and demeanor, not your own feelings.
- Declare any conflict of interest, or even the appearance of a conflict.
- If strong feelings about a certain issue affect your impartiality, declare the problem and decline or withdraw from the assignment, even if all parties urge you to stay.
- Decline any assignment where you feel your impartiality cannot be maintained due to strong personal bias, beliefs or relationships.

Non-judgmental attitude. It is important not to allow your biases to temper your respect for all parties present. Everyone is the interpreted encounter, like you, is human, and therefore worthy of your respect. To the extent that you deliberately adopt a non-judgmental attitude, you will find that the neutrality of your behavior is easier to maintain. Feeling less internal emotion will also enhance your ability to focus on interpreting accurately and well. If you are unable to maintain a non-judgmental attitude, you should withdraw.

Conflicts of interest. In the event of a conflict of interest, decline the assignment, withdraw from the session, or allow the parties to decide what to do.

If you enter the room and realize that you know the client in a personal way, follow these steps:

a) Inform all present that there is a conflict of interest and state it clearly.

b) Offer to withdraw.

c) If, and only if, all parties present urge you to stay, and you feel certain that you can interpret for all present with complete impartiality, you may remain and interpret the session. (For legal interpreting, simply withdraw politely.)

However, be aware that the client may not really want you to stay but does not dare to cause difficulties or hard feelings by telling you to go. Try to be sensitive to what is best for the client and provider, not for you.

Often, interpreters believe that if they maintain a professional demeanor, a client they know personally will feel comfortable. This is not always true. Many clients will not say they are ill at ease, but your presence will hinder their ability to fully discuss their concerns with the providers.

Role Boundaries

The interpreter maintains the boundaries of the professional role, refraining from personal involvement.

Maintaining boundaries. In general, even bilingual employees *should not conduct their regular job while interpreting.* In other words, during an interpreted session a bilingual employee may act either as an interpreter *or* as a caseworker (or nurse, social worker, parent-teacher liaison, receptionist, etc.), but <u>not both at the same time.</u> To perform one's job while interpreting blurs professional roles, erodes boundaries and leads to potential conflicts of interest. It is also difficult if not impossible to concentrate on interpreting accurately while performing in another role.

Avoid personal involvement. In addition, bilingual employees and community interpreters often develop close ties with clients. In some cases interpreters are even expected to accompany clients to their next appointments, drive them to other services and support clients outside regular working hours. This type of personal involvement is damaging for the interpreter's role boundaries and can undermine impartiality. Strive to establish and maintain appropriate professional boundaries and, if you are a bilingual employee, educate your workplace about the reasons why boundaries are important for interpreters.

Role boundaries and colleagues. If you are a bilingual employee who interprets, your colleagues may know nothing about interpreting. They may therefore not understand why you cannot answer questions during an interpreted session or otherwise "help out" as usual. That's how they know you: you are a colleague. As a result, you may have to explain to them beforehand that during the interpreted session you will not be able to act as their colleague but only as their interpreter because you must adhere to professional interpreter ethics and standards of practice while interpreting. Ask them to choose if they would like you present as an interpreter or as a colleague (e.g. as a case manager, co-therapist, teaching assistant) because you cannot perform both types of work at the same time. Inform them that interpreting involves highly complex, demanding skills that take up an immense amount of the interpreter's concentration. Then let them decide if they will need to bring in someone else to interpret so that you can continue to assist them in your primary role.

Guidelines. In general:

- Decline gifts, except where organizational policy dictates a specific gift policy.
- Refrain from socializing with clients.
- Refrain from making purchases from clients (handcrafts, foods, etc.).
- Refrain from touching clients except in special circumstances (e.g., prior to life-threatening surgery, at the death of a family member, or when acting no longer as an interpreter but a bilingual employee who is permitted to touch clients for specific reasons, for example, a bilingual nurse or physical therapist).
- Refrain from performing unnecessary services for clients.
- Refrain from performing services for clients that they are able to perform for themselves.
- If appropriate and permitted, bilingual employees may refer clients as needed to relevant human and social services. (Most contract interpreters, however, should not engage in referral services. The issues of legal liability both for you and for the interpreter agency are potentially serious, and there may be other legal concerns.)

In addition, engage in no sexual contact of any kind with clients or clients' families.

Gifts. Grateful clients often offer gifts to interpreters. Some organizations allow their employees, including bilingual employees, to accept gifts. A policy that gifts of food may be accepted if shared with all employees may seem like a harmless policy. However, in reality, any gifts from clients to interpreters can cause problems.

Factors to consider:

- Can low-income clients really afford to offer gifts?
- If you accept a gift, are you sending the message, "All interpreters should be given gifts"?
- If you provide an even bigger service, will the client who gave you a gift in the past think s/he must bring a bigger gift this time?
- If the gift is food, can you be certain it was prepared under appropriate sanitary conditions?
- Are you really impartial after a client has given you a gift?
- In giving you something, will the client expect something extra in return?

If, for any reason, the interpreter feels compelled to accept a gift (for example, when cultural norms make refusing gifts appear to be an insult), the interpreter should state firmly that it is a duty to provide competent interpreting for no additional compensation or reward. In no case will the community interpreter accept money from any client or from any companion of a client but only from the organization, typically in the form of remuneration for work performed (which may be a salary in the case of bilingual employees).

Both the authors have been offered gifts from clients who clearly expected some "additional service" that was not ethically acceptable. Be careful.

Organizational gift policies. Gift policies should be dictated by the employer, but the interpreter can make the employer aware that most professional interpreter ethics discourage accepting gifts. If you are a bilingual employee who finds it difficult to decline gifts for cultural reasons or because you fear causing the client offense, and your organization permits gifts from clients, here is a solution: sit down with a supervisor, explain the problem, and ask the organization to adopt a special no-gifts policy for bilingual employees who interpret

What to Say When Declining a Gift. Remember, the client wants to show gratitude. Thank the client graciously for his or her kindness, emphasize that you are already paid to interpret, and then (if it seems helpful) add a kind and culturally appropriate remark, such as "Helping you is my reward." At that point, *offer another way for the client to show gratitude* without giving you a gift. For example, the grateful client could:
- Let a supervisor know that the interpreting service is helpful.
- Write a thank you note to the agency.
- Donate the gift to a nonprofit that helps families.
- Consider volunteering for others.
- Spread the word that this agency offers interpreters at no charge.
- Let other LEP residents know they have the right to an interpreter at no charge in public services.

Cultural Awareness

The interpreter continually strives to develop awareness of his/her own and other (including biomedical) cultures encountered in the performance of their professional duties.

Controversy. While most codes of ethics and standards of practice around the world do not include or address cultural awareness, most interpreters recognize that in order to interpret accurately, they must know and take into account the cultural context. The controversy arises over whether the interpreter is permitted to articulate that knowledge during the encounter if a cultural barrier arises. In the U.S., the community interpreter is permitted to do so.

Risks of inappropriate involvement. It is one thing to develop cultural awareness, and another thing altogether to provide cultural information. The risks of providing cultural information to either the provider or client are so high that in some countries, including Canada, community and general interpreters are prohibited from performing cultural mediation. (This issue is addressed in detail in Unit 3 of this manual.)

Cultural competence. The community interpreter strives to embody the highest degrees of cultural competence and respect for all. Recognizing your central role in mediating communication between parties of different cultures, you should make every effort to:
- Develop cultural awareness.
- Model cultural sensitivity.
- Examine your own cultural biases and attitudes, recognizing that all of us harbor such biases.
- Allow no bias, belief or subjective feelings to color the work of interpreting.
- Display no personal cultural beliefs while interpreting.
- Practice transparency (make certain that everyone present understands what the interpreter is doing and feels included, not excluded).
- Use cultural knowledge to promote mutual respect among all parties.

Any act of mediation, including advocacy (see below), should take into consideration:
- The culture of the client's native country/region, religion, ethnic group.
- The organizational and professional culture of the agency providing a service (e.g., biomedical culture or the culture of domestic violence services, public libraries, K-12 schools, etc.).
- The client's literacy and education level.
- The degree of the client's cultural assimilation.
- Cultural gender differences.
- The culture of the region where the service is provided (e.g., rural, urban, mid-western, southern).

Respect

The interpreter treats all parties with respect.

The rationale for respect. Treating all parties with respect is central to the work of the community interpreter. It is important to recall that in many areas of life, the LEP client may have been insulted, hurt or humiliated due to racial prejudice and anti-immigrant bias. Clients report that even an accent seems to invite discrimination.

Therefore, it is vital to help establish an atmosphere of trust that helps to ensure that the client will provide information openly and honestly so that the best quality of services can be provided. To help accomplish this, the interpreter should display and model respect. Sometimes it may also be helpful to explain cultural indicators of respect to providers and administrators. It is not unusual, for example, to hear a young doctor or other service provider address an older LEP client by his or her first name. In many cultures using a first name among strangers is shockingly rude behavior. Sometimes a provider may touch a client when doing may be culturally offensive. (For example, in many cultures a number of women do not shake hands with men.)

The provider is often unaware that he or she is acting disrespectfully. Many providers welcome information from interpreters about where to find cultural information to learn helpful ways to interact beneficially with clients from other cultures. Such resources, however, are best communicated outside the session during a pre-conference (discussed in Unit 2). Be careful to refer providers to trusted resources that do not make cultural overgeneralizations or promote stereotypes.

Client trust. Respect promotes trust. Without trust, clients may withhold critical information or fail to follow through on a treatment plan or service delivery plan. They may not adhere to follow-up instructions or provider recommendations, jeopardizing their access to a needed service. Many LEP clients have left a service after an encounter with a rude provider (or with a rude interpreter) saying, "I will *never* go back." The interpreter can help to prevent such events from taking place.

Client autonomy. There are many ways to show respect—or lack of respect. An interpreter who helps out clients, even after work hours, often behaves in condescending ways without realizing it. Even if the interpreter has a big heart, it is important to allow clients to do for themselves what they can. Respect for the client's autonomy allows clients to acquire the skills they need to function independently in the U.S., develop self-sufficiency and eventually thrive in their new culture. Keep in mind that most western cultures value independence and promote self sufficiency.

Displaying respect. Here are a few simple examples of ways that interpreters can show respect to both clients and providers:

- Greet the client using a culturally appropriate title or formula.
- Show that you are listening attentively to all parties.
- Pay attention to turn-taking.
- Note how body language can influence a client's trust.
- Smile and show warmth when you are not interpreting. (When you are interpreting, let your face and body language model the emotions of the speaker for whom you are interpreting.)
- Use your introduction to display a respectful, kind demeanor.
- During your introduction, address any issues that might help to show respect, e.g., "You may see me taking notes, but only to help me be accurate. I'll destroy my notes before I leave this building out of respect for your privacy and confidentiality."

Advocacy

When the patient's health, well-being, or dignity is at risk, the interpreter may be justified in acting as an advocate. Advocacy is understood as an action taken on behalf of an individual that goes beyond facilitating communication, with the intention of supporting good health outcomes. Advocacy must only be undertaken after careful and thoughtful analysis of the situation and if other less intrusive actions have not resolved.

The need for advocacy. Community interpreters in the U.S. (and in some other countries, such as Belgium and Switzerland) are not required to limit their work to interpreting the content of a message but may, as needed, provide mediation to remove cultural and institutional obstacles to communication, or to support equal access to services.

Mediation refers to any act or utterance of the interpreter that goes beyond interpreting and is intended to address barriers to communication or service delivery. Advocacy is a form of mediation, and it is addressed in Unit 3 of this manual.

It is critical to note that advocacy is the *riskiest and least practiced form of mediation*. Few interpreters clearly understand what advocacy is, and therefore how to practice it safely. Advocacy is explicitly prohibited for community interpreters in Canada's *National Standards Guide for Community Interpreting Services* (Healthcare Interpretation Network, 2009). Advocacy may require the interpreter to address:

- An unresolved communication barrier (e.g., at the end of a medical appointment, the interpreter feels sure that the patient has no real understanding about the pre-surgery instructions).
- Discrimination against LEP clients.
- A lack of understanding by the client about important next steps.
- A client's fear or lack of trust.
- Any other barrier that may hinder clients' access to services.
- Any other problem that is potentially injurious to the client's health, safety or well being.

Institutional barriers. Interpreter advocacy is often considered a particular form of mediation that focuses on overcoming institutional barriers to services. Confusion surrounds the issue of whether the interpreter who advocates is biased. The profession takes a larger view: the interpreter is biased only in the direction of striving to facilitate communication and promoting equal access to services to support the beneficial outcomes sought by providers and clients. The interpreter should never express, or act on, bias toward a particular individual or institution.

Risks of advocacy. Experts in the profession agree that advocacy should never be undertaken lightly. Advocacy involves many risks: for the client, the interpreter and the institution. Before engaging in advocacy, seek guidance from a supervisor or from other interpreters. Try to find appropriate mechanisms within the institution through which to pursue advocacy.

Safest form advocacy. Sometimes simple solutions are the safest. To practice "safe advocacy," simply report any critical incident to the relevant supervisor.

Client autonomy. It is sometimes stated that if the client does not wish the interpreter to act on his or her behalf, the interpreter should do not do so. (E.g., do not file a civil rights complaint with the Office of Civil Rights on behalf of a client without his or her permission.) However, you always free to report a critical incident to the appropriate supervisor. Indeed, if a health or service outcome is at risk, it is *your* decision whether or not to report it, not the client's, as both the agency and the interpreter have legal liability to consider, among other factors.

Professional development

The interpreter strives to continually further his/her knowledge and skills.

Strategies for professional development. Community interpreters will pursue opportunities to increase their knowledge, skills and understanding of languages, interpreting and culture. Interpreters should maintain language skills, including the ability to render register accurately in either language (from formal to slang), by reading, monitoring radio or television shows, conversing with others who speak the language, attending language conferences, teaching the language (e.g., at community colleges or for faith-based organizations) and in other practical ways. As the field of interpreting evolves, interpreters should continue their professional education in various ways, for example:

- Courses and seminars.
- In-services for interpreters.
- Conferences.
- Professional associations.
- Books, periodicals and other literature.
- Glossaries and dictionaries (whether in print, online, electronic or in phone applications).
- Courses on related subjects such as intercultural communication, sociolinguistics, medical terminology or language access laws.
- Self-help materials, e.g. interpreting manuals and practice CDs.
- DVDs about interpreting.
- Websites and Internet resources.

Information about a number of resources for professional development can be found in the resources section of this book.

UNIT 1

JUST SAY NO!

Professionalism—An Ethical Challenge

(Accept no assignment for which you are not qualified.)

Professionalism

The interpreter must at all times act in a professional and ethical manner.

The community interpreter will exhibit utmost professionalism in appearance, manner and conduct. You should also strive to respect the highest standards of professional competence for language proficiency, interpreting skill and communication. To achieve this:

- Decline any assignment for which you are not qualified.
- Prepare for assignments.
- Correctly represent your qualifications.
- Maintain a pace or flow which promotes successful interpreting.
- Check for understanding as needed to ensure communication.

> **How to Decline a Request Professionally**
>
> 1. Decline graciously: I honestly wish I could help out because I can see how important this is for the client and I know it's time sensitive.
>
> 2. Give an alternative: However, I think it will be much safer for you to [e.g., call a legal interpreter, call a telephone interpreter, or ask Houda down the hall].
>
> 3. Give reasons: I really don't know the kind of terminology for this assignment, and I don't think my skills are up to it. If anything bad happens because the client didn't understand or I interpreted the wrong information, the agency would be legally liable for my mistakes, and so would I.

Bilingual employees and freelance community interpreters who are asked to perform interpreting or translation for which they are not qualified shall respectfully decline to do so. However, bilingual employees are frequently asked to perform written translation. *If you decline to perform the translation and a supervisor or colleague insists you do it, make clear that <u>the ethics of the profession require interpreters to decline assignments for which they are not qualified.</u>*

> **Other examples of professionalism include:**
>
> • Be punctual or early. Plan to arrive at least 15 minutes ahead of the appointed time.
> • Dress appropriately. Formal dress is encouraged. At a minimum, "business casual" dress code should be respected.
> • Be courteous and amicable.
> • Cancel with proper notice and only when truly necessary.
> • Accurately represent one's credentials (e.g., do not call yourself certified after training unless you are court-certified or certified by a government or professional body).

UNIT 1

Core Values

The NCIHC National Code of Ethics also makes reference to the core values that underlie this code of ethics. They are:

1. *Beneficence. The interpreter seeks to support the health and well being of the patient and her/his family and community and to do no harm.*

2. *Fidelity. Interpreters remain faithful to the original message.*

3. *Respect for the importance of culture and cultural differences. First, interpreters must understand the cultural context of a message to grasp its meaning and interpreter it accurately. Second, the interpreter must always be aware how cultural differences of perspective and worldview can lead to critical miscommunication that could have an adverse impact on the encounter and its outcome.*

Purpose of Interpreting

According to NCIHC:

> *The purpose of interpreting is to enable communication between two or more individuals who do not speak each other's languages.*

This purpose statement from NCIHC guides the ethics and practice of community interpreting in the U.S. The purpose of *enabling communication* distinguishes medical (and by extension community) interpreting from other areas such as conference or legal interpreting.

Community interpreters must constantly monitor the flow of communication to help all parties present understand each other. This is a complex task. As we will see, the need to monitor the quality and success of communication influences every aspect of the community interpreter's conduct and practice.

UNIT 1

Applying Ethics

Objective 1.2 (c) Develop strategies to apply ethical principles in real-life settings.

When a situation arises that is not a clear "textbook" case of ethics, it is not always clear what the interpreter should do. For example, you are alone with the client and the client confesses that she has committed a serious crime. She adds hastily, "But don't tell anyone." What would you do?

The answer will depend on a number of factors beyond confidentiality. There is no one answer that is "right." The interpreter does not have to imagine every problem that can arise. Instead, the interpreter should know the appropriate code of ethics well, understand his or her own values and learn how to integrate ethics and values in any individual situation. The interpreter should also consider the core values of the NCIHC code: beneficence (to promote a good outcome); fidelity (to preserve the accuracy of the message) and respect.

> *The community interpreter must always look carefully at the question of how to apply professional interpreter ethics, skills and standards to the real world of the community interpreter.*

Ethical Guidelines

Confidentiality

Question: If a client shares information with me in a waiting area and asks me not to disclose it to the provider, what should I do? (E.g., A patient says, "I have HIV, but don't tell the doctor!")

Answer: There is no simple answer to this question. However, most experts (including NCIHC) agree on the first step: *try to have the client disclose this information to the provider*. If the client refuses, NCIHC urges the interpreter to balance the value of beneficence with the interpreter's right to provide relevant information to the "treating team" (the team of healthcare professionals and staff who provide services to the patient, typically within a single institution). In particular, if the client's disclosure may affect the outcome or the patient's safety or well being, even if the client does not want to share that information with the doctor or nurse, the correct course of action for the interpreter may be to disclose that information. However, such a decision may be difficult for the interpreter and may involve personal conscience and values that go beyond professional ethics.

Question: If clients often disclose personal information to me, can I ask them in advance not to do so?

Answer: Yes. During introductions, for example, or a pre-session, you may emphasize that everything said during the session will be interpreted and that no information should be shared if anyone does not want you to interpret it. If a client approaches you outside the encounter you may also add (if desired) that you may be obligated to share with the provider any important information heard outside the encounter. However, try not to be alone with clients outside the interpreted session unless you are a bilingual employee. (If you are a legal interpreter, do not speak with clients outside the courtroom or the attorney's office. Direct the client immediately back to the relevant attorney or court staff.)

Question: If I have to make an ethical decision on the spot, and later feel I made an error, what should I do?

Answer: Sit down with a supervisor at the interpreter agency or at your workplace to discuss the incident. Then plan together how to proceed if similar situations arise.

Question: If I live in a state where interpreters are mandated to disclose suspicions of child abuse or vulnerable adult abuse—does that mean I should also report domestic violence?

Answer: No. Typically there is *no legal obligation* to report domestic violence if minors are not involved, if there is no *imminent* danger and if disclosing may be a violation of interpreter confidentiality. Such laws may change, however, and if the client's safety is a concern, the interpreter *may* be permitted to disclose such information to the team that works directly with the client. This is a "gray zone" of confidentiality where you will have to consider client safety issues, legal concerns, core values, and your own conscience. In general, bilingual employees are usually permitted to discuss sensitive issues with colleagues who provide services to the same client.

UNIT 1

ACCURACY

Question: If the client doesn't understand the provider's language, why can't I simplify it?

Answer: Simplifying the provider's language (lowering the register) is unethical and dangerous. If you are not a doctor or teacher or social worker (etc.) you may make a very serious error that could compromise the service. Even if you *are* a doctor or service provider, you are not the provider for this client, only the interpreter, and you have no right to make decisions about what information is important and how to convey it. If you are worried about the client not understanding the provider, instead of lowering register you can simply say, "Excuse me, as the interpreter I'm concerned the information I am interpreting isn't clear. Perhaps if you rephrase in simpler language, I can interpret it clearly." This technique is discussed in Unit 3.

Question: Should I interpret body language?

Answer: Yes, if body language, tone of voice or gestures contribute to the meaning of the message. Interpret gestures and other body language only if their meaning would otherwise be missed or lost. (Note that in legal interpreting, body language should not be interpreted or addressed. See Unit 4 for more information about legal interpreting.)

Question: Do I *really* have to interpret the "bad words"?

Answer: Yes. Study them. Memorize them. Interpret them. Do not omit them.

Question: What if the language is so offensive that I just can't bring myself to interpret it?

Answer: Withdraw from the session.

Question: What if the provider or client says something racist or bigoted? If I interpret something like that, won't it cause a big problem?

Answer: There is some controversy on this issue. First, if the language is intentionally bigoted or mean, interpret it. On the other hand, if the person (usually the provider) is not trying to be offensive and does not appear to realize the possible distress or offense that might be caused to the client, opinion is divided. Some experts say: simply interpret what is said. Others feel the interpreter should provide a cultural mediation and point out to the speaker the possible impact of such talk, offering the speaker an opportunity to rephrase. Complex issues of this kind are discussed in Units 3 and 5. When in doubt, <u>*interpret what is said*</u>.

UNIT 1

Question: If the provider asks the client a question and the client rambles on and on about unrelated matters, can't I just cut it short?

Answer: No. Telling the client to "get to the point" is the provider's job. The interpreter must interpret everything, no matter how long the client rambles.

IMPARTIALITY

Question: If I'm a bilingual employee and part of my job is to counsel the client or give advice, can I still do that when I interpret?

Answer: No. Not during the session. When you interpret, you take off your other "hat" (e.g., social worker, nurse, income support specialist, clerical staff, caseworker or parent-teacher liaison) and put on the interpreter hat. During an interpreted encounter, you cannot advise the client. Only the provider may do so.

Question: Being impartial seems a bit cold. Do I have to be so distant?

Answer: No. You can be both friendly and professional. As long as you adhere to the ethics of impartiality and do not allow your personal feelings, opinions or judgments to influence the encounter, you may display kindness, warmth and empathy at appropriate moments, e.g., during introductions and at the end of the session.

UNIT 1

ROLE BOUNDARIES

Question: What if my workplace expects me to do things that involve being an interpreter and performing other tasks for LEP clients?

Answer: There are three issues here. First, you may have to educate you colleagues about the professional role of the interpreter. Second, the ethics of interpreting require you to remain within the interpreter role while interpreting. Third, outside the session, as the interpreter you are often expected to perform tasks (such as health education) for which you have never been trained and for which you may have no professional qualifications. Although this situation is common, it is unacceptable for an interpreter to perform a provider's role without the appropriate training and qualifications. During the session, simply interpret. Outside the session, politely decline all tasks for which you are not trained, qualified and competent.

> **Remember: the job of the interpreter is to interpret.** Declining a request does not indicate disrespect or rudeness. Staying within your role boundaries protects you, the client and your agency from legal liability.

Question: How do I know if I'm working against client autonomy or patient self-determination?

Answer: There is a simple rule of thumb to protect client autonomy. Decline to do anything for a client that the client can do for him- or herself.

Question: If a client sees me in the street or at the market and wants to chat, what should I do?

Answer: Try to avoid a conversation. A quick, friendly "fly-by" greeting may suffice.

Question: What if the client is in my church (or mosque or temple)?

Answer: Try to avoid social contact. If that is not possible, you may have to clarify your professional role and ethical obligations to the client. Otherwise, decline further interpreting assignments for that client and make sure the client understands that confidentiality is respected indefinitely (forever).

UNIT 1

Cultural Awareness/Cultural Competence

Question: Why is cultural mediation (also known as culture brokering, intercultural mediation, cultural interpreting, etc.) forbidden in other areas of interpreting, like legal and conference interpreting?

Answer: Many risks arise when you address cultural barriers. Except for advocacy, which is rarely practiced, cultural mediation is probably the single most complex skill for community interpreters. It may take years to master. Many experts question the wisdom of allowing interpreters to address culture while interpreting. For example, in Canada, national standards of practice for community interpreters published in 2007 explicitly prohibit community interpreters from performing culture brokering (cultural mediation) because interpreting specialists in Canada saw so many community interpreters perform inappropriate cultural mediation. This decision was not made lightly and reflects a national concern about the risks. In general, most community interpreters receive little training on cultural mediation, making it difficult for them to execute it effectively.

RESPECT

Question: If I use an informal type of address (such as calling an adult "*tu*" in Spanish or French or using his or her first name) in daily life, why can't I do so when I interpret?

Answer: Using the informal mode of address or first name undermines role boundaries and impartiality. Except for children, keep a respectful distance and use the formal ways of addressing a client.

One last question...

QUESTION: If I am a bilingual employee or a volunteer, should I also respect the ethics and standards of practice for professional interpreters?

ANSWER: <u>Yes</u>. *If you interpret in any community setting, whether you are a bilingual staff member, a volunteer or a contract interpreter, <u>respect the ethics and standards of practice appropriate for community interpreters in your own country</u>.*

THE COMMUNITY INTERPRETER

UNIT 1

REVIEW

UNIT 1 REVIEW EXERCISES

The Interpreting Profession

Circle one answer.

1. Community interpreters usually perform:
   - (a) Medical interpreting.
   - (b) Social services interpreting.
   - (c) Interpreting in schools.
   - (d) Any or all of the above.

2. Community interpreters most often work:
   - (a) For big companies.
   - (b) As telephone interpreters.
   - (c) In health, education or human service settings.
   - (d) In the courts.

3. National certification exists for:
   - (a) Community interpreters.
   - (b) Conference interpreters.
   - (c) Business interpreters.
   - (d) Medical interpreters.

4. An adjunct or dual role interpreter is:
   - (a) A full-time staff interpreter.
   - (b) A medical interpreter.
   - (c) A bilingual employee who also interprets.
   - (d) None of the above.

History of Interpreting

When was the profession of interpreting in general first established?
_____

In what nation was the profession of community interpreting first born, and when?
_____

When did community interpreting emerge as a profession in the U.S.?
_____

What driving forces shaped the profession?
_____

Are there any international standards for community interpreting?
_____

UNIT 1

Qualifications and Skills

Decide whether each point below represents a "qualification" (Q) or a "skill" (S) and identify them by writing "Q" or "S" beside each of the following points:

Hold a certificate for professional interpreter training, at least 40 hours. _____
Adhere to relevant ethics and standards _____
Interpret with approximate accuracy _____
Be 18 years or older. _____
Hold a high school diploma or equivalent. _____
Interpret 2-3 sentences without requesting repetition. _____
Demonstrate bilingualism and literacy. _____
Interpret in first person. _____

What are the minimal qualifications for community interpreters?
_____
_____
_____

What are the minimal skills required to perform community interpreting?
_____
_____
_____

Why should bilingual staff and all other community interpreters be tested to see if they are truly proficient in both languages?
_____
_____
_____

What may happen if someone who is not truly proficient in a language interprets in that language?
_____
_____
_____

THE COMMUNITY INTERPRETER

UNIT 1

Interpreter Certification

1. List three basic types of interpreter certification:
_____
_____
_____

2. If you successfully complete a 40-hour interpreter training, are you a certified interpreter? Why or why not?
_____
_____
_____

3. In what state(s) are community interpreters certified by the state government?
_____

4. Give the names of two national medical interpreter certification programs.
_____
_____

5. If you are not certified, but you hold a certificate of successful completion for an interpreter training program of 40 hours or more, how should you describe your qualifications?
_____

UNIT 1

Language Access Laws

1. What does "LEP" stand for?
   _____

Circle one answer:

2. Who makes language access laws?
   - (a) The federal government.
   - (b) Some state governments.
   - (c) Some local governments.
   - (d) All of the above.

3. A language access law
   - (a) Helps improve the access of LEP clients to government-funded services.
   - (b) Prohibits posting signs in English in certain neighborhoods.
   - (c) Requires the use of English in legal and other settings.
   - (d) None of the above.

4. Why is it important for an interpreter to know about Title VI?
   _____
   _____
   _____

UNIT 1

Self Monitoring and Self-Assessment

Listen to the recording you made in class or record yourself while you interpret a text or scripted dialogue from your workbook. (Do not interrupt the recording at any time.) Then, from the following list, put a checkmark beside those points that seem to describe your own performance.

1. My delivery was smooth.
2. Sometimes I stumbled or hesitated. ✓
3. I interpreted with overall accuracy.
4. I omitted some words. ✓
5. I added some words that weren't in the original text.
6. I changed the meaning of some words.
7. I captured the spirit and emotion of the speaker. ✓
8. I interpreted in a neutral voice (instead of conveying the speaker's tone).
9. My interpreting reflected the meaning of the message. ✓
10. My accent was easy to understand. ✓
11. My accent may need some work.
12. I felt at ease in both languages. ✓
13. I found one language much easier than the other.
14. I felt confident.
15. I felt nervous and somewhat insecure. ✓
16. My performance was professional.

Now look at all the points you checked off. What do they tell you about your own performance—your strengths and weaknesses, and the areas in which you may need to improve?

_____
_____
_____

UNIT 1

Ethics and Standards

Answer the following questions:

1. What is a code of ethics?
   _____
   _____
   _____
   _____

2. What are standards of practice?
   _____
   _____
   _____

3. Describe the differences between a code of ethics and standards of practice.
   _____
   _____
   _____

4. Give five principles from a code of ethics for interpreters:
   _____
   _____
   _____

UNIT 1

Applying Ethics

Write "true or false" beside each statement.

1. A code of ethics lays down rules to help the interpreter know right from wrong in professional situations. _____

2. It is acceptable for an interpreter to accept a gold bracelet from a grateful client. _____

3. Ethical situations are always simple and clear (right or wrong). _____

4. Standards represent the strictest rules of a profession. _____

5. If a client tells the interpreter privately that she is a victim of domestic violence, the interpreter is required to report this. _____

6. Where possible, the interpreter should try to avoid being left alone with the client to discourage the sharing of private information from the client. _____

7. If the provider is speaking at a high register, in words that the client may not understand, the interpreter may simplify the language. _____

8. Community interpreters in the U.S. should adhere to the NCIHC Code of Ethics. _____

9. The interpreter may use informal modes of address (such as *tu* in Spanish or French, or a client's first name) for clients he or she sees on a regular basis and feels comfortable with. _____

10. There are international standards of practice for medical interpreters. _____

UNIT 2
INTERPRETER SKILLS

Unit 2 Objectives

OBJECTIVE 2.1
Execute an interpreted session.
2.1 (a) List the steps to execute an interpreted session.
2.1 (b) Discuss and select appropriate modes of interpreting.
2.1 (c) Practice interpreting in consecutive and simultaneous modes.
2.1 (d) Demonstrate basic sight translation skills.

OBJECTIVE 2.2
Analyze and practice basic interpreter skills.
2.2 (a) Describe the differences between ethics and standards of practice.
2.2 (b) Develop message analysis, note-taking and memory skills sufficient to interpret two to three sentences without asking for repetition.
2.2 (c) Practice basic interpreting skills in simple role plays.

OBJECTIVE 2.1

Execute an interpreted session.

Introduction

Unit 2 looks at the interpreted session from beginning to end. It considers the basic skills required of an interpreter before, during and after each session. It also considers how these skills intertwine with interpreter ethics and conduct.

Unit 2 focuses above all on the skills needed to execute a professional interpreted encounter. In order for the entry level interpreter not to interrupt the flow of communication too often, it will be important for you to be able to <u>accurately interpret two to three sentences without requesting interruption</u>, a minimal requirement for professional community interpreting. Unit 2 will help you accomplish this basic goal.

2.1 (a) List the steps to execute a successful interpreted session.

2.1 (b) Discuss and select appropriate modes of interpreting.

2.1 (c) Practice interpreting in consecutive and simultaneous modes.

2.1 (d) Demonstrate basic sight translation skills.

THE INTERPRETED SESSION

OBJECTIVE 2.1 (a) List the steps to execute a successful interpreted session.

The Steps

In order to execute an interpreted session successfully, the interpreter moves through a series of basic steps which include:

- Preparation
- Pre-conference (optional)
- Introductions
- The interpreted session
- Mediation (optional)
- Ending the session
- Post-session

KEY QUESTIONS

What are the interpreter's "working languages?
These are any languages from and into which you interpret.

What is a "source language"?
This is the language <u>from</u> which you interpret at any given moment.

What is the "target language"?
This is the language <u>into</u> which you interpret at any given moment.

How is community interpreting delivered?
Community interpreting may be delivered in person, on the phone or by video.

1. Preparation

Information gathering
First, before any assignment, find out the following details if possible:

- Language needed
- Regional variation (e.g., Taiwanese, Moroccan Arabic or Brazilian Portuguese)
- Type of meeting
- Sensitive issues to be addressed
- Date and time of the session
- Name of the contact person to ask for when you arrive
- Telephone number/email of the contact
- Length of the meeting
- Place of the session, including an exact address with a suite or office number
- Possibly the client's phone number (but only if you are asked to contact the client to confirm or give instructions about the appointment)
- Any documents or forms that will be sight translated
- Any documents with terminology that will be helpful for you to study

General preparation
To be sure that you convey information during session accurately and appropriately, take some time to prepare for an assignment and familiarize yourself with the subject area, especially if it is new to you. Gather any information you can about the nature of the session (some providers are more helpful than others), select appropriate dictionaries and research any professional jargon in the field (e.g., "Individualized Education Plan," "SSI" or "Medicaid Waiver"). Make sure you know how to convey the meaning of common terms in that field in your working languages.

Research
As needed, consult the Internet, speak with service providers, find or develop specialized glossaries, or ask other interpreters or bilingual staff for guidance. If possible, request and study any documents that may be used during the session, especially if you are expected to sight translate them. Be careful not to waste the time of others: one provider reported that she and an interpreter spent a long time on the phone before a session trying to decide on the best way to interpret "post-traumatic stress disorder." But you are the language specialist. It is your job, not the provider's, to find out the correct way to convey such information.

Terminology
To research terminology related to the assignment, the Internet is often a valuable resource. It is possible to find or create one's own glossaries for medical, social services, educational and other specialized vocabulary. This topic is discussed in Unit 4 of this manual. Excellent resources, specialized glossaries and phone applications appear in a variety of languages almost daily. See the Resources section of this manual for examples. However, the interpreter must keep in mind that any glossary can contain errors, and that context will always influence the best word choice. Sometimes it is preferable to consult other interpreters, interpreter listservs or translator forums.

Special note
If you know that you must leave at a certain time, notify the interpreting agency, the organization where the session is held and/or the provider (as appropriate) ahead of time.

2. Preconference

A preconference is a "sit-down" time, usually a few minutes, where you can talk alone with the provider about the coming session. (If you are a bilingual employee, you will probably not need to do so.) A preconference is not common in community interpreting, but it is *very* helpful. At this time, the provider can share any details, sensitive issues or particular concerns that might affect your interpreting. You, in turn, can let the provider know anything that might help the session to go more smoothly. If you are interpreting in any area that relates to trauma (such as torture and trauma services, domestic violence, sexual assault, mental health, asylee interviews or crisis intervention), then *try to hold a preconference.*

Many providers have never worked with a professional interpreter and do not know how to communicate effectively when an interpreter is there. A preconference is your opportunity to educate them, which will help them not only for that session but in the future. Even a quick, informal chat in the hallway with a provider can help the session go more smoothly.

What to tell the provider during a pre-conference
Here are some things that interpreters who are working with a provider for the first time often like to share during a preconference:

- During the session, you will interpret everything.
- The provider should speak directly to the client, not to you.
- The provider should not speak to you or ask you questions during the session, since you will have to interpret them.
- You will interpret in first person (discussed later in Unit 2).
- You will take notes only to enhance your accuracy: those notes will be destroyed before you leave the building .
- If you notice a barrier to communication, e.g., you hear a term you don't understand, or the client does not appear to understand, you may interrupt the session.
- Although it is not your job to provide cultural information, you will try to alert the provider if you observea cultural barrier. That way the provider can ask the client helpful questions to determine what might be going on.

Use your best judgment. One main point of the preconference is to share with the provider anything you feel will help the session go more smoothly. *If there is general cultural information about the coming session that might be helpful to the provider, you are permitted to share it during a preconference, but be very, very careful not to over-generalize.* Every client is culturally unique: you could easily mislead or misinform the provider. Do not share cultural information too freely. Be cautious about culture. Try not to foster stereotypes.

What is a pre-session—is it the same as a pre-conference?
Pre-session is a confusing word. It can mean a preconference or a professional interpreter introduction.

3. Introductions

Purpose of the introduction
The interpreter's professional introduction should be short, but it is very important. Your introduction lays down the parameters for the interpreter session. It makes clear how you will do you your job.

The introduction is important because most providers and clients in community interpreting have not worked with a professional interpreter. They may have worked with untrained interpreters and picked up poor communication habits that make your work harder. Your introduction will guide the provider and client to conduct a successful session even if they have never worked with a professional interpreter before. This introduction is particularly important if you have not had a preconference with the provider.

First, find out if the parties have worked with a professional interpreter before. If not, emphasize each part of your introduction firmly and clearly. Be assertive (calm, authoritative and direct). How to perform your introduction and what to say will be discussed later in Unit 2.

4. The interpreted session

During the session, you will:

- Take appropriate positioning.
- Interpret in consecutive mode (i.e., everyone pauses to let you interpret).
- Use first person.
- Interpret everything.
- Interpret as accurately as possible.
- Avoid summarizing.

Each of these elements will be discussed in detail in this unit.

> **MEDIATION**
>
> Mediation refers to any act or utterance of the interpreter that goes beyond interpreting and is intended to remove barriers to communication between two or more individuals who do not share a common language.

5. Mediation

Sometimes the interpreter may have to interrupt the session to address a barrier to communication. This type of intervention is known as mediation. During the session, either you are interpreting or mediating.

Mediation is, without a doubt, the single most complex skill expected of community interpreters. It is so important, and so challenging, that an entire unit of this manual has been devoted to mediation skills (Unit 3).

6. Ending the Session

The rule is that you leave only when the provider and client have terminated the session. However, it is not rare in community interpreting (and is in fact rather common) that the session goes on longer than planned. Often, the interpreter has another assignment to go to, or a bilingual employee has an important task to attend to right after the session.

THE COMMUNITY INTERPRETER

The end of the session is not the time to address these problems. Determine the length of the appointment ahead of time. If you can stay longer as needed, there is no problem. If you know that you must leave at a certain time, clearly indicate that time *before* accepting the appointment, and then repeat your departure time when you arrive so that everyone is aware you must leave by an appointed time.

7. Post Session

After the session, many things can happen.

a) *The client may want to ask you questions.*

If you are a contract interpreter, resist the temptation of answering a client's questions. Instead, refer the client back to the agency by taking the client to the receptionist's desk or a provider and interpreting the client's question for that person. Remember: you are there to interpret, not to serve as the client's social worker. If, on the other hand, you are a bilingual employee, do exactly for that client what you are expected to do for any of your clients. In general, however, when the session is over, leave. Do not linger with the client.

b) *The provider may want to ask you questions.*

You may answer a provider's questions after the session, and doing so may be helpful for you. For example, if traumatic information was shared during the session, you can debrief with the provider. In addition, if the session was culturally complex the provider may feel confused and need guidance. In general, if the provider wishes to speak to you post-session and you have time, do so. (If you are a contract interpreter, this is billable time.)

c) *You may need to report a critical incident.*

Perhaps the provider said something racist or bigoted about the client. Perhaps the client grew violent and uncontrolled. Perhaps the doctor left before the patient correctly understood the treatment plan or next steps. If you have concerns, report the incident to the appropriate supervisor.

d) *You may be upset.*

Most community interpreters love their work, but they hear many difficult and painful stories. After a difficult session, you may need to care for yourself. How to do so is discussed in Unit 5.

e) *You can evaluate your performance.*

Examine the session in your mind. What went well? What caused you difficulties? What words did you not know? How accurate was your interpreting? Analyze what might have made the session proceed more smoothly and what might improve your performance in the future.

MODES OF INTERPRETING

OBJECTIVE 2.1 (b) Discuss and select appropriate modes of interpreting.

There are three principal modes in community interpreting:
- Consecutive
- Simultaneous
- Sight translation

In addition, there is a fourth, somewhat disputed mode:
- Summarization

Many legal interpreters do not consider summarization a true "mode" of interpreting, perhaps because summarization is prohibited in legal interpreting.

> **MODES OF INTERPRETING**
>
> **Consecutive mode:** Rendering a message into another language when a speaker or signer pauses.
>
> **Simultaneous mode:** Rendering a message into another language while a person is still speaking or signing the message.
>
> **Sight translation:** The oral or signed translation of a written document. (For example, an interpreter takes a patient education brochure and reads it aloud to the patient in another language.)
>
> **Summarization:** Rendering the gist of a message into another language.

Consecutive Mode

The default mode

In consecutive mode, one party speaks or signs, then pauses while the interpreter interprets the message. Consecutive is the default mode in community interpreting. *You should, unless there is a compelling reason to do otherwise, interpret in consecutive mode.*

There are several reasons why consecutive is the default mode in community interpreting:
- Some research shows consecutive is more accurate than simultaneous.
- Simultaneous involves higher-level skills.
- Most community interpreters cannot perform in simultaneous mode accurately and well.
- Consecutive is often less confusing and distracting than simultaneous.

All interpreters should be able to work in consecutive mode. Only highly skilled, experienced interpreters should work regularly in simultaneous mode.

In community interpreting and also in legal interpreting or virtually any other interpreting sector, consecutive mode is the default mode in liaison or dialogue interpreting (also known as interview interpreting), that is, consecutive is usually required for any conversations that involve *questions and answers*.

Accuracy

Accuracy is critical in community interpreting to ensure safety and equal access to services. Interpreting accurately is not the same as interpreting literally. You must convey the spirit and meaning of the message. Accuracy also helps to protect the agency (and the interpreter) from legal liability resulting from errors. Consecutive allows you more time to render meaning accurately. That is the single most important reason that consecutive is the default mode in community interpreting.

Managing the flow

In consecutive, the interpreter is responsible for managing the flow of the communication. If a speaker goes on too long and exceeds the interpreter's ability to remember and interpret accurately, the interpreter should interrupt the speaker. However, the interpreter should strive to develop the memory skills to interpret at least two to three sentences accurately before interrupting a speaker, and preferably more, because sometimes people are too emotional or engaged in what they are saying to interrupt themselves regularly.

Mediation

Consecutive mode facilitates accuracy by allowing more time to process various dimensions of the message. It therefore helps the interpreter to assess whether there is a need to mediate by giving the interpreter more time to:
- Assess whether there is a linguistic, social or cultural barrier to communication.
- Observe participants and the cultural nature of their interaction.
- Address concerns that could affect service outcomes.
- Make appropriate, ethical decisions.

Simultaneous Mode

Conference and court interpreting

Simultaneous interpreting takes place at the same time the speaker is speaking, with a slight delay or lag in the timing of the rendition. As a result, simultaneous mode is preferred for most types of conference interpreting and for diplomatic meetings. It is often used in court interpreting when the whole court is being addressed (for example, during opening remarks by a judge), or when an interpreter throughout a trial interprets everything that is being said for a defendant.

However, even in court, consecutive interpreting is preferred for question-answer sessions such as witness interviews.

Simultaneous in community interpreting

Occasionally the community interpreter must resort to simultaneous interpreting. This should occur only when truly necessary. Cases where simultaneous mode may be necessary in community interpreting include:

- When people speak too quickly.
- In emergencies or times of danger (e.g., in emergencies rooms or during 911 calls).
- When people are so upset they refuse to pause.
- With small children[1] who don't understand they must pause.
- For people with mental illness or dementia who speak incoherently without pausing.
- With individuals who are intoxicated or abusing drugs.

Simultaneous interpreting is best performed by experienced interpreters. A short training program is not adequate to prepare interpreters for simultaneous interpreting. Until you are skilled and experienced, do not attempt simultaneous interpreting unless a compelling emergency arises.

Whisper interpreting

Whispered simultaneous interpreting (also known as chuchotage or whisper interpreting) is a variation on simultaneous mode. In whisper mode, the interpreter has to interpret for one or a few people who speak a minority language in a larger group while a speaker addresses the whole

---

[1] Interpreting for children involves so many specialized skills that it is nearly its own sector of interpreting.

group. The interpreter has to render the message by whispering it to the small group. The interpreter then stands or sits close enough to whisper the interpreting to that individual or group.

Simultaneous equipment

Recent reductions in the cost of purchasing simultaneous interpreting equipment have led schools, health departments, libraries and other community services to purchase it. This equipment allows the interpreter to remain at a distance while individuals in a large group who do not speak the language of the session's speakers —can sit anywhere with a headpiece.

The interpreter listens to the public speech or message through headphones and interprets through a microphone. The headphones reduce extraneous noise and facilitate concentration. Equipment sets for simultaneous interpreting (which are in essence microphones for interpreters and earpieces for clients) have come down in cost to such a degree that even many freelance interpreters now purchase them.

However, if you purchase this equipment, *do not bring it to your interpreting assignments for client-provider sessions.* Consecutive mode, not simultaneous, is the default in question-answer sessions. Use the equipment for public settings.

When to perform in simultaneous mode

Community interpreters often perform in simultaneous mode for:

- Schools (for example, special events, multicultural conferences, and Board hearings)
- Libraries (e.g., storytelling, orientations, public talks)
- Community conferences
- Health education
- Seminars on tax or immigration issues
- Legal clinics
- Public education events
- Town hall meetings

Sight Translation

What is sight translation?

In sight translation, the interpreter reads a document in the source language and renders an oral translation into the target language. Essentially, the interpreter takes a document and "reads it out loud" into another language. Community interpreters should only translate short documents of one to two pages.

Sight translation is often used for brochures, releases, intake forms, prescriptions, financial forms, correspondence, documents that require signatures, consent forms, education plans, discharge papers and other vital documents in community services. However, in most cases it is not appropriate for community interpreters (unless they are also trained, qualified, and preferably certified legal interpreters) to sight translate legal documents.

Steps for sight translation

To perform effective, skillful sight translation, decline any text that is too long or complex (or ask the provider to explain it and interpret the explanation). Then:

> **Who Performs Sight Translation: The Interpreter or the Translator?**
>
> Sight translation is a common duty assigned to community interpreters. It is part of the work of an interpreter, not a translator.

- Make certain the provider remains in the room.
- Read the *whole text* first.
- Identify unfamiliar concepts and potential language barriers, such as complex sentence structure and vocabulary.
- Ask for any necessary clarification or consult a dictionary/electronic device or phone.
- Analyze the register and language patterns.
- From the beginning of the text to the end, render the entire document with no additions, changes or deletions, maintaining the grammar and register of the source text.
- Maintain the flow and style of the document.

Challenges in sight translation

Sight translation is difficult due to the challenges that a written text presents. Most documents are written in a higher register (i.e., a more formal level of language) than oral speech, and they have more complex syntax (word order). Sentences are longer, and may be convoluted. For example, a document in English is often written in the passive voice. In many languages, it is difficult to maintain passive voice while sight translating because the passive voice is not commonly used.

Documents for community services also tend to use the third person, while spoken interpreting is usually rendered in the first person. The grammar of documents may be difficult and complex, while most oral statements are brief and simple. The register of a written document may be so formal that the syntax and vocabulary are too complex for many immigrant or native-born clients of community services to understand easily, and the interpreter often feels tempted to simplify the register of the document. (Resist this temptation.) Many documents in community services include culturally complex concepts, for example, advance directives in health care or Individualized Education Plans in schools.

What not to sight translate

In community interpreting, sight translation may sometimes be used for *short* documents of one to two pages written in *simple* language. Ideally, the interpreter should not perform sight translation for:

- Long or complex documents.
- Legal documents (including consent forms)
- Technical documents using terminology unfamiliar to the interpreter.

Instead, ask the provider to explain the document and interpret the explanation.

Alternatives to sight translation

If there is the slightest doubt in your mind about whether or not to perform a sight translation, ask the provider to:

- Read the document out loud (you can interpret what is spoken).
- Explain the document (you can interpret the explanation).
- Summarize the document (you can interpret the summary).

> **Questions**
>
> *Question*: Should the interpreter herself summarize the document?
> *Answer*: No. Only the provider should summarize a document.
>
> *Question*: Is it permissible to sight translate a brief technical document?
> *Answer*: Yes, but only if the interpreter has sufficient skills to do so accurately.

A strict requirement

During a sight translation, the provider *must remain* with the interpreter to answer client questions. Otherwise, the client will ask the interpreter questions and may share information that the interpreter feels the provider should know, putting the interpreter in a difficult situation.

To remedy the common problem of the provider who wants to leave the interpreter alone to perform a sight translation, some organizations, including hospitals, have developed a strict policy: if the provider leaves the room, the interpreter must also leave the room.

Handling requests to summarize

Summarizing a document involves judging and screening the information that will be conveyed to the client. That is not the interpreter's role. It is required that the provider, not the interpreter, explain or summarize the content of a document or video. The interpreter should make sure that the provider explains the text, not the interpreter. Here is an example of how to decline a sight translation (you may recall these three steps from Unit 1):

1. *Decline graciously:* e.g., "I really wish I could help you out because I can see this document is important."
2. *Give an alternative:* e.g., "However, I think it will be much safer for you to explain the document and for me to interpret it."
3. *Give reasons:* e.g., "You know what's important in the document and what the client needs to know. I don't, so I might miss important information that puts the client's [Special Education plan, treatment plan, benefits, next steps, etc.] at risk. If anything bad happens, the agency would be legally liable for my mistakes, and so would I. Having you explain summarize the document reduces all these risks."

"Explaining a form"

It's a common request. The provider hands the interpreter a form and says, "Here, you explain it. You've done this a million times. You know it better than I do!" But the interpreter should never explain a form or other document (unless you are a bilingual employee and explaining such forms is part of your job). Explaining forms is the *provider's* role. Nor should the interpreter offer a client a descriptive statement about the document, e.g., "This is a release of information form. You need to sign it." Unless the interpreter typically provides the same service as the provider who gives the form (and is professionally trained to do so), the provider should be present each time a document is handed to the client.

UNIT 2

Summarization

Summarization is prohibited in legal interpreting. In community interpreting in general, it may sometimes be used a *last resort*. However, if interpreting in consecutive mode becomes difficult for any reason, first :

- Try to manage the flow.
- Interrupt parties as needed.
- If these strategies fail, try simultaneous.
- For emergencies, incoherent speech, several people speaking at once, or other exceptional cases, then and only then, resort to summarization.

Summarization (or summary) is not a true mode of interpreting but a technique. In community settings, summarization may *sometimes* be used if all other interpreting modes have failed for :

- Minute-to-minute emergencies (e.g., military interpreting in community settings, 911 calls, emergency surgery, etc).
- Situations when too many people speak at once.
- Special situations of mental illness, crisis, inebriation, substance abuse or other cases where a speaker may be incoherent.
- Aging clients or children who do not speak articulately enough for the interpreter to perform either consecutive or simultaneous interpreting.
- Long, rapid or technical videos (e.g., those used for health education).

In community settings, summarize only when the session has become so out of control that you have no choice.

MODES AND SKILLS

OBJECTIVE 2.1 (c) Practice interpreting in consecutive, simultaneous and sight translation modes.

Before practicing modes, let's look at the skills involved for each of the three primary modes.

Consecutive skills

To perform at a professional level in consecutive mode, you will need to:

- Remember everything that is said and the sequence of the message.
- Control the pace of the dialogue in order to encourage appropriately-timed pauses without disrupting the session. (Sometimes a discreet hand gesture is enough to remind the parties that it is time to pause.)
- Be ready to take meaningful notes.
- Convey the intent of the message and its emotional content and cultural nuances through tone, volume, emphasis and emotional coloring.

Challenges when performing in consecutive mode include the following:

1. Consecutive mode requires note-taking skills.
    a) Because introductory programs in community interpreting spend very little time on note-taking, community interpreters are often weak in note-taking skills. (Note-taking is discussed later in Unit 2.)
    b) Poor note-taking skills undermine accuracy in consecutive mode.

2. Consecutive mode requires more memory skills than any other mode.
    a) Again, introductory programs in community interpreting have very little time to spend helping interpreters develop memory skills.
    b) Typically, interpreters must work independently to enhance their memory skills after the training has ended.
    c) Enhancing memory skills is a lifelong process.

3. Community interpreters often fail to manage the flow.
   Many community interpreters come from cultures where people assert themselves in ways that are different from American culture. Interpreters must learn to interrupt as needed in order to manage the communication flow.
    a) If you do not interrupt when speakers go on too long, *you will not be able to maintain accuracy.*
    b) When community interpreters do not manage the flow, they typically resort to summarizing when they should not do so.

4. Speakers often do not wish to pause, which makes consecutive interpreting difficult or impossible.
   a) Sometimes managing the flow is difficult in community interpreting because so many situations get emotional and intense.
   b) It is common that clients come with a family member or friend, or even several people, and/or children. They may all speak at once.
   c) Speakers may not understand the concept of taking turns.

Simultaneous skills

To perform at a professional level in simultaneous mode, you will need to:

- Show a strong capacity for focus and concentration.
- Dismiss outside distractions (crying babies, blinking lights, pneumatic drills...)
- Remember everything that is said and the sequence of the message, even when you have not yet heard the end of the message.
- Remember *and* forget: remember what you are interpreting and at the same time forget what you have just interpreted in order to render the message.
- Still convey the intent of the message and its emotional content and cultural nuances through tone, volume, emphasis and emotional coloring.

Challenges when performing in simultaneous mode include the following:

1. Simultaneous is a higher level skill
   a) To perform accurately in simultaneous dictates an even higher level of language proficiency in all working languages than consecutive.
   b) Simultaneous requires more practice and experience than consecutive to perform well.
   c) Simultaneous demands an intensely strong ability to concentrate.

2. Most community interpreters receive inadequate training in simultaneous.
   a) They really should not perform in simultaneous, lacking the skills, but are often forced to.
   b) They lack programs where they can go to improve their simultaneous skills.
   c) Few programs have the language laboratories that can truly help develop these skills.
   d) Not enough mentorship programs are available to support community interpreters.
   e) Community interpreters typically lack funds to travel to parts of the country that offer intensive simultaneous interpreting classes.

3. Simultaneous interpreting is exhausting.
   a) After about 15 minutes, accuracy goes down. After 30 minutes, accuracy is seriously undermined.
   b) Interpreters who perform in simultaneous for any length of time report feeling completely drained.
   c) Providers have no concept how exhausting simultaneous can be.

4. Simultaneous interpreting requires working in teams of at least two interpreters.
   a) Unfortunately, except for legal and sign language interpreting, very few agencies consider bringing in two interpreters for simultaneous community interpreting.
   b) As a result, sessions are scheduled too long for one interpreter to perform well.
   c) Accuracy is eroded, interpreters burn out, but if they complain they are often told, "Well, so-and-so does it—why can't you?"

A great deal of education is needed so that providers and community service agencies understand the intensive demands that simultaneous mode places on interpreters.

Whispered simultaneous skills

To perform at a professional level in whispered simultaneous mode, you will need to:

- Speak clearly and not mumble the message.
- Stay focused: it is easy to forget to maintain the sequence of the message when whispering.
- Make sure that the client can hear the message without drowning out the speaker or distracting other participants.

Challenges when performing in whispered simultaneous mode are roughly the same as those for performing in regular simultaneous.

Sight translation skills[1]

To perform at a professional level in sight translation mode, the interpreter will need to:

- Develop a strong capacity for focus and concentration.
- Be highly proficient in both languages.
- Have excellent literacy and reading skills in both languages.
- Know the skills and steps for sight translation.

---

1 Grateful acknowledgement is made to Katharine Allen for her expertise and contributions to this section.

Challenges when performing sight translation include the following:

1. Sight translation involves making a written text oral.
   a) Normally we do not speak aloud using the same syntax as a written text. (Doing so can feel odd or uncomfortable at first.)
   b) Because you are used to interpreting spoken speech, you may not have a mental plan about how to translate more formal sentence structures

2. You are more likely to fixate on a problem in sight translation than in consecutive or in simultaneous.
   a) When you read a word or phrase that is difficult to render, you are more like to stop and think about it than when you are rendering speech.
   b) It feels harder to find an equivalent meaning and move on.
   c) Long sentences can cause you to freeze, slow down or get confused.

3. It is very hard to sight translate into your weaker (B) language.
   a) Sight translation requires a very high level of literacy in both languages.
   b) If you are sight translating into your A language (your primary or native language), you are typically more confident, at ease and fluid in your performance, whereas you may stumble and hesitate when you sight translate into your B language.
   c) This delivery actually affects the ability of the listener to comprehend what you say.
   d) You usually know fewer synonyms, alternatives and "workarounds" for difficult or complex concepts in your B language than your A language.

4. English is often a difficult language to sight translate into.
   a) In some languages, like Spanish, a certain flexibility about syntax (sentence structure and order) means that you can start a sentence in one structure and change it halfway through.
   b) In other languages, like English and German, there is less flexibility. You may start sight translating a sentence and then have to start over again, not continue.

   As a result, unlike consecutive or simultaneous interpreting, you may have to think consciously about syntax and how it affects your performance.

OBJECTIVE 2.2

Analyze and practice basic interpreter skills.

2.2 (a) Describe the differences between ethics and standards of practice.

2.2 (b) Develop message analysis, note-taking and memory skills sufficient to interpret two to three sentences without asking for repetition.

2.2 (c) Practice basic interpreting skills in simple role plays.

Basic Interpreter Skills

The Big Picture

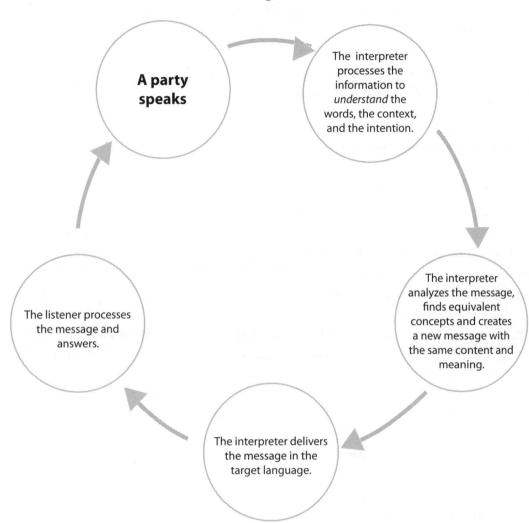

Examples of Basic Interpreter Skills

- Select the appropriate mode of interpreting.
- Use first person.
- Adopt effective positioning.
- Foster direct communication between the client and provider.
- Capture and communicate the meaning of the message accurately.
- Interpret the tone, intent, spirit and nuances of the message.
- Monitor to see if both parties understand.

Introductions, Positioning and First Person

OBJECTIVE 2.2 (a) Demonstrate professional introductions, positioning and use of first person.

Professional Introductions

Purpose of the introduction

The primary purpose of a professional interpreter introduction is to lay down clear parameters for the session. It is also an opportunity for the interpreter to establish a warm rapport, display a professional demeanor and "set the stage" for the session.

Should you always perform an introduction?

You should always conduct a professional introduction. Determine ahead of time if the provider and client have worked often with professional interpreters, in which case your introduction may be shorter. (Remember: in community interpreting in the U.S. and most other countries, the majority of providers and clients have not worked with trained, professional community interpreters.

What should the introduction include?

The interpreter may state anything in the introduction that could be helpful for the provider and/or client. However, when starting out, use this model as the basis on which to build your introduction.

A BASIC INTRODUCTION

Two disclosures
1. "Everything that is said in the session will be interpreted."
2. "Everything said in the room will be kept confidential."

Two requests
1. "Please speak directly to each other."
2. "Please speak slowly and pause so I can interpret everything."

UNIT 2

Interpreter Introductions: The Next Level

Adding other elements

After you are comfortable with the four basic elements of a professional introduction, if time permits you may wish to add other elements.

Here are a few examples of statements that many professional interpreters add to their introductions:

- "I'll be speaking in first person." (You may need to explain briefly what first person means: first person is discussed below.)
- "Please use simple language and explain any technical terms clearly."
- "If I give a hand signal, please pause so I can interpret."
- "You may not wish to say anything you don't want me to interpret, since I am obliged to interpret everything."
- "I'll be taking notes to help me interpret accurately, but they'll be destroyed or given to the provider before I leave."
- "If I say anything you don't understand, please say so."

Creating rapport

The interpreter can also use the introduction to establish a positive rapport. During the session, you must adopt the emotional tone of the speakers. During an introduction, you may speak as yourself.

A smile, a warm voice, an authentic handshake and an appearance of interest in the client and provider help to establish a relationship of professionalism and trust. The tone of the introduction, while professional, should not seem overpowering.

The importance of brevity

Keep introductions brief. Have a quick routine. Providers are often rushed and may interrupt you.

Effective Positioning

The Goal

The goal of effective positioning is to promote direct client-provider communication.

Why it matters

The seating or standing arrangement that the interpreter selects is very important for a successful outcome. If the interpreter gets all the attention, then the client and provider are not focused on each other. In that case, the client may not develop a relationship of trust with the provider and may not open up to that provider. *Unless the client feels comfortable enough to share all relevant information that the provider needs in order to provide the service, the outcome of that service could be at risk.* Therefore, the community interpreter, like the legal interpreter, must adopt an *unobtrusive* (background) position.

The problem with the triangle

When an untrained interpreter works with a provider who is not trained to work effectively with interpreters, the client, provider and interpreter tend to fall into the "triangle" position. To this day, in Europe, parts of the U.S. and many other parts of the world, many professional interpreters think the triangle position is excellent. A number of interpreting specialists in the U.S., however, including the authors of this manual, strongly disagree and recommend that you do not interpret in a triangle position. The reason for advocating against the triangle position in spoken community interpreting is that in a triangle, provider and client have a very strong tendency to look at, and speak to, the interpreter—not each other.

Other challenging positions

In many healthcare settings, there is almost no room for the interpreter, and very limited choices about positioning. Bilingual employees are often asked to sit next to their colleagues, at a distance from the client, or even across a table from the client. In some time types of meetings, e.g., special education meetings in schools, there may be a long or round table with many people sitting around it.

Safety considerations may also play a role, especially in certain settings such as mental health, police work, homeless shelters, psychiatric hospitals and crisis intervention.

Positioning Choices

An "ideal" position

Every community interpreting session is unique and will require thoughtful consideration about the best position to adopt. However, if you can do so, the position that many specialists recommend is slightly behind the client.

Why behind the client?

There are many reasons to position yourself slightly behind the client, if possible:
- You are unobtrusive.
- Provider and client can face each other.
- Provider and client will tend to focus on each other.
- The client can hear you easily.
- The client cannot easily look at you.
- The client feels supported by you ("like there's someone on my side").
- The client is the most vulnerable person in the room due to language and cultural barriers. Helping the client feel supported can help to foster feelings of trust and openness in the client.

Why not take a position behind the provider?

Many interpreters do sit behind the provider. After all, the provider's agency is paying for the interpreter, who often is a bilingual employee. In that case the provider may be your colleague and even your friend.

However, the authors of this manual discourage taking a position behind the provider for the following reasons:

- It appears that you have aligned with the provider.
- The client will look at you, not the provider.
- The client often feels intimidated ("two against one").
- The power dynamics place all the power and confidence on the side of the provider, when it is the client who is more likely ill at ease and at a disadvantage.

Additional considerations

To complicate this picture, in schools, social services, police stations and other community settings, you may be involved in meetings of more than two persons. Several people may be sitting around a table, standing in a spacious area, or hunched together inside a crowded room. Many times, a session takes place in a hallway or a cubicle. In certain medical appointments or Emergency Room visits, to respect a patient's privacy you may need to turn your back or stand outside a curtained area.

During home visits, the client may invite you to sit down on a sofa and you may feel too shy to refuse, even if that position is not ideal for interpreting. Interpreters in many settings may have little choice about their position.

Positioning challenges

In cases where you cannot position yourself behind the client, you face two key challenges: intrusiveness and distance. A position that puts you directly in the line of vision of both client and provider can feel intrusive because you are inviting attention when you should play a low-key role. Yet if you are physically distant, the client may feel vulnerable. They often perceive you as an ally, the person in the room who shares the same language and culture (or at least understands the culture). Your presence may feel reassuring.

However, a position that makes you stand out and draws attention to you often does not allow the provider to address the client directly. So it is important to find a position that draws the attention of the provider and client to each other, not to you, while also making the client feel supported.

Alternative approach

Here is the basic default approach to take when you consider positioning:

- Always adopt the least intrusive position.
- Try, if possible, to stay out of the client's sight-line while interpreting.
- Try, if possible (and safety permits), to stay closer to the client than the provider.

Remember: there is no absolute consensus on positioning for community interpreters because there are so many different settings and constraints. For a working paper on this topic by NCIHC, consult *Guide to Interpreter Positioning in Health Care Settings,* available at www.ncihc.org.

Positioning and Eye Contact

Think a moment about the kind of work you do. You are there to interpret, not to engage in a conversation with the provider or client. What happens, however, when you make eye contact with either of them while you interpret? They look at you. They speak to you.

Any position you adopt is important, but eye contact is often just as important. Again, the goal is to promote direct client-provider communication. Optimal positioning helps to put the provider and client in charge, not the interpreter. Eye contact can do the same. *If you break off eye contact while you interpret, provider and client are much more likely to look at each other, not you.*

How it feels to break off eye contact

Breaking off eye contact feels strange. It can feel rude. Most interpreters are polite and feel as if they should make eye contact. Resist this temptation. Interpreting is not about what makes you feel good but the best ways to promote accurate communication between the client and provider.

An effective strategy for breaking eye contact

Every community interpreter should come to the session with a pad and pen or pencil to take notes as needed. Use your note-taking equipment to make breaking off eye contact feel more natural. You can even pretend to take notes without actually doing so.

Don't I need to look at body language?

It is true that a great deal of information and meaning is gleaned from body language. So as soon as the provider and client are looking at and speaking to each other, you can look up to observe body language. If anyone meets your eyes, look down quickly at your pad.

Other benefits of breaking eye contact

Eye contact is a distraction. When you are focused on interpreting, not having eye contact makes it is easier to concentrate on interpreting accurately. When you make eye contact and feel you are connected to the speakers, those feelings require neural processing, which undermines the intense focus and concentration you need to make your interpreting as accurate as possible. Focus on language. Your job is not to connect to the speakers. Your job is to connect them to each other.

UNIT 2

First Person: Direct Speech

Direct vs. Indirect Speech

Direct speech means reporting what is said as it is said. For example, if the client says (in any given language), "My wife is crazy," you will say in English, "My wife is crazy," and not, "He said his wife is out of her mind." The use of direct speech is usually called "first person."

However, most providers and clients who have never worked with a professional interpreter will automatically turn to the interpreter and say things like "Tell her to..." or "Ask him ..." For example: "Ask him if he has come here before," or "Have her fill out this form." This kind of statement is indirect or reported speech. It is often referred to as "third person."

Why first person is required in interpreting

Professional interpreters interpret in first person. (In fact, one of the quickest ways to tell an untrained from a trained interpreter is to listen and see whether or not the interpreter is interpreting in first person.) Some of the reasons why first person is required include:

- First person is direct and more accurate than third person.
- First person is shorter and simpler to interpret.
- First person is up to 50 percent faster than third person.
- First person fosters direct client-provider communication.

Interpreting in first person identifies the source of the statement and makes it clear that whatever is said does not come from the interpreter but from the speaker. This technique also puts the responsibility of the discourse on the speaker, and not on the interpreter.

Problems with third person

- Third person takes longer and is more difficult to interpret than first person.
- Third person creates a barrier of distance between the provider and the client.
- Third person is often convoluted: it has more complex syntax, which takes a toll on the interpreter's memory and makes accuracy more difficult.
- Third person often leads the interpreter to change and add to the message.

UNIT 2

> **Example of third person (Indirect speech)**
> Client says, "We need food stamps. Can you help us?"
> The interpreter says in English, "She says they need food stamps. She's wondering if maybe your office could help this family."
> **Example of first person (Direct speech)**
> Client says, "We need food stamps. Can you help us?"
> The interpreter says in English, "We need food stamps. Can you help us?"

Do I need to explain that I'm interpreting in first person?

In order to make interpreting as accurate as possible, during the introduction you may want to ask the provider and the client to use first person. You might also need to explain what first person means. That decision is up to you.

Exceptions to the rule

Avoid communicating in third person for community interpreting. It creates confusion and undermines the relationship between the provider and the client. However, in some cases it may be necessary to use third person. For example, in some languages it may be inappropriate for social, linguistic or cultural reasons to interpret in first person. Here are a few other examples of situations where third person may be needed:

- Interpreting for children (especially under eight years old)
- Interpreting for the mentally ill
- Interpreting for patients with dementia or confusion
- Interpreting during emergencies
- Interpreting in any situations where you must resort to summarizing

UNIT 2

Example of First Person

Notice that the interpreting below is not literal. Interpret for meaning.

Provider: What is the reason for your visit today?
Interpreter: *What is the reason you've come to visit today?*
Client: Euh, I'm here because I need to renew my insurance. You see, it expired about a month ago and now that woman says the doctor can't see me until I get a new one. Do you believe it?
Interpreter: *Well, I came here because I have to renew my insurance. About a month ago it expired, you see. And now that woman says the doctor can't see me until I get a new one. Can you believe it?*
Provider: I'm so sorry to hear that! Let's see, what can we do here?
Interpreter: *I'm very sorry to hear that! Let me see. What can we do for you?*
Client: You know, you're very good looking, and nice too.
Interpreter: *You know, you are very good looking, and kind too.*
Provider: Thank you. Um. When were you born?"
Interpreter: *Thank you. Euh… What year were you born?*

The interpreter here has maintained the first person. By doing so, she has been able to convey the message and emotion in the message in a clear and accurate way.

Note that verbatim interpreting is impossible. To interpret word for word would change meaning because not all words mean the same thing in the context of two languages. Interpreting touches on the complexity of language, culture, meaning and social relationships.

Message analysis, note-taking and memory skills

OBJECTIVE 2.2 (b) Develop message analysis, note-taking and memory skills sufficient to interpret two to three sentences without asking for repetition.

In community interpreting, you work hard to promote accurate, meaningful communication. Remember that the purpose of interpreting is to facilitate communication between two or more individuals who do not share a common language.

An entry-level interpreter will need to manage the flow to maintain accuracy yet not interrupt the session too often. Interrupting the session could undermine the development of a relationship and sense of trust between the provider and client. Too many interruptions are also distracting.

This tension between the need to maintain accuracy and the need to maintain an even flow means essentially one thing: the interpreter must build strong skills that include analyzing the meaning of a message, short-term memory skills and note-taking skills.

UNIT 2

Message Analysis

The steps in message analysis

Whole books have been written on how to analyze a message. It is impossible to adequately summarize all the research in this field. Instead, this section of the manual offers a basic introduction to the concept of message analysis within the pragmatic framework of four steps:

1) Comprehend the message.
2) Parse (break down) the message into its concepts and linguistic structures.
3) Find conceptual equivalents in the target language.
4) Reframe and reconstruct the message.

Your goal is to find words, concepts and structures that constitute *equivalents* of the original message in a target language. To accomplish this, break the message down into component parts to find the best way to interpret them accurately.

Comprehension

It sounds so easy: "First, understand the message." But this step is harder than it appears, because even for a simple sentence like, "You have no idea!" the interpreter must take into account:

- *Context*. Social, professional, personal, cultural and even religious context can all affect the meaning of the message.
- *Body language and gestures*. While it is not formal responsibility of the interpreter to interpret body language (and legal interpreters should not try), the meaning inherent in body language and gestures must be constantly assessed by the interpreter.
- *Long term memory*. The interpreter must bring a great deal of life experience, factual knowledge and social awareness to the encounter in order to analyze a message skillfully. In this sense, older interpreters may have some advantages over younger ones.[1]
- *Intent*. Is the speaker being sarcastic? Is she angry or upset? Does he intend to educate someone or simple express his feelings? Are certain words in the message (e.g., "You have *no* idea?") emphasized more than others? The speaker's intent informs the interpreter's understanding of the message.

---

[1] It goes without saying that younger interpreters have other advantages. For example, they are often much more comfortable than older interpreters with the increasing number of electronic applications and tools that assist interpreters in their day-to-day work.

UNIT 2

Other aspects of language and communication that can influence your understanding of a message include regionalisms, dialects, individual style, register, literal and figurative language, idiomatic meaning, power dynamics and cultural protocols.

Remember that most of a message is not contained in words but in the speaker's body language, voice, gestures, nuances and context.

Parse the message

Whether the message is long or short, you may need to break it down into smaller parts in order to be able to render it faithfully into another language. Take the sentence, "We may need to consider having a CT-scan and MRI done to find out what's really going on." Here are a few examples of breaking that message down:

- *"We may need to..."* Who does "we" refer to?
- *"CT-scan and MRI"* These are two well-known medical tests in the U.S. However, if you interpret them into a non-western language, do the names for these medical tests even exist in the target language? Would the patient know about them if you interpreted them literally or would the patient understand better if you kept the English name for the test? Then again, if translations for those terms did not exist 20 years ago in the target language when you left your country of origin, perhaps those terms *do* exist in the language now and the patient might know them. Does your language have medical dictionaries or glossaries available in print or online to verify?
- *"—consider having a CT-scan and MRI done..."* This is a passive sentence structure, which is very common in written English and also in the spoken English of educated persons. But passive is not a common sentence structure in many other languages. What is the best way to restructure the syntax of this sentence in the target language?
- *"...to find out what's really going on."* What is the best way to express the meaning of this English sentence, given that it could be understood in so many different ways?

There is no one answer to any of these questions because the answers depend on the target language, the context and many other factors. The interpreter will have to make an on-the-spot decision.

Find conceptual equivalents in the target language

In many languages, there may not be a conceptual equivalent that is readily available or that you know. Until recently, even concepts like radiation therapy were unknown in many languages. One teenager who was asked to interpret for his mother that she was going to have radiation treatment dutifully reported, "They're going to put fire in you" while another boy whose mother was about to be X-rayed told his mother, "They're going to microwave you." (This leads one to wonder about the likelihood of the patient agreeing to the recomended test or treatment plan...)

Understanding the intent and purpose of a message is also critically important. We can't, on the fly, all suddenly become perfect interpreters. If we get caught up worrying about our mistakes and weaknesses and start "beating ourselves up" while we interpret, we'll only get lost and further behind. Do not fixate on challenging concepts: simply ask for clarification. (How to request clarification is discussed in Unit 3.) Then do your best to find a reasonable equivalent and move on.

Reframe and reconstruct the message

After all these steps, when you mentally put the message back together in the target language, try to:

- *Respect the register.* Create a new message that conveys the same register (level of language). Do not simplify or change the register.
- *Imitate the style and diction.* Diction (word choice) means choosing just the right words and phrases to convey the same style and reproduce the impact of a message.
- *Convey the tone and affect.* Find language the captures the emotional expressivity of the speaker.
- *Use appropriate syntax.* The sentence order will be different in the two languages, but your rendering should reflect the same level of complexity as the original message. If the original long sentence in English had many subordinate clauses, for example, do not divide them the message up into five separate sentences when you interpret.
- *Prioritize the key components.* In French and many other languages, one does not put emphasis on particular words in a sentence the way English speakers often do. Yet there are other ways to convey emphasis in such languages that may include word order, diction, tone of voice, etc.

It is quite typical for a community interpreter to think, "Oh, no, if I just had a little more time I *know* I could say this better!" However, we don't have that time. Simply do your best.

UNIT 2

Memory Skills

First, manage the flow!

Developing strong memory skills is critical for an interpreter. But first, manage the flow of information. When people get excited, sometimes their words flow like rivers. The interpreter must be the dam. Each interpreter knows his memory limits, and it is important to interrupt the speaker with a gesture or signal as needed. Control the pace.

Meantime, also try to develop your memory skills.

Very short-term, short-term and long-term memory

Here is a simple table to help you grasp a few basic concepts about memory skills.

MEMORY

Type of Memory	Characteristics	Mode	Techniques
Very short term	Instantaneous (a few seconds) Helps you remember a few words or string of numbers.	Simultaneous and sight translation modes (for context); whisper interpreting	Concentration, practice, or "parroting" a recording or radio/television program.
Short term	Active. Helps you remember ideas, concepts, images.	Consecutive mode	Analytical skills, breaking down messages into parts, note-taking, memory games.
Long term	Passive. The critical areas of knowledge (intellectual, social, emotional and pragmatic) that you have acquired over a lifetime.	All modes (you need background knowledge, skills, cultural understanding, experience to perform accurately in all modes)	Continuing education in language and interpreting. Self-recording and vocabulary exercises, word games and manuals for self study.

Remember: summarizing is not permitted in most community interpreting. Yet many community interpreters summarize when they should not do so.

The three most common reasons for summarizing are:
- Use of third person (which contributes to memory overload)
- Failing to manage the flow (which again leads to memory overload)
- Lack of training and practice to develop memory skills.

UNIT 2

Strategies to Enhance Memory Skills

Key strategies

There are many strategies to improve your memory skills. Here are a few:

- Concentration and focus
- Chunking
- Visualization
- Classic memory exercises
- Word games
- Practice
- Note-taking

Let's consider these strategies, one by one.

Concentration

In order to maintain your focus and enhance your memory:

- Avoid distractions.
- Avoid eye contact, which may distract you.
- If possible, ask for distractions to be removed (e.g., change room if lights flicker or a baby is crying next door).
- Enter the "flow" or rhythm of interpreting so that it feels smooth and nearly automatic.

Chunking

If the messages you are interpreting are long sentences and not simple pieces of information, break the message down into its component concepts. Mentally organize those concepts into chunks that you can identify by a simple mental subject header, for example,
- "Next steps"
- "Documents [to bring to the next appointment]"
- "Contact information"

When you break the information into shorter chunks:
- Look for sequence.
- Try to see the relationships between chunks.
- Pay attention to main ideas, key words and relevant details.

UNIT 2

Visualization

Many books have been written about the importance of visualization as a memory aid going back at least to the ancient Greeks. In concrete terms, if the sanitation department official is explaining changes in county recycling procedures to the LEP owner of a restaurant, the interpreter[1] could imagine (to keep track of the old system vs the new system for recycling in mind) an old woman next to a series of bins and a young child next to the bin that says "commingled." However, real visualization exercises are far more sophisticated, though they do tend to focus on very concrete images. Many of the classic memory exercises that go back hundreds of years work with visualization training. (Mind mapping is another famous variation of visualization, a tool to enhance memory skills.) For a popular and readable look at some of these exercises, see a recent article and book by Joshua Foer (2011a and b) in the bibliography.

Word games

Many interpreters love words games. Some interpreters hate them. But if you enjoy them, they can be a wonderful tool to enhance memory skills. There are so many word games online that they are very easy to find. Here are only a few examples:

Merriam-Webster provides a free online dictionary, thesaurus, audio pronunciations, Word of the Day, word games, and other English language resources. http://www.m-w.com/game/

Vocabulary University participants learn English vocabulary in context (grades 5-12) with free word puzzles. Thematic word games and creative activities. www.vocabulary.com/

---

1 This is a real example from a community interpreter training participant in Maryland.

UNIT 2

Learn about word origins and etymology with a tough and educational word game. www.etymologic.com/

Free on-line interactive word games, boggle, anagrams, puzzles, crosswords, cryptograms, cryptoquotes, jumble. Play and solve word games. Word plays. www.wordplays.com/

Vocabulary University® recommended word-related web sites. www.vocabulary.com/

Internet Park is an interesting and friendly place to play word games live on the Internet. One game, Ready Mix is very popular and addictive. www.internet-park.com/

A word a day with Wordsmith.Org, the home of A.Word.A.Day, Internet Anagram Server, wordserver. www.wordsmith.org

Previous Cryptograms and Hangman. Solve the phrase by guessing each word Previous Hangman Games. www.dictionary.reference.com/fun/

Practice

Here are a few of the many practice exercises that interpreters have used to enhance their memory skills:

- Practice with sentences or numbers. Have a partner read a longer and even longer number of sentences and/or strings of numbers out loud to you. See how many sentences you can interpret accurately. Keep striving to break your previous record. Make it a game.
- Add distractions when you practice (e.g., music, noise, background conversation).
- Have a partner recite a story to you (e.g., something that happened to her) for a couple of paragraphs. Take notes. See how much you can accurately interpret back.
- Interpret what is said on radio or television programs or taped books, either simultaneously or consecutively (by lowering the volume when you interpret).
- Keep reading in both languages.
- Assess your memory weaknesses (e.g., numbers, lists, complicated syntax) and work on those.

UNIT 2

Note-taking

The authors wish to express our thanks and acknowledgements to Katharine Allen for her cogent and thoughtful contributions to this section on note-taking for interpreters.

Why take notes?

Sometimes it is difficult or impossible to interrupt the speaker, which may stretch the memory limits of the interpreter. Perhaps the speaker is too emotional. Perhaps the situation has turned into an emergency. Taking notes is one way of enhancing interpreter accuracy in situations where the pace is fast, the terminology is technical, the syntax is complex, or in any situation where the interpreter is unable to control the flow of communication.

What is the best system for note-taking?

The note-taking system considered most effective for consecutive interpreting is based on techniques developed for conference interpreters[1]. The trick is to take the most useful elements of that system and make them work for the short consecutive used in dialog settings where community interpreting takes place. Once the basic system is mastered, you will see that every interpreter finds his or her own unique note-taking style. For community interpreting settings, the interpreter may wish to restrict note-taking to basic concepts, abbreviations and symbols and should never attempt verbatim note-taking (such as shorthand). In particular, the interpreter may wish to consider noting down:

- Numbers
- Dates
- Addresses
- Technical terms
- Acronyms
- Proper nouns
- Lists or steps (e.g., procedures, symptoms, medications, instructions)

Note-taking basics

First, notes should be *simple and legible* to the interpreter. They must be destroyed after the session or given to the provider. Notes contain confidential information and should not be left anywhere. The interpreter should not take detailed notes and instead note down only those elements of the message that might be difficult to recapture or recall. Remember, the notes are there to jog your memory, not replace it!

---

[1] *Note-taking in Consecutive Interpreting,* Rozan, Jean Francois, (1956 Geneve, Georg), 2005 Tertium, Cracow.

UNIT 2

Note-taking Principles and Elements

Fundamentals of note-taking

- Write the concept, not the words
- Keep your notes short
- Capture a whole idea with a symbol
- Use abbreviations wherever possible
- Use strike-out for negation (e.g., ~~insur~~ for "no insurance")
- Use your margins for large categories
- Use arrows (for increase/decrease, directions, time, etc)
- Chunk information into sub-categories

Visuals

Avoid writing whole lines of text. Instead structure your notes either vertically (top to bottom for most interpreters) or diagonally (left to right or right to left, depending on your native language).

If you write horizontally, it may interfere with your ability to keep the two syntax systems for your working language separate, which may confuse you when you use your notes to render the message in the target language.

Into which language?

Some interpreters prefer to take notes in their native language, regardless of who is speaking. Some take notes in whatever language is spoken, and others mix languages in their notes regardless of which language the concept is expressed in. Find the system that works for you, there is no right or wrong.

Subject-verb-object

Always keep track of "who did what to whom." While sentence structures for these grammatical elements vary from language to language, all languages include them, and they are the critical information to remember.

UNIT 2

Things to note down

Some important elements to note may include:

- Essential ideas. Experienced note-takers can capture a whole idea with a symbol.
- Links. The relationship between different parts of an utterance (like next steps) can be confusing if they are mixed up. Arrows, lines, and placement on the page are useful for indicating how concepts are linked.
- Causality. If one thing causes the next, this connection must be clear in the interpreter's mind and notes. (Again, arrows or a standard abbreviation for "because" may help, for example "bc")
- Transcodable terms. Some words should not be interpreted but simply rendered "as is" into the other language (e.g., terms with no conceptual equivalence in the target language). These may be referred to as "transcodable" terms and followed by a paraphrase, a request for clarification or a mediation (discussed in Unit 3),

A Word About Shorthand

Interpreters often ask about shorthand and believe that note-taking is a form of shorthand. That is incorrect: shorthand is a symbolic writing method intended to record entire conversations. (Before electronic recording devices became common, shorthand was used by secretaries and administrative assistants who took dictation.) If an interpreter tries to record a whole conversation, he or she will be unable to interpret, because the goal is not a word-for-word literal recap of dialog into the same language, but rather rendering the *meaning* of what is said idiomatically into another language. It is both impossible and dangerous to attempt shorthand while interpreting.

Symbols in Note-taking

Why use symbols?

Using symbols during note-taking can be a powerful tool for ensuring accurate and complete renditions because they represent *meaning* rather than words. They embody the essence of what the speaker says, but they free interpreters from the actual words used, allowing them to capture that same meaning using the appropriate terminology in the target language. In addition, symbols are visual and compact. They often express many ideas in little space and take less time to write down than words. In short, symbols help to anchor what was said in your mind and to jog your memory when the time comes to render that idea.

UNIT 2

Typically, interpreters mix symbols with words and abbreviations in their note-taking, Don't fixate solely on symbols. Rather, have a mental map about how to take down and diagram your notes. Symbols will come later. They should be the symbols that make most sense to you. Unless your note-taking system is clear, simple and coherent, symbols will never help you.

How to use symbols

- *Make them easy to draw.* Two or three pen-strokes are enough.
- *Keep them meaningful.* The symbol should have some connection to your experience.
- *Use them consistently.* One symbol should always have the same meaning.

Typically, interpreters have a set of symbols developed *ahead of time* for expressing commonly repeated concepts (such as time, place, connectors, people, emotions) that are used over and over again regardless of the specific assignment. These symbols are unique to each individual interpreter. In addition, interpreters will often improvise symbols specific to the session at hand. For example, they might use a capital D for "diabetes" in a patient-doctor exchange. But be careful, it can be dangerous to improvise symbol systems on the spot, because the interpreter may incorrectly remember what the symbol means and make an important error. Symbols used in note-taking should be simple and clear for the interpreter. Use them for:

- Common concepts (e.g., forms that the interpreter sees often).
- Technical terms that recur frequently.
- Instructions that are common in a particular service.

Examples of symbols

Common symbols used by interpreters can include such symbols as the ones below (with any meaning that the interpreter wants to assign to a given symbol):

1. Text message abbreviations. Good texters may become good note-takers! The best abbreviations use letters from the beginning and end of the word, so that it can't be mistaken for a similar word and misinterpreted (ply for policy, pltcn for politician, and plcal for political, etc).
2. Arrows. Arrows can be used to indicate direction but they may also show an INCREASE (arrow goes up) or a DECREASE (arrow goes down): ↔←↑→↓. Also: come back, reverse, rise/fall, etc.
3. Basic math symbols, e.g., >, <, =, ~, ± can be used with their usual meaning
4. Science/mathematical symbols may be helpful, e.g., Σ, °, Ψ, Ω, ς, α, Θ, Ξ, ∴ Π
5. Symbols in common usage can be co-opted for special meaning, e.g., √, φ, ♣,♦,♥,♠,*,☼, ○, ♂
6. Shapes (squares, circles, trapezoids, triangles, etc.) can mean what you want them to
7. Punctuation marks, e.g. ? ! ( ) " :
8. Keyboard symbols such as *,&, ^, %, $, #, @ can be used with their usual or another meaning.

9. Emoticons, like smiley-faces and sad faces, are helpful.
10. Use underlining, bold, italics and double-underlining of words to create emphasis, e.g., needs vs *needs* vs underline{needs} vs **__NEEDS__** etc to denote urgency of need.

Common Errors in Note-taking

Remember, new skills only feel comfortable when they are practiced frequently enough to become automatic. When you begin taking notes, it is likely to feel awkward and may cause your interpreting performance to actually degrade temporarily as your mind adjusts to the new cognitive task it is learning.

It is natural, therefore, that when interpreters begin taking notes, many of them commit a few basic errors.

Errors during note-taking

Often, interpreters may:
- Write down too many notes.
- Forget to listen while they write notes.
- Get confused while note-taking.
- Become muddled between the two languages.
- Write illegibly.

Errors during the rendering of notes.

In many cases, when you look at you notes and try to render the interpretation, you may;

- Spend too much time or effort trying to decode your notes.
- Render the notes awkwardly.
- Forget the audience and how to interpret for them.
- Read too literally instead of creating a flowing delivery.
- Fail to deliver the emotional tone or affect of the message.

But just like learning to ride a bike, driving a car or learning a new language, once you have the basics mastered, your new skill becomes automatic and you will perform it without thinking about it.

UNIT 2

A Brief Review of Unit 2

This unit has covered many skills. All of them are important. However, as you are starting out, here are the skills to *prioritize* and *remember*.

Steps

The steps to execute an interpreted session are:

1. Preparation
2. Pre-conference (optional)
3. Introductions
4. Session
5. Mediation (optional)
6. Ending the session
7. Post-session

In particular, you should try to:

- Prepare for the session
- Collect critical information (address, contact information, sensitive issues, technical terminology, etc)
- Ask for any forms you might have to sight translate (be prepared to decline graciously if they are too long or complex).
- Let the agency know what time you have to leave.
- Review your own performance afterward for improvements

Modes

There are three accepted modes in community interpreting, and a fourth mode that is somewhat disputed:

- Consecutive
- Simultaneous
- Sight translation
- Summarization (disputed)

Of the three modes, consecutive is the default mode that you should use to interpret unless:

- The speaker is too excited to pause.
- The session is so intense you do not wish to interrupt it.
- A client has dementia, a mental health condition or substance abuse problem and cannot interrupt his or her own speech.
- A child is too young to pause for you to interpret.

If you cannot interpret in consecutively, try simultaneous mode. If simultaneous is impossible (e.g., an emergency, too many people speaking at once) then and only then—as an absolute last resort—consider summarization. Legal interpreters should not summarize, however.

Whispered simultaneous (also known as whisper interpreting or *chuchotage*) is a variation of simultaneous that involves the interpreter whispering to an individual or small group of people who do not speak the language of a public speaker.

Introductions

At a minimum, state your name ("I am so-and-so and I'll be interpreting for you today") followed by:

- Everything said will be interpreted.
- Everything will be kept confidential.
- Please speak directly to each other, not to me.
- Please speak slowly and pause often so I can interpret.

You may add anything else that will help the interpreted session go smoothly, provided that what you add is both professional and appropriate.

Positioning

While there is no universal agreement about positioning, we urge you to:

- Avoid the triangle position.
- Try to sit beside and slightly behind the client.
- If the client looks at you, sit even further behind the client.
- If this is not possible, adopt a position that is unobtrusive and lets the client and provider speak directly to each other.
- Where feasible and safe, position yourself closer to the client than the provider.

> Remember: the goal of effective position is to promote *direct client-provider communication*.

UNIT 2

First person

Interpret in first person as a default because:

- Professional interpreters are required to interpret in first person.
- Doing so supports accuracy.
- First person is faster than third person (up to 50 percent faster).
- First person is less taxing on memory than third person.
- The syntax of third person is more convoluted and harder to interpret.

It may however be difficult or impossible to interpret in first person when:

- Too many people speak at once.
- Everything happens too fast (an emergency).
- Speech is incoherent (dementia, mental illness, substance abuse).
- Small children are confused by first person (too abstract).

Accuracy

- Interpret everything.
- Maintain the spirit, tone and style.
- Keep the same register.
- Reflect the emotions of the speaker, not your own.
- Interpret in first person (this may feel artificial at first).
- Manage the flow.
- Adopt effective positioning.

> **THIRD PERSON**
>
> If the provider or client speak in third person, *do not change their speech to first person.* Instead, gently remind them to use first person. Try the following techniques to help provider and client speak to each other in first person.
>
> - Avoid eye contact. This reminds them to focus on each other.
> - Give a brief reminder, e.g., *Please speak to the [provider/client], not to me.*
> - Give a hand signal to direct them back to each other. If all else fails, perform a mediation (how to mediate is discussed in Unit 3) to explain why it is important to speak in first person (.e.g., first person is faster, easier to interpret, more accurate, etc).
> - After the session briefly chat with the provider to explain the importance of speaking in first person.

However, do not mimic the speaker to such a degree that anyone feels mocked.

UNIT 2

Message analysis

Try to:

1) Comprehend the message.
2) Parse (break down) the message into its concepts and linguistic structures.
3) Find conceptual equivalents in the target language.
4) Reframe and reconstruct the message.

Memory Skills

Work on your short-term memory.
Remember: summarizing is not permitted except as a last resort (and not at all permitted in legal interpreting). The three most common reasons for summarizing are:
- Use of third person (which contributes to memory overload)
- Failing to manage the flow (which again leads to memory overload)
- Lack of training and practice to develop memory skills.

To improve your memory skills, work on:

- Concentration and focus
- Chunking
- Note-taking
- Visualization
- Classic memory exercises
- Word games
- Practice

Note-taking basics

- Write the concept, not the words
- Keep your notes short
- Capture a whole idea with a symbol
- Use abbreviations wherever possible
- Use strike out for negation (e.g., ~~insur~~ for "no insurance")
- Use your margins for large categories
- Use arrows (for increase/decrease, directions, time, etc)
- Chunk into sub-categories

UNIT 2

Some interpreters prefer to take notes in their native language, regardless of who is speaking. Some take notes in whatever language is spoken,

Avoid writing whole lines of text. Instead structure your notes either vertically (top to bottom for most interpreters) or diagonally (left to right or right to left, depending on your native language). If you write horizontally, it may confuse you.

Things to note down

Some important elements to note may include:

- Essential ideas.
- Links.
- Causality.
- Transcodable terms. (e.g., terms with no conceptual equivalents in the target language).

Symbols in note-taking

Remember to:

- *Make them easy to draw.* Two or three pen-strokes are enough.
- *Keep them meaningful.* The symbol should have some connection to your experience.
- *Use them consistently.* One symbol should always have the same meaning.

Use them for:

- Common concepts (e.g., forms that the interpreter sees often).
- Technical terms that recur frequently.
- Instructions that are common in a particular service .

Avoid errors during note-taking

If you are still new to note-taking, try not to:
- Write down too many notes.
- Forget to listen while you write notes.
- Get confused while note-taking.
- Become muddled by the two languages.
- Write illegibly.

UNIT 2

REVIEW

UNIT 2 REVIEW EXERCISES

The steps of an interpreted session

Put these seven steps in the correct order:

Mediation (optional)
The interpreted session
Preparation
Ending the Session
Introductions
Pre-conference (optional)
Post Session

_____
_____
_____
_____
_____
_____
_____

Preparation

Strike out those details in the list below that an interpreter does NOT need to know or prepare ahead of time:

- Language needed.
- Location of session.
- Type of session.
- Sensitive issues to be addressed.
- Name of client.
- If client is HIV positive (for medical interpreting).
- Approximate length of session.
- Telephone number of client.
- Contact information for agency/provider.

UNIT 2

Modes of Interpreting

Circle one answer.

1. Community interpreters usually perform:
   (a) Consecutive interpreting.
   (b) Simultaneous interpreting.
   (c) Whisper interpreting.
   (d) Summarization.

2. Circle the situation where it is not appropriate to practice simultaneous interpreting.
   (a) At the United Nations.
   (b) At a social services conference.
   (c) When the interpreter is new and inexperienced.
   (d) For a corporate meeting.

3. What mode of interpreting should community interpreters rarely—if ever—use?
   (a) Consecutive.
   (b) Simultaneous.
   (c) Sight translation.
   (d) Summary.

4. Community interpreters may need to switch to simultaneous mode if:
   (a) An emergency situation occurs
   (b) One or more of the parties becomes so excited that they refuse to pause to allow the interpreter to interpret.
   (c) An elderly person or client with mental illness does not understand the need to pause for the interpreter.
   (d) Any of the above.

Which mode of interpreting would you adopt in the following situations? Fill in the blanks with one of the following: simultaneous, consecutive, sight translation, summary, whisper.

At a Back to School Night, the principal welcomes the auditorium of families with a speech. You interpret for 5 LEP parents.

_____

The clinical dietician has developed a nutrition program for a patient with gall-bladder disease and explains it to the patient.

_____

The social worker is performing intake for a food stamps application when four family members grow upset and begin talking all at once.

_____

UNIT 2

The senior center's Information and Referral specialist offers a woman a bulletin of the county's services in English and suggests that you read certain parts of it aloud while she remains there to answer the client's questions.

_____

The doctor is speaking on the phone with the patient's oncologist about a recent marker test, CT-scan and upcoming surgery. The patient is in the room. The doctor speaks quickly and uses very technical language that you don't understand.

_____

The librarian summarizes a library policy document about leaving children unattended, and the interpreter interprets her summary.

_____

Introductions

List at least four or five things you would say during an introduction to the provider or the client:

_____
_____
_____
_____
_____
_____

Positioning

What is the *primary* goal of effective positioning in community interpreting?

_____
_____
_____
_____
_____

UNIT 2

First and Third Person

Describe some of the differences between interpreting in first and in third person.
_____
_____
_____
_____
_____

Why does using third person typically result in a longer message?
_____
_____
_____
_____

Interpreter Skills

True or False

1. The provider should speak directly to the client. _____
2. The interpreter should remain in the background. _____
3. All interpreters should use first person at all times. _____
4. Interpreters should maintain the register, tone, spirit and language style of the speaker and the message. _____
5. Interpreters should maintain a neutral tone of voice. _____
6. Interpreters should interpret literally at all times. _____
7. If a provider is mistaken, the interpreter may give advice. _____
8. Note-taking is rarely needed in community interpreting. _____
9. Avoiding eye contact while interpreting is rude. _____
10. A professional introduction is always necessary. _____
11. If the doctor uses third person, the interpreter should interpret in first person. _____

UNIT 2

Memory Skills

1. Why are memory skills important for community interpreters?
_____
_____
_____
_____

2. What can interpreters do to improve memory skills?
_____
_____
_____
_____

Note-taking

Have someone read the following paragraph out loud for you. (Do not look at it yourself.) Take notes according to the information provided in this unit. Afterwards, try and render an interpretation based on your notes.

The District of Columbia Housing Code (DCHC) is enforced by the D.C. Department of Consumer and Regulatory Affairs' (DCRA) Housing Regulation Administration (HRA). DCRA publishes a "Tenant's Guide to Safe and Decent Housing," which is a 30-page booklet that summarizes the D.C. housing code and the Rental Housing Act of 1985, which is the city law covering rent-controlled apartments. To obtain a copy of this booklet, go to the Housing Regulation Services Center in Room 700 at 614 H Street, N.W., Washington, D.C., 20001, telephone (202) 727-7395, or send the office a self-addressed, stamped envelope to receive the guide by mail. You may also find it on the DCRA web site at www.dcra.dc.gov on the "Housing Regulation" page under rent control.

Now look at the text and your own notes. Do you feel your rendition was roughly accurate? What could you do to improve your note-taking skills?

___
___
___
___
___
___

UNIT 3
MEDIATION AND CULTURE

Unit 3 Objectives

OBJECTIVE 3.1
Demonstrate effective mediation skills.
3.1 (a) List and practice the steps for mediation.
3.1 (b) Practice strategic mediation.
3.1 (c) Define and compare interpreter roles.

OBJECTIVE 3.2
Develop and practice cultural mediation strategies.
3.2 (a) Define culture and cultural competence.
3.2 (b) Apply ethical decision-making to a communication barrier.
3.2 (c) Practice non-intrusive cultural mediation.
3.2 (d) Show awareness of stereotypes and bias.

OBJECTIVE 3.1

Demonstrate effective mediation skills

Introduction

This unit centers on an important aspect of community interpreting: how to address barriers to communication, including cultural differences. In Unit 3 we consider practical aspects of the community interpreter's work that go beyond words and the literal message. Many specialists around the world call this critical dimension of the interpreter's work "mediation."

The reason that mediation is often necessary in community interpreting is that even if a message is interpreted accurately and competently, the client or provider may not understand what is said. Such barriers to understanding put the outcome

3.1 (a) List and practice the steps for mediation.

3.1 (b) Practice strategic mediation.

3.1 (c) Define and compare interpreter roles.

of the service at risk. In addition, it is difficult to speak of "equal access" to a service in cases where the client does not understand what is taking place. (For example, is informed consent truly informed if the client does not understand what he or she is agreeing to?)

Sometimes the problem of understanding is on the provider's side. If the client is not responding for cultural reasons, the provider may sense that something is wrong but have no idea what to do about the problem. Sometimes the client feels lost because the service system is so different from the equivalent system in the client's country of origin.

To remedy this type of challenge, *community interpreters may need to interrupt the session to address a barrier to communication*.

> **Mediation and Culture**
>
> **Mediation:** Any act or utterance of the interpreter that goes beyond interpreting and is intended to address barriers to communication between parties who do not share a common language.
>
> **Cultural awareness:** Recognition of the importance of cultural differences.
>
> **Cultural sensitivity:** A willingness to accept and value cultural differences.
>
> **Cultural competence:** The ability to provide services effectively across cultures.

Conference interpreters can usually do little or nothing to address misunderstandings that take place while they interpret. Court interpreters are also very restricted in what they may do to address barriers to communication. Community interpreters in the U.S. and other countries have more freedom to intervene—but that freedom itself carries risks and dangers.

Unit 3 helps to prepare the community interpreter to address barriers to communication safely, effectively and competently, including barriers of cultural misunderstanding.

Steps for Mediation

OBJECTIVE 3.1 (a) List and practice the steps for mediation

Understanding mediation

Mediation is an international term used in many countries to describe any speech and actions of the interpreter that go beyond interpreting. Mediation can take place during or outside the interpreted session.

It is important to understand that the community interpreter has essentially two jobs: to interpret, or to mediate. There are many types of mediation. But in your work, you are either interpreting or you are mediating, and these responsibilities entail two very different skill sets.

Interpreting involves taking an oral or signed message and rendering its meaning into another language. Mediation involves interrupting the session when there appears to be a misunderstanding or a barrier to service delivery in order to facilitate successful communication.

Many communication barriers are cultural in nature. For example, in a nursing home a Haitian woman became mentally ill. She put a belt around her own neck but said that her husband did it. She believed that, because she had initiated the divorce, her husband had put a spell on her to make her ill. But she did not inform the health care staff about her beliefs. Without an interpreter or a cultural mediator to help nursing home staff address the cultural barrier, those who were caring for her might never have found out what she believed was causing her illness. Without knowing what a patient thinks about her illness can make it difficult to provide appropriate care.

Interpreting is usually about language.

Mediation is often about culture.

Yet in truth, no one can separate language from culture.

Steps for Mediation

When to mediate
The first rule of mediation is to mediate only when you must. *Only a significant barrier to communication or service delivery justifies the time and risk involved in mediating.*

The steps

The steps for mediation are simple, though often hard to remember in real life.

How it works
Let's look at an example to see the steps in actions.

> **STEPS FOR MEDIATION**
>
> 1. Interpret what was just said.
> 2. Identify yourself as the interpreter.
> 3. Address one party briefly.
> 4. Interpret what you said to the other party.
> 5. Return to basic interpreting.

Preschool Teacher: We're concerned about your daughter's fine motor skills, and we'd like to refer her to Child Find for assessment.

1. Interprets what was just said
The interpreter interprets what the teacher says into Cantonese, leaving the term "Child Find" in English. Then she turns to the teacher, leans forward and makes eye contact.

2. Identifies herself as the interpreter.
The interpreter begins the mediation by saying, "Excuse me, as the interpreter...."

3. Addresses one party briefly. The interpreter continues, "I'd like to clarify what Child Find means."

4. Interprets what she said to the other party. Turning to Mrs. Wong, the interpreter says in Cantonese, "Excuse me, as the interpreter I just asked the teacher to clarify what 'Child Find' means."

5. Returns to basic interpreting. The interpreter returns to an unobtrusive position. The teacher responds (to the interpreter), "Oh, sure. Child Find is a national program that runs in each state and county. It's a great program that helps us identify children who need special help. And it's free." *Instead of answering the teacher, the interpreter interprets what the teacher has just said*, breaking off eye contact with both parties.

THE COMMUNITY INTERPRETER

Guidelines for Mediation

Transparency

Transparency means that you must interpret everything that is said during the session, including anything that is said to you or anything that you say to anyone in the room when you mediate. In this way, everyone in the room knows what is going on.

Transparency is easy to forget. If the provider asks you, "Do you think she needs more time to make a decision?" your immediate and natural response will be to answer the question. Resist the temptation. No doubt you are a polite person. But when you are interpreting, the rules of polite conversation do not apply. If someone asks you a question during the session, *interpret it*.

> **Transparency**
>
> Transparency requires interpreting everything that is said or signed, including remarks addressed to the interpreter, any intervention by the interpreter, or any rude language or aggressive comments made by any party.

(However, if you don't understand what some parties are saying "offline" because it is too technical—for example, when a doctor consults on the phone with a radiologist—you may summarize what is said for the client.)

Remember: When mediating with one party, *always inform the other party what you are doing*.

Why transparency matters

Transparency is necessary for community interpreting. Transparency is an ethical requirement under respect and accuracy and also a national standard of practice. (See Unit 5, where standards of practice are discussed in detail.)

Lack of transparency may make the ignored party feel suspicious, scared, upset, angry or confused. Providers and clients may lose trust in an interpreter who engages in side conversations.

The single most common complaint that the authors of this manual hear from providers about interpreters is side conversations between interpreters and clients. Such conversations make the provider feel excluded and concerned.

Always respect transparency while interpreting.

Effective Mediation Techniques

To keep your mediation simple, here are a few helpful details. Try to burn them into your mind, because these remarks will help you avoid the most common pitfalls of interpreter mediation.

The Basics

- *Interpret what was just said.* This is usually the first thing that interpreters forget when they mediate.

- *When you interrupt the session, identify yourself as the interpreter.* This is a second very common thing that interpreters forget to do.

- *Remember to interpret what you say for both or all parties.* Forgetting to mediate with both parties is a widespread problem among community interpreters. Often they get distracted when they mediate and speak to one party only.

- *Keep your mediations brief.* It is easy to launch a long, complicated mediation. Don't. Long mediations lead to side conversations. Keep your mediations short, simple and to the point.

- *If someone speaks to you after your mediation*, do not answer. Instead, just interpret what is said, even if the person is speaking to you. Otherwise, you will get locked into a side conversation. If there's a misunderstanding, you can always mediate again.

- Repeat in English any term or phrase that you do not know how to interpret if you plan to request clarification of that term immediately.

> **Eye Contact**
>
> Remember: when you interpret, you must be unobtrusive. Do not gesture or draw attention to yourself. Avoid eye contact to avoid getting involved in a conversation. But when you mediate, everything changes because you enter the conversation (briefly).
>
> While mediating, make eye contact with either or both parties. Lean forward and speak assertively, but only during the mediation.
>
> As soon as you have finished mediating, break off eye contact and return to your unobtrusive position and behavior. You may wish to glance down at your notepad.

Special Guidance

1. Try to mediate as little as possible.

2. Never give advice, even if someone asks for your opinion.

3. Do not get caught in the middle. You are not there as a case manager, a co-therapist or a social worker. You are there to interpret.

4. Break off eye contact after you mediate, because after a mediation *there is a much greater tendency for the provider and client to look at and talk to you*. Use eye contact and body language to signal the fact that you are back to your main job: interpreting.

Avoiding Side Conversations

Side conversations

Side conversations take place when the interpreter begins talking to one party. The other party (or parties) in the room do not know what is taking place. Side conversations are prohibited in community and legal interpreting. They violate transparency.

Why side conversations happen

Interpreters often end up in a side conversation when they mediate. Typically they get trapped in side conversations for one of two reasons:

- The interpreter performs a mediation that is too long and complicated; and/or

- When someone asks the interpreter a question, the interpreter answers the question instead of interpreting it.

Let us look at how to handle these challenges.

Avoid a long mediation: The only solution to a long mediation is a short one. The reason that performing a long mediation gets you trapped into a side conversation is that a long mediation already feels like a conversation. For example, many interpreters say things like this:

Long Mediation

"Excuse me, as the interpreter I'm really worried that the client doesn't understand because in her country social services don't exist in the same way they do here and they don't have something like food stamps, and besides, I'm not even sure she's literate. So the forms you're talking about may be very confusing."

All of which may be true. But by the time you finish this long mediation, you may not remember what you said, may not want to interpret all of it for the client (in case you offend her) and you've established so much eye contact and rapport with the service provider that the provider will have questions for you that typically engage you to keep talking. Meanwhile, the client sits there with no idea what is going on. So try this instead:

> **Short mediation**
>
> "Excuse me, as the interpreter I'm concerned because social services are so different in the client's country that what I'm interpreting does not make sense in [Punjabi]."

Then interpret your mediation for the client. In this way, the provider (a) understands the problem; (b) knows what to do; and (c) leaves you free to interpret.

Plan your mediations ahead of time. Certain common situations occur again and again. Prepare mental scripts in your head about what to say.

Don't answer questions. It is very common during a session that the provider or client will turn to you and ask you a question, e.g., a client asks you, "What do you think I should do?" or a provider asks you, "I don't think she's following me. Can you tell me whether she understands?" Simply interpret the question. Often, interpreting the question solves the problem because the other party will answer it, leaving you out of the middle.

UNIT 3

Client Support

In some countries, mediation outside the session is encouraged. In the U.S., mediating outside the session is often discouraged for contract interpreters but routinely expected of adjunct interpreters (bilingual staff), who perform many types of client support.

> **Examples of Client Support**
> (Ouside the Session)
>
> - Making phone calls and follow-up appointments for a client.
> - Explaining forms, next steps or procedures.
> - Case management.
> - Client follow-up
> - Coordinating with other agencies about the client.
> - Giving directions, accompanying or driving clients to other services.
> - Contacting a family member to provide an update.

Contract interpreters do not usually engage in client support because it is (a) not part of interpreting; (b) inclined to create bias in favor of the client (as opposed to impartiality); (c) risky, since the client may confide in the interpreter and ask the interpreter not to reveal that information. However, for adjunct interpreters, such duties may be part of their job description and a major reason they were hired in the first place. Client support of this kind may be everyday work for many bilingual employees.

> Mediation outside the encounter is often considered an unacceptable activity by professional interpreters. Yet if a bilingual staff member is hired to perform such duties, it is necessary to do so. However, be careful not to perform these duties while interpreting.

Strategic Mediation

OBJECTIVE 3.1 (b) Practice strategic mediation

Mediation involves a tremendous risk that the interpreter will engage in behaviors that undermine the session's goals. For example, it is *extremely common that when you mediate you may:*

- Forget to interpret the last thing said.
- Forget to interpret what is said during the mediation to all parties.
- Forget to clearly identify yourself as the interpreter.
- Enter a side conversation.
- Give opinions without realizing it.
- Provide erroneous information.
- Develop a relationship with the client or provider (taking sides).
- Undermine clear client-provider communication.
- Undermine the client-provider relationship.
- Derail the session.
- Put beneficial outcomes at risk.
- Unwittingly foster a situation where, after the mediation is over, all parties will tend to look at and speak to you, not each other.

To avoid these risks, master the basic steps for mediation and have a few mental scripts rehearsed to address common communication barriers.

Scripts for Mediation

The single best way to practice strategic mediation is to have mental scripts ready for common mediation situations. The more you practice basic mediation scenarios, the more comfortable you will feel about tackling more challenging communication barriers.

Here are examples of some common barriers to communication that community interpreters address often, including examples of what to say. However, every interpreter's experience is different. You will need to develop your own scripts. You should write them down. Create scripts that reflect your language, your personality, and the types of communication barriers that you commonly encounter in your areas of service. Then memorize and practice your scripts.

1. CLARIFICATION:

Situation: The interpreter does not understand something said by the provider or client.

Script: *(To provider)* "Excuse me, as the interpreter I wanted to ask the client what he means by *cochinillas*."

(To client) "Excuse me, as the interpreter I wanted to ask what you mean by *cochinillas*."

2. CHECKING FOR UNDERSTANDING:

Situation: The client appears not to understand what the provider says, but the provider seems unaware of this problem.

Script: *(To provider)* "Excuse me, as the interpreter I sense a break in communication that might be caused by a misunderstaning about what consent forms are."

(To client) "I just informed the provider that I sensed a communication problem that might be caused by a misunderstanding about what consent forms are."

3. HIGH REGISTER

Situation: The provider is using PhD English with a client who has little education.

Script: *(To provider)* "Excuse me, as the interpreter I'm not sure that what I am interpreting is clear. If you would like to rephrase in simpler language, I may be able to interpret it more clearly."

(To client) "Excuse me, as the interpreter I just informed the provider that what I am interpreting may not be clear. I suggested she rephrase in simpler language, so that I can interpret it more clearly."[1]

4. CULTURAL-LINGUISTIC BARRIER

Situation: The provider is using the client's last name as their first name and vice versa.

Script: *(To provider)* "Excuse me, as the interpreter I'm concerned there may be an inaccurate record for this client's name due to a different naming system in the client's country. You may wish to ask the client about this issue."

(To client) "Excuse me, as the interpreter I just informed the provider that there may be an inaccurate record for your name due to the different naming system in our country. I suggested she might want to ask you about this."

---

[1] Notice how this type of mediation is not insulting the client's education or literacy level. It is very important that whatever you say to the provider be something that you can also say to the client without sounding condescending or offensive.

5. BASIC CULTURAL BARRIER

Situation: During a parent-teacher interview, a child's father has no idea what is going on and you suspect the problem is that he has never even heard of, much less seen, a report card.

Script: (*To provider*) "Excuse me, as the interpreter I'm concerned there may be a misunderstanding about the purpose of a report card."

(*To client*) "Excuse me, as the interpreter I told the teacher I'm concerned there may be a misunderstanding about the purpose of a report cards."

6. COMPLEX CULTURAL BARRIER

Situation: During a child protective services investigation, a parent shuts down and the interpreter senses a serious cultural barrier.

Script: (*To client*) "Excuse me, as the interpreter I'm concerned there may be a cultural misunderstanding related to family roles between husband and wife. Service providers often find it helpful to hear cultural information. Is there anything you'd like to share with the provider?"

(*To provider*): "Excuse me, as the interpreter I'm concerned there may be cultural misunderstanding related to gender roles. I asked the client if there anything he'd like to share with you about this topic."

(Note: *it is often preferable to address the provider first unless the interpreter senses an important cultural barrier that is causing tension. In that case, addressing the client first may help to defuse the tension.*)

7. SERVICE DELIVERY BARRIER

Situation: The service provider, during intake, is asking many questions which appear intrusive and culturally upsetting, e.g., past sexual behavior and partners. The interpreter watches the session derail and fears that the patient will not take the necessary tests or adhere to a treatment plan.

Script: (*to provider*) "Excuse me, as the interpreter, I'm concerned that some of these questions may appear upsetting or culturally intrusive to many people from the patient's culture."

(*to patient*) "Excuse me, as the interpreter, I shared with the provider that some of these questions may appear upsetting or culturally intrusive to many people from our culture."

THE COMMUNITY INTERPRETER

8. CLIENT SPEAKS TO INTERPRETER

Situation: The client tells the interpreter, during the session, "I'm not sure about this. Do you think the provider is giving me good information?"

Script: No script. Simply interpret the mediation and let the provider answer the question.

9. PROVIDER SPEAKS TO INTERPRETER

Situation: The provider asks the interpreter, "Do you think my client understands?"

Script: First, interpret the question. Then remind the provider:
(to provider) "Excuse me, as the interpreter I want to remind you that I must interpret everything you say and that I'm not permitted to answer questions during a session."
(to client) "Excuse me, as the interpreter I just reminded the provider that I must interpret everything he says and can't answer questions during the session."

One Final Note

Many interpreters fail to respect transparency when they mediate because, in the privacy of their own minds, they know that what they have just to one party would sound offensive to the other party. The mediation, literally interpreted, might come across as patronizing, demeaning, offensive or inappropriate. This type of "discrepant mediation" (where what is said to one party is very different than what is said to the other party) is understandable but not acceptable. The interpreter must at all times be vigilant to say to one party only what can be respectfully interpreted for all parties present.

Challenges in Mediation

Practice and prepare

The steps of mediation look simple. However, it takes a great deal of practice to avoid the common pitfalls of mediation.

The importance of planning ahead

If the interpreter does not have a plan about what to say when he or she mediates, mediation becomes difficult. The interpreter, lacking confidence, usually says something that is too long, inadvertently offensive, or unclear. As the interpreter familiar with the culture of your clients, you know that certain situations arise often. These common types of communication barriers should be planned for ahead of time—not during the encounter.

Whom to speak to first

There is no rule in community interpreting about which party to address first when mediating. The authors recommend that, unless there is a compelling reason to speak to the client first, develop the habit of addressing the provider first, and then the client, for the following reasons:

- Having a simple mental pattern (first the provider, then the client) helps keep your mediation process simple. Anything that simplifies mediation will be helpful to you.

- In legal interpreting, you are supposed to address the provider first, so having this habit in place will be less confusing if you also do legal interpreting.

- The provider always likes to know what is going on.

- Providing a quality service is the provider's responsibility. If your mediation indicates a concern or problem with service delivery, the provider will want to know immediately.

- If you notify the provider first, it gives the provider time (while you mediate with the client) about how to change course, if that is needed.

- Some providers, including doctors and other professionals, prefer to feel in control of their vital service. They appreciate it very much if the interpreter speaks first to the provider during mediation.

Always start a mediation by saying, "Excuse me, as the interpreter..."

We recommend that you develop the habit of beginning all your mediations with the words, "Excuse me, as the interpreter...." for the following reasons:

- You will develop the habit of always identifying yourself in both languages as the interpreter.
- The words "Excuse me" act as a natural conversation break in most languages, which helps to make clear that you are speaking as the *interpreter*.

UNIT 3

Mediating Offensive Questions or Remarks

One of the most delicate questions in community interpreting is how to handle an offensive question or remark.

If someone is angry and uses bad or offensive language, the official ethical requirement is: "Just interpret it." (However, it is often very emotionally difficult for the interpreter to do so.[1]) To add to this challenge, sometimes people say something during a session that isn't meant to be offensive. For example, often a provider will turn to the interpreter to ask something like: "Do you think my client is mentally competent?"

Imagine if you were the client and you heard the interpreter accurately interpret that question. How would you feel about the provider? The client-provider relationship would be broken.

In delicate cases such as these, the interpreting field is divided. Some experts say, "Accuracy is required. Just interpret the question." Others say, "The provider didn't mean to destroy the relationship. She was just speaking to the interpreter. Give the provider another chance!"

The authors of this manual make the following observations.

- Try to avoid this problem before it starts by emphasizing in your introductions (or a pre-conference) that you are ethically bound to interpret **_everything_** that is said.
- Some providers are bigoted or racist (a certain percentage of any population is). If the provider's remarks were intentionally nasty or mean-spirited, interpret them. After all, if you were the client—wouldn't you want to know if your provider was a racist or a bigot? If the provider's intentions are *benevolent* and the provider is speaking to *you* (not the client), take the following into consideration as you decide whether or not to interpret the remarks:
    o Will interpreting these remarks irreparably damage the client-provider relationship?
    o Would it be feasible for the client to find another provider who is more sensitive?
    o Is the provider otherwise acting in a competent, professional and caring manner?

---

[1] There are, however, a growing number of bilingual dictionaries and glossaries, in print and online, that can help to interpret curses, rude slang and other offensive terms that are often missing from conventional dictionaries and glossaries.

UNIT 3

- If you decide not to interpret the remarks, you can remind the provider gently, "Excuse me, as the interpreter I need to remind you that I am obliged to interpret everything and these remarks would be very awkward to interpret." Then tell the client, "Excuse me, as the interpreter I informed the provider that her remarks were difficult and awkward to interpret and suggested she might want to rephrase them."

Be careful, though. Sometimes the client understands the provider, and may not trust you if you do not interpret the provider's awkward remarks.

UNIT 3

Third Person and Mediation

Use of third person

Often you may hear the following expression used in mediation: "The interpreter requests clarification of..." In other words, the interpreter is referring to herself in the third person.

This custom of using third person while mediating probably began in courts, where written records are kept of court proceedings. In such cases, interpreters *must* use third person when they mediate to clarify for the written record that the interpreter is speaking as himself.

Use of the third person is not required in community interpreting. However, if you also perform court interpreting, you may wish to use third person when you mediate to avoid any confusion when you go back and forth between community and legal interpreting.

The following phrases are all perfectly appropriate ways to begin mediating:

- Excuse me, as the interpreter I want to clarify....
- The interpreter would like to ask for clarification of....
- Excuse me, the interpreter requests clarification of....

A REVIEW: POINTS TO REPEAT AND REMEMBER AGAIN AND AGAIN

You may note that this section contains repetitions and redundancies. They are intentional. We include them because the interpreter who mediates makes the same mistakes over and over before getting it right. So as one last review, because these errors are so widespread, please remember:

- Before mediating, interpret the last thing said.
- Identify that you are speaking as the interpreter.
- Respect transparency: mediate with all parties.
- Keep the mediation short.
- As soon as anyone speaks, don't answer. Return to an unobtrusive position, avoid eye contact and continue to interpret.

Interpreter Roles

OBJECTIVE 3.1 (c) Define and compare interpreter roles

Around the world, the question of the interpreter's role has become a controversial one. In a nutshell the controversy boils down to:

- Should interpreters only interpret or also mediate?
- If interpreters mediate, what should they be allowed to do?

Different countries have different answers to these questions. In some countries, interpreters may not engage in cultural mediation or advocacy. In the U.S., cultural mediation and advocacy are standard practice. In Europe, one country may prohibit cultural mediation while other countries allow interpreters to engage in many types of mediation (during and outside the encounter) sometimes allowing interpreters to function as de facto caseworkers.

A Story From Switzerland

In Switzerland, an interpreter worked with a young Muslim patient who was pregnant and would not accept a male doctor for prenatal appointments. No female obstetricians were available, so the interpreter (whose job title was "cultural mediator") introduced the patient to a pious older woman who had made the pilgrimage to Mecca. The older woman justified having her own baby delivered by a male obstetrician in the context of her faith. After meeting with her, the younger patient agreed to see a male doctor.

Within the U.S., legal interpreters *may not* engage in cultural mediation or advocacy. On the other hand, medical interpreters are routinely taught to perform culture brokering and advocacy. Some mental health therapists encourage the interpreters to act as co-therapists while others ask their interpreters to restrict their activities to interpreting. In short, the field of community interpreting is somewhat confused about the issue of interpreter roles. In this section, we will :

1) Examine the historical roles of community interpreters in the U.S.
2) Address common concerns about these roles.

Make clear recommendations.

UNIT 3

Interpreter Roles

The term "roles" is often a confusing one, because this word is widely used in medical interpreting in the U.S. but not so widely used in other interpreting professions (such as legal or conference interpreting) even within the U.S.

Discussions about interpreter roles essentially center on a continuum between interpreting and various forms of mediation. Even within community interpreting in the U.S., a tension has long existed between those who believe an interpreter should restrict his or her activities primarily to interpreting and those who believe an interpreter should intervene as needed to "help out" when misunderstandings arise. One of the best and most sophisticated discussions of this topic is found in Beltran Avery (2001), a NCIHC working paper, called *The Role of the Health Care Interpreter: An Evolving Dialogue*. This paper is the fruit of a national dialogue and national work meetings on the topic and describes the following dichotomy:

> **The "neutral" interpreter**
> According to the neutral interpreter perspective, the sole function of the medical interpreter is "message passing." The interpreter's only responsibility in the encounter is to provide accurate and complete transmissions of messages conveyed in one language into another language, allowing the patient and provider to interact, as nearly as possible, as if they are engaged in a same language exchange. From this perspective, the interpreter is not an active player in the social encounter occurring between patient and provider. The ideal interpreter presence is unobtrusive and non-relational. …. Establishing a relationship with the patient is discouraged.
>
> **The "active" interpreter**
> In contrast is the active interpreter perspective, in which the interpreter is someone who is likely to hold a variety of responsibilities, beyond that of "message passing." This perspective is championed by interpreters who come from small, closely-knit cultural communities and by those who interpret for communities in which relational ties form the foundation of trust and credibility. The fact that they are bilingual and can negotiate both cultures — theirs and the mainstream culture — often casts them into a position of assuming many other tasks and functions that their community needs to survive. …. If a cultural factor such as a belief, assumption or value is creating a misunderstanding that affects the goals of the encounter, the interpreter would be expected to intervene. In such situations, the interpreter has the legitimate option of alerting both parties to the miscommunication, offering suggestions as to what could be impeding mutual understanding.
>
> Beltran Avery (2001:4)

Interpreter Roles and Responsibilities

Three Interpreter Responsibilities

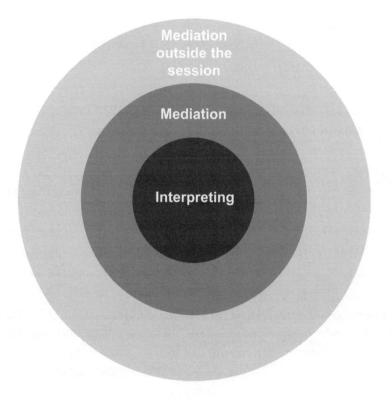

Interpreting: Rendering an oral or signed message into another language, orally or in signed language.

Mediation: Any act or utterance of the interpreter that goes beyond interpreting and is intended to address barriers to understanding between parties who do not share a common language. Examples: clarification, checking for understanding, cultural mediation (culture brokering).

Mediation outside the session: Client support and advocacy. Examples: making phone calls to clients, accompaniment, referrals to other services, reporting a critical incident.

Contract interpreters

Most of the contract interpreter's work will consist of interpreting with relatively small little mediation, during or outside the session.

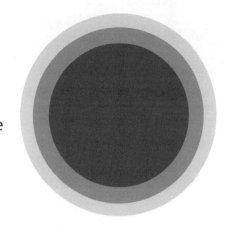

Adjunct interpreters

For adjunct interpreters, community advocates and volunteers, interpreting may constitute a very small portion of their work and they may perform extensive mediation outside the session, often in the form of client support or de facto case management.

Concerns about mediating

In general, community interpreters often spend a great deal of time mediating, during and outside the session. Some of these mediation activities are appropriate for community interpreters. Some are not. The community interpreter will have to think carefully about whether or not to mediate.

SHOULD YOU MEDIATE?

All interpreters will have to carefully consider whether the mediation they perform is truly necessary. In general, outside the session, they should follow a simple rule mentioned in Unit 1 that promotes client autonomy and self-sufficiency: Never do anything for a client that the client can do for him- or herself.

UNIT 3

Mediating Outside the Session

Most mediation outside the session should be restricted to bilingual staff, community advocates and (in some cases) staff interpreters. Contract or agency interpreters should not typically engage in mediation outside the session.

Before mediating outside the session, the adjunct interpreter should carefully consider:
- Is the service I am providing part of my job description?
- Am I trained and qualified to perform it?
- Do I have time to assist the LEP client and still meet my job requirements?
- Does my supervisor know I am performing this sort of service for our LEP clients?
- If not, would he or she approve this sort of service?
- What could I do instead?

In general, many and perhaps most supervisors of bilingual employees are unaware of the degree to which clients seek help from interpreters and bilingual staff after an interpreted session. The adjunct interpreter should discuss this subject openly with a supervisor in order to establish policy and guidelines. For example, a list of appropriate referral agencies could be drawn up. Rather than helping the client directly, the interpreter could then refer the client to an appropriate service.

If supervisors expect the interpreter to make phone calls for follow-up appointments, accompany clients to appointments, help clients with forms or perform other duties for clients outside the session, such services would ideally be written into the interpreter's job description (if they are adjunct interpreters) or added to the interpreter's billable hours (for contract interpreters).

> **What May Bilingual Employees Do?**
>
> The role of the bilingual employee who interprets may confuse you. But remember: during the session, you are an *interpreter*, bound by interpreter ethics. After the session, you are a regular bilingual employee.
>
> If you are trained and qualified to perform a certain task that is in your job description, and you do it for native-born clients, you may also perform it for LEP clients, as long as you are not performing that task *during* the interpreting assignment.
>
> If you are not sure what you are allowed to do, first ask yourself the question: *Which hat am I wearing, my interpreter hat or my bilingual employee hat?* If you are wearing your bilingual employee hat, ask yourself the question: *Is this task something I would normally do for my English-speaking clients?* If so, you may perform that task, even for a client for whom you were just interpreting.

Incremental Intervention

The model of incremental intervention

The NCIHC working paper discussed above was based on a national discussion of interpreter roles that identified various approaches to addressing the dynamic tension between the interpreter as conduit (i.e., the interpreter who "only interprets") and the interpreter as an active participant in the encounter. Among the many approaches the paper discussed was a model that has since become famous: the model of incremental Intervention.

In the U.S., four roles of medical interpreters were elaborated in some detail by Cross-Cultural Health Care Program in Seattle in the mid-1990s, and these four roles have now become widely known. Today a community interpreter working in the U.S. cannot be considered an informed and educated interpreter without knowing about these roles.

The famous "four roles"

The four roles promulgated by CCHCP are

1. Conduit: i.e. basic interpreting
2. Clarifier: clarify linguistic misunderstandings
3. Culture broker: address cultural barriers
4. Advocate: address systemic barriers

In other words you are either interpreting (conduit role) or mediating (clarifier, culture broker and advocate roles).

How the model of incremental intervention works

The "incremental intervention" concept is as follows. Of these four roles, restrict the interpreter's role to basic interpreting wherever possible, but mediate when a clear barrier to understanding arises. Clarification, culture brokering and advocacy are all forms of mediation. However, the more distant a role is from basic interpreting, the less often it should be performed. Hence the model's pyramid shape (see the next page), with the conduit role serving as the base of the pyramid and other roles growing progressively smaller as you move up that pyramid.

How this model is unique

This model delineates interpreter roles and their respective risks in a simple, visual format that has helped to shape the profession of medical interpreting. Today, the terms conduit, clarifier, culture broker and advocate are common. Every community interpreter should know the names of these four roles.

"INCREMENTAL INTERVENTION"

Model created by Cynthia Roat, author of Bridging the Gap, and the Cross Cultural Health Care Program

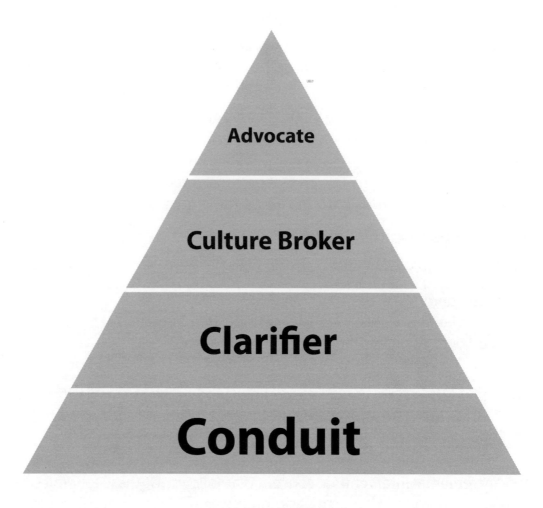

This famous "pyramid" has exerted considerable influence on medical and community interpreting in the U.S.

Conduit: Interpret the message faithfully. Interpret everything that is said, as it is said: add nothing, omit nothing and change nothing.

Clarifier: Check for understanding and adapt the interpreting to ensure understanding (e.g., ask the provider to rephrase in simpler language).

Culture broker: Overcome "cultural bumps" by offering information.

Advocate: Take an action on behalf of a patient that does not deal with the message that one person is trying to pass on to the other.

UNIT 3

Challenges in Mediation

The situation today

The tension between interpreting and mediation still exists in community interpreting today. The model of incremental intervention was a good-faith effort intended to resolve that tension and lay down clear guidance for interpreters. But concerns and challenges remain, for example:

1. Faced with a communication barrier, most community interpreters do not know what to say or do about it.
2. Interpreters are not adequately trained on *how* to perform mediation. During a typical 40-hour training, little time is spent guiding interpreters what to say or do when they mediate.
3. Lack of practice. Relatively few mentoring, shadowing and internship programs exist today for community interpreters (although a growing number of programs have been established for medical interpreting—an encouraging trend). This lack of guided real-world practice and observation means that interpreters are not getting the guidance they need on how to perform mediation safely and effectively.

Problems observed in the field

Whenever specialists, trainers and interpreters collect and share anecdotal stories, common threads emerge. What we see across the country are well-intentioned interpreters with good hearts who are genuinely trying to help out. However, too often they:

- Tell the provider one thing and the client another—a lack of transparency.
- Take over the encounter.
- Give advice when they mediate.
- Stereotype clients. ("In her country, no woman is going to make a decision without her husband here.")
- Tell providers what to do.
- Mind read. ("She's never going to sign a form like that.")
- Inform providers that the client is illiterate, uneducated, or "doesn't understand." (Typically, the interpreters don't tell the client that they said this to the provider.)
- Answer questions during the session.
- Get locked into side conversations.
- Offer inaccurate cultural information.

Strategic Mediation

The model of strategic mediation accepts and endorses the incremental intervention model, i.e.:

- Community interpreters should largely restrict their work to interpreting.
- When mediating, the interpreter should engage in progressively fewer interventions of higher risk.

The model of strategic mediation helps to operationalize the model of incremental intervention by offering specific strategies for safe, effective intervention.

The concept underlying the model of strategic mediation is that, instead of providing information, the interpreter alerts all parties to the nature of a communication barrier and lets them resolve it.

To perform strategic mediation, proceed as follows:
1. Interpret as long as all parties appear to understand each other.
2. If, and only if, they do not understand each other, mediate.
3. Mediate by identifying the nature of the communication barrier, not explaining it.

> **REALITY CHECK**
>
> One Ethiopian community interpreter in Canada put it best: "Telling community interpreters not to do culture brokering is like telling teenagers not to have sex."
>
> The strategic mediation model offers interpreters safe ways to perform mediation.

Effective Mediation Strategies

A number of former practices are changing across the U.S. as new approaches to mediation emerge. Here are a few concrete examples of strategic mediation.

Observe how, in every case, the interpreter does not "jump in" to solve the problem. Instead, the interpreter alerts everyone to the fact that there is a communication barrier and invites them to address it.

Clarifier role

1. *Old practice.* Adjust register (e.g., simplify the provider's language) to facilitate understanding. *This practice is not permitted under NCIHC national standards of practice due to the risks involved if the interpreter tries to change the register.*
New practice. Do not adjust register. If a term is unclear, instead of explaining it, request a clarification and interpret the clarification.

2. *Old practice.* Make "word pictures" of terms that have no linguistic equivalent (e.g., the term "fine needle biopsy" might be impossible to render briefly into many African, Asian or Indian languages).
New practice. A word picture is a paraphrase. Make only short paraphrases (e.g., a sentence). Any long paraphrase is considered unsafe—and it is also a de facto side conversation. Instead, if there is no linguistic equivalent for the concept, invite the client or provider to explain the concept, and interpret their description. This is a much safer practice.

3. *Old practice.* Check for understanding. Often the interpreter sees the client has not understood, while the provider does not notice the problem.
New practice. Invite the provider to check for understanding. (E.g., "Excuse me, as the interpreter I'm concerned there may be a break in communication and that what I'm interpreting is not clear.") It is the provider's job, not the interpreter's, to check for understanding.

Culture broker role

1. *Old practice* "Provide a necessary cultural framework for understanding the message." This guidance assumes that the interpreter is both culturally knowledgeable in all cultures relevant to the encounter (e.g., Californian, American, Hmong and Cambodian cultures, war and refugee culture, hospital culture,

biomedical culture, culture of different educational systems and life experiences, etc). The old practice suggests the interpreter is culturally competent to provide a framework for understanding all those cultures during the encounter. Sadly, these assumptions about the interpreter's competence to navigate complex cultural interactions have proved incorrect.
New practice. Alert provider and client to the existence of the cultural barrier, identify it (e.g., a naming practice, traditional medicine, a different cultural understanding about who makes decisions for a family) and let them address it. (E.g., "Excuse me, as the interpreter I sense a possible miscommunication related to family decision-making and the person who is expected to make medical decisions in the family. You may wish to ask the patient about this.")

2. *Old practice.* Share "appropriate information" about the culture.
Emerging practice. Do not speak directly about the culture. If the barrier is significant, invite the parties present to explore it. (E.g., "Excuse me, as the interpreter I think there may be a serious misunderstanding here about what levels of crime and violence are considered normal in the client's country. You may wish to explore this.")

Advocate role

1. *Old practice.* Intervene when you perceive the patient is not getting appropriate care (e.g., help the client to file a complaint with the Office for Civil Rights or take a patient to visit the hospital ombudsman.)
Suggested Practice. Unless you are a professionally trained advocate, report any critical incident to the appropriate supervisor.

2. *Old practice.* Always make sure the client knows if you propose to advocate and agrees to it.
Standard practice. You do not need a client's permission to report a critical incident, nor should the interpreter engage in such a discussion under normal circumstances. Avoid speaking to the client outside the encounter if possible. Simply report the critical incident. You and the agency may be legally liable for the consequences of a critical incident that you do not report.

OBJECTIVE 3.2

Develop and practice cultural mediation strategies

Introduction

Culture is perhaps the most complex area of the community interpreter's work. Principles from some codes of ethics or standard of practice for community or medical interpreters in the U.S. require the interpreter to address culture while interpreting. This section of the manual explores practical strategies to perform effective cultural mediation. Let's begin by looking at how NCIHC national ethics and standards address culture.

3.2 (a) Define culture and cultural competence.

3.2 (b) Apply ethical decision-making to a communication barrier.

3.2 (c) Practice non-intrusive cultural mediation.

3.2 (d) Show awareness of stereotypes and bias.

NCIHC Ethics and Culture

Several principles from the 2004 NCIHC National Code of Ethics for Interpreters in Healthcare (available at www.ncihc.org) address culture:

- Principle of Accuracy: "The interpreter strives to render the message accurately, conveying the content and spirit of the original message, taking into consideration its cultural context."

- Principle of Cultural Awareness: "The interpreter strives to develop awareness of his/her own and other (including biomedical) cultures encountered in the performance of their professional duties."

- Principle of Respect: "The interpreter treats all parties with respect." (By implication, the interpreter needs cultural knowledge to know how to treat all parties respectfully.)

- Principle of Professional Development. "The interpreter strives to continually further his/her knowledge and skills." Interpreters are responsible for continually deepening their understanding of the socio-cultural context of the populations served (e.g., beliefs about illness and the impact of assimilation and acculturation).

NCIHC Standards of Practice and Culture

Principles from the 2005 NCIHC National Standards of Practice for Interpreters in Healthcare (available at www.ncihc.org) also address culture.

- Standard 11. "The interpreter uses professional, culturally appropriate ways of showing respect. For example, in greetings, an interpreter uses appropriate titles for both patient and provider."

- Standard 14. "The interpreter strives to understand the cultures associated with the languages he or she interprets, including biomedical culture. For example, an interpreter learns about the traditional remedies some patients may use."

- Standard 15. "The interpreter alerts all parties to any significant cultural misunderstanding that arises. For example, if a provider asks a patient who is fasting for religious reasons to take an oral medication, an interpreter may call attention to the potential conflict."

Grateful acknowledgement is made to Julie Burns for her collaboration on these issues.

Culture and Cultural Competence

OBJECTIVE 3.2 (a) Define culture and cultural competence

Culture can be defined in many ways. Here is one way to consider culture:

> The ways of a people.
> *Robert Lado*

Anthropologists, who are the professional specialists of culture, have developed hundreds of definitions of culture. Most of these definitions address the ways of being and understanding shared by a social group. Many of them speak about the knowledge, attitudes, beliefs, values, traditions, customs, education and worldview passed down to others. Here is another definition:

> You can also think of culture as 'our learned humanity.'
> -Center for Cross-Cultural Health, Minnesota

Elements of Culture

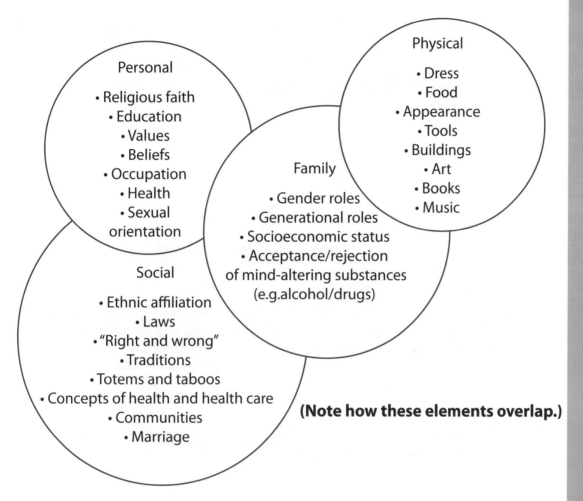

(Note how these elements overlap.)

Cultural Competence

Cultural competence is a field that focuses on how to provide services effectively across cultures. It is an important dimension of the work of community interpreters.

Cultural competence refers to the knowledge, attitudes and skills we need to effectively mediate cultural differences in public settings and promote equal access to services. Like culture itself, cultural competence has been defined in many different ways. Here are a few definitions.

Definitions of Cultural Competence

> A set of attitudes, skills, behaviors, and policies that enable organizations and staff to work effectively in cross-cultural situations.
>
> Cross et al, Toward a Culturally Competent System of Care, 1989.

> An ability by health care providers and health care organizations to understand and respond effectively to the cultural and linguistic needs brought by patients to the health care encounter.
>
> DHHS Office of Minority Health

> Understanding and appreciating the cultural differences and similarities within, among, and between groups. [...] Cultural competence helps prevention practitioners avoid stereotypes and biases that can undermine prevention efforts. It promotes a focus on the positive characteristics of a particular group, and instills prevention activities with an appreciation of cultural differences.
>
> Indiana Prevention Resource Center

> The knowledge and interpersonal skills that allow providers to understand, appreciate, and work with individuals from cultures other than their own. It involves an awareness and acceptance of cultural differences; self-awareness; knowledge of the patient's culture; and adaptation of skills.
>
> Bureau of Primary Health Care, DHHS

> The ability of individuals and systems to respond respectfully and effectively to people of all cultures, in a manner that affirms the worth and preserves the dignity of individuals, families, and communities.
>
> Center for Cross-Cultural Health, Minnesota

CORE CONTENT UNIT 3.2

UNIT 3

Cultural Competence: A Collective Responsibility

Culture competence is the responsibility of both individuals who provide a service (including interpreters) and the organization that offers the service.

However, organizations cannot change until people do. People cannot change their behavior effectively unless organizations support them, e.g., by allowing adjunct interpreters extra time to finish their main job after interpreting.

Cultural competence becomes possible only if all of us work together to provide services effectively across cultures. This is true of all organizations, in every area of community services. Cultural competence is the responsibility of the interpreter—but not only of the interpreter. We must all work together to support quality services to culturally diverse populations.

Culture Iceberg

Culture is often compared to an iceberg because icebergs are only partly visible. What lies beneath the surface is often much larger — and more significant — than what we see above the water.

On the next page, we can see how the iceberg analogy is used in discussions about culture to point out those elements of culture that are conscious or visible and those elements that lie underneath the surface and may not be conscious. Yet often it is the "invisible" aspects of culture that have the greatest impact on the interpreted session.

UNIT 3

Cultural Iceberg

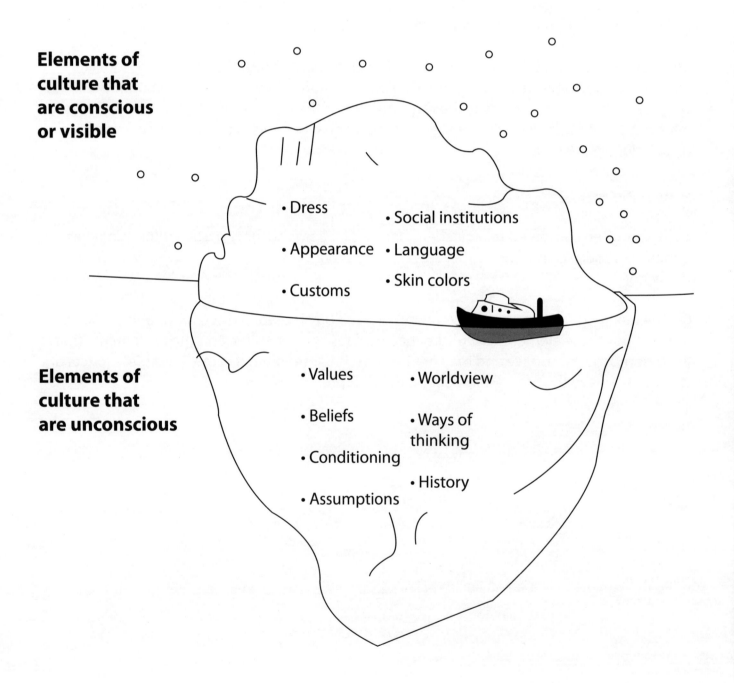

Culture: the Garden

It may also be helpful to think of culture as a garden. The word culture comes from a French word meaning to cultivate, to grow. The words agriculture and horticulture both include "culture" in them.

Culture is alive. It is not static or cold. Created by human beings, culture changes, evolves and grows.

Gardens, like cultures, come in all colors, forms and sizes. Many are filled with useful nourishment. Gardens, like cultures, may include things that we do not always appreciate, such as bees and worms, which help our garden grow, and even snakes. But all the aspects of a culture are part of that culture, even if we do not like them.

Sometimes gardens, and cultures, are filled with works of art and astonishing variety. Gardens and cultures may contain things that seem exotic to those who do not live there—such as the cactus gardens of Arizona. Often the result of hard work over many years, gardens and cultures are the fruit of the creativity, dedication, skill, passion and caring by individuals, groups and nations, who treasure their national parks and gardens just as they treasure their cultural heritage sites.

Gardens and culture can be large (like "American culture") or small: we can speak about the culture of a small state, the culture of a city, and even the culture of a rural county or a suburb. Culture, like a garden, can be social or individual, public or private. Compare the culture of a doctor in a small town with the culture of a migrant laborer in the same town. Even within families, the culture of parents is often quite different from the culture (or cultures) of their children.

Culture is complex, beautiful and unique. Above all, it is always changing. That is why no interpreter can be considered a cultural expert.

UNIT 3

Cultural Constructs

We think we "see" reality. But we do not. Research shows that we perceive only a small part of the sensory and social information available to us. We unconsciously "select" what we see or hear, taste, feel or smell, and we unconsciously filter out the rest.

The reason for this filtering process is that the world offers us too much information to absorb at once. As a result, we notice what we unconsciously think may be important. We "see" or sense only a small part of reality present, yet out of that limited stream of sensory information we build a construct: a picture or a story about what we think is happening. Our culture heavily influences these constructs. *We all have our own culturally influenced constructs of reality. We are, in this sense, all biased, because we are all human.*

This perceptual and cultural reality affects interpreters in many different ways. For example, in any interpreted session, there are at least three different constructs of the same situation. In a triadic encounter, the provider, interpreter and client may look at the same situation but draw different conclusions.

A common example is child discipline. What is considered appropriate discipline in many cultures is often considered child abuse in the U.S. The investigator from Child Protective Services may see bruises on a child and think: "Abuse." The parent may think: "I love my family, and to be a good parent I *must* physically discipline my child." The interpreter may note the perspectives of both parties and use her understanding to provide effective mediation.

SITUATION: Investigation of child abuse.

(Triangle diagram with vertices labeled Interpreter, Client, Provider)

Effective mediation in this case does *not* mean talking about the child or parent. Instead, the interpreter might intervene to inform the provider, "Excuse me, as the interpreter I sense a serious cultural misunderstanding about child discipline. Perhaps Mrs. Wong might be willing to discuss how people in her community look at disciplining children." She would then interpret what she said for Mrs. Wong. In this model, the interpreter *alerts* the parties present to the cultural barrier—but allows them resolve it.

Culture and Cultural Competence

OBJECTIVE 3.2 (b) Apply ethical decision-making to a communication barrier.

Intervention skills

Keep it simple: here are the basic intervention skills

INTERVENTION SKILLS
1. Assess the situation.
2. Identify the problem.
3. Make a decision.
4. Interrupt the session, if needed.
5. Mediate.
6. Return to basic interpreting.

Ethical decision-making

The interpreter must make many decisions quickly, both before and during mediation. These decisions can be challenging. Cultural barriers often involve the most complex decisions.

The two biggest decisions are *whether* to mediate and *how* to mediate. To help interpreters face the challenges of real-life interpreting in a professional and ethical manner, the California Healthcare Interpreting Association (CHIA) created important, practical guidelines. Published in 2002 as part of the CHIA standards of practice discussed in Unit 1, these guidelines constitute an ethical decision-making protocol. They are available at www.chiaonline.org.

CHIA guidelines

Many interpreters in health care were confused about how to respect codes of ethics. CHIA established a list of questions that would help guide interpreters as they made ethical decisions. These same questions also help guide interpreters to make decisions about whether and how to mediate.

UNIT 3

The CHIA Ethical Decision-making Guidelines
The six questions

The CHIA guidelines come in the form of six questions:
1. Ask questions to determine whether there is a problem. (Before mediating, the interpreter may ask these questions silently, in his or her own mind.)
2. Identify and clearly state the problem, considering the ethical principles that may apply and ranking them in applicability.
3. Clarify personal values as they relate to the problem.
4. Consider alternative actions, including benefits and risks.
5. Decide to carry out the action chosen.
6. Evaluate the outcome and consider what might be done differently next time.

These steps may seem like a lot to think about when one is trying to decide whether or not to mediate. But unless the interpreter thinks carefully about when to mediate, she may mediate too often—and inappropriately.

The Guidelines in Action

Let us consider a real-life situation and apply the ethical decision-making guidelines. Here is another common scenario related to child abuse. A child at school is feeling unwell and goes to the sick room, where a school nurse notices that the child has strange red marks on his chest. When the child's mother arrives, the interpreter, who is a Vietnamese parent-teacher liaison working in that school district, is called in to interpret for the nurse. The interpreter often sees these distinctive marks and knows that they are indicators of a healing technique called coining, which involves rubbing hot coins over a sick person's body to help the person heal. Should the interpreter interrupt the session to say anything about coining?

> 1. **Ask questions to determine whether there is a problem.**
> The interpreter may ask questions out loud or silently, to herself. In this case it may be preferable to ask questions silently: *Does the nurse think this case is about child abuse? If so, is it better for me to say something about coining, or just interpret?* If the nurse is suspicious of child abuse, she may be legally required to report the parent to Child Protective Services within 24 hours. This phone call could lead to terrible consequences for the parent, including arrest. Many innocent parents have been arrested for coining (or similar healing practices). One Cambodian father, age 47 and father of two, was arrested for child abuse and committed suicide while in jail for a similar practice. So the interpreter may wish to interrupt in case the nurse is unfamiliar with these kinds of marks, because if she is not, the nurse may report an innocent parent for suspicion of child abuse, leading to potentially very serious consequences.

UNIT 3

2. Identify and clearly state the problem, considering the ethical principles that may apply and ranking them in applicability.
Here are some of the NCIHC ethical principles involved in this situation:

> a) *Cultural awareness*. It is part of the interpreter's responsibility to consider and address cultural differences while interpreting if they are relevant to the encounter and of potential importance.
>
> b) *Advocacy*. The interpreter has a responsibility to speak out to protect an individual from serious harm. An inappropriate investigation for child abuse and possible arrest would be serious harm.
>
> c) *Impartiality*. The interpreter's loyalty is not to the individual client or provider. The interpreter must consider the best interests of the school, the parent, the child and the service outcome. All may be compromised if the interpreter does nothing about this situation.
>
> d) *Professionalism*. The interpreter is accountable for her professional performance. Ignoring the cultural context in this case, since it could sabotage the encounter, is potentially unprofessional.
>
> e) *Respect*. To put a parent at risk of being arrested for perhaps no valid reason when the interpreter has knowledge that might help to avoid that situation could be disrespectful to that parent's well being and human dignity.

3. Clarify personal values as they relate to the problem.
The interpreter may feel a loyalty both to the organization and the parent's culture which makes her feel strongly that she must do "the right thing." She may also feel that her spiritual beliefs require her to prevent harm if possible.

4. Consider alternative actions, including benefits and risks.
If the interpreter is silent, unless the school nurse asks the right questions and gets clear answers about what caused the marks, the nurse may make a report to Child Protective Services. Since hundreds of unnecessary child abuse reports have been filed about coining and similar healing practices, the risk that the nurse will report on the parent is significant. A thorough medical examination can easily determine whether the marks are from bruises or coining.

UNIT 3

5. Decide to carry out the action chosen.
The interpreter waits to see if the nurse is concerned about child abuse. Soon the nurse's expression grows dark and clouded: the nurse appears to have concerns about the parent. The interpreter then interrupts the session and asks the nurse, "Excuse me, as the interpreter I wanted to ask if you are you familiar with coining" (she interprets this question for the parent). When the nurse responds, "No, I'm not. What is coining?" the interpreter does not answer—she interprets the question and lets the *mother* answer it. The mother explains coining. The nurse asks the mother many questions about coining and thanks both the mother and the interpreter for this information. She does not report the mother to Child Protective Services.

6. Evaluate the outcome and consider what might be done differently next time.
The outcome was excellent. Perhaps the interpreter could have handled the situation a little differently, but this course of action proved simple, effective and safe.

CULTURAL MEDIATION TECHNIQUES

OBJECTIVE 3.2 (c) Practice non-intrusive cultural mediation.

Perhaps the most fundamental rule in cultural mediation is : "First, do no harm." In other words, the best way to practice non-intrusive cultural mediation is not to mediate at all unless it's necessary. To avoid unnecessary interventions, the interpreter will need to monitor the situation closely.

Before the Session

Prepare for session.

- Research the culture if needed.
- Research terminology.
- Prepare for special needs of session.

During the Session

Monitor the session.
1. Do the client and provider seem to understand each other?
2. Is the provider aware when the client does not seem to understand? If not, why not?
3. Is the provider's register appropriate to the education and understanding of the client?
4. Is the provider's terminology too technical?
5. Does the client make obscure cultural references?
6. What other barriers to understanding do you see?

After the Session

Post-hoc assessment
Did you successfully bridge misunderstandings? Why or why not? What worked? What could have helped?

How to Perform Non-Intrusive Cultural Mediation

The concept of non-intrusive cultural mediation

The concept underlying the model of non-intrusive cultural mediation is that it is critical to intervene as *little* as possible, as *briefly* as possible, while still addressing a cultural barrier to communication. In other words, instead of explaining a cultural barrier, you *identify* it.

Steps to follow for cultural mediation

1. Follow all steps for basic mediation.
2. Identify the cultural barrier.
3. Alert all parties to the nature of the cultural barrier.
4. Invite them (implicitly or explicitly) to explore the issue.
5. Return to basic interpreting.

Example

> **Librarian:** So now everyone in your family has a library card. I'm so glad. Was everything clear?
> **Interpreter:** (Interprets)
> **Father:** Yes, thank you.
> **Interpreter:** (Interprets "Yes, thank you," then turns to the librarian) Excuse me, as the interpreter I'm concerned that the information I interpreted about library fines wasn't clear, especially the expensive fines for late videos. (Interprets this mediation for the client and returns to the unobtrusive position.)
> **Librarian:** I'm happy you mentioned that. Thank you. You're quite right, sometimes people get confused about the system for fines. Basically, here's how it works... (Interpreter interprets.)

Note how this interpreter handled the situation:

- She had a strong feeling that the father hadn't understood the fine system for late video returns.
- When the librarian asked, "Was everything clear?" and the father answered yes, the interpreter was aware that the father, for cultural reasons, was saying yes to be polite—not because he understood.
- She sensed that the family was not wealthy and had heard stories of families in her community building up fines of $40 or more because they had not understood the policy.
- She did not say, "The client doesn't understand" (which would have been condescending and perhaps offensive). She said she was concerned "that the information I interpreted wasn't clear." This statement is unlikely to offend anyone.

UNIT 3

Wise Words from IMIA

The International Medical Interpreters Association (IMIA) makes a vital observation in their seminal document, *Medical Interpreting Standards of Practice*. These standards, adopted in 1995 and available at www.imiaweb.org, have influenced medical interpreting practice around the world. The wise words are as follows:

> Interpreters, therefore, have the task of identifying those occasions when unshared cultural assumptions create barriers to understanding or message equivalence. Their role in such situations is not to 'give the answer' but rather to help both provider and patient to investigate the intercultural interface that may be creating the communication problem.
>
> Interpreters must keep in mind that no matter how much 'factual' information they have about the beliefs, values, norms, and customs of a particular culture, they have no way of knowing where the individual facing them in that specific situation stands along a continuum from close adherence to the norms of a culture to acculturation into a new culture.
>
> IMIA Standards of Practice (pp. 15f)

UNIT 3

Using Cultural Skills in Mediation

Personal culture:
Age, gender, social status, beliefs, fears, eye contact, relationship to authority figures, degree of acculturation, etc.

Linguistic concerns:
Titles, terms of address and respect or honorifics; special prefixes and suffixes for certain age groups; use of verb tenses (concepts of time differ from culture to culture); etc.

Social culture
Ethnic groups, customs, taboos, social groupings, gender roles, family structures, tribalism, etc.

- Respect the knowledge of all parties.
- Resist seeing client in "deficit" terms and provider in "asset" terms.
- Provide information to both parties only if needed.
- Allow client's knowledge of what is best for the individual or family to emerge and be sure that the provider can assess that knowledge.
- Do not explain any aspect of culture if the client can explain it.

Respect the Client's Right to Self Determination

- Never influence a client's decision: use information to support accurate and clear communication.
- Use mediation to promote client autonomy, not dependency.
- Use cultural mediation to support the provider's goal of quality care or services and client well being.

UNIT 3

Culture and Mediation Around the World

EUROPE

Roles of the Interpreter: In some countries (e.g., Belgium and Switzerland), interpreters mediate both within and outside the interpreted encounter.. In other countries, interpreter roles may be restricted to basic interpreting. However, a shadow profession of community interpreting may have evolved, with community interpreters (often untrained) performing general and cultural mediation. There is no consensus across Europe on issues of mediation.

Names for the community interpreter: Public service interpreter, cultural mediator, intercultural mediator, health advocate, liaison interpreter, dialogue interpreter.

AUSTRALIA, NEW ZEALAND and CANADA

Roles of the Interpreter: Interpreter roles are still evolving. Community interpreting was established in Canada by the 1960s and Australia in the 1970s. Community interpreting in Canada was often referred to as cultural mediation. Historically, a great deal of cultural mediation occurred. Today, interpreter roles in all three countries are often restricted to basic interpreting and clarification, especially in courts. In Canada, national standards of practice for community interpreters prohibit culture brokering and advocacy.

Names: Community interpreter, cultural mediator, cultural interpreter, institutional interpreter.

OTHER PARTS OF THE WORLD

Roles of the Interpreter: Interpreter roles are still evolving worldwide, with encouraging developments However, in most countries no consensus on interpreter roles or mediation in community interpreting has emerged.

Names: Community interpreter, liaison interpreter, contact interpreter.

U.S.

Roles of the Interpreter: Rapidly evolving. Culture mediation/culture brokering and advocacy are widely accepted in community interpreting but generally prohibited in legal and conference interpreting.

Names: Community interpreter, cultural interpreter, ad hoc interpreter (i.e., an untrained interpreter who has not been tested or assessed and may not be qualified to interpret).

Challenges in Cultural Mediation

Many risks arise when interpreters perform mediation, particularly cultural mediation (or culture brokering). Both trained and untrained interpreters make common mistakes while mediating that fall into four broad categories: basic errors; stereotyping and personalization; taking over the encounter; and interpreting non-equivalent concepts.

Basic mediation errors

- The interpreter forgets to respect transparency.
- The interpreter forgets to fall back into basic interpreting as soon as the mediation is completed.
- The interpreter answers for the client.

Stereotyping and personalization

1. *Over-generalizing*: The interpreter sometimes makes overly broad statements, such as, "Everybody in Vietnam uses coining if someone in their family gets sick."

2. *Stereotyping*: The interpreter may make statements that paint everybody in one culture with the same brush, e.g., "Women in Mexico won't do anything unless their husband agrees," or "Nobody in China says, 'No,' because that's rude."

3. *Personalizing*: Interpreters speak about a client's beliefs when they do not know the client, e.g., the interpreter may say, "This client would never agree to organ harvesting." (In many cultures, the idea of having a loved one's body mutilated by organ harvesting might be devastating, but this particular family member might feel differently.)

Sometimes interpreters make broad assumptions, such as, "Oh, you know how these people are," or, "She thinks it's okay if her husband beats her up. That's just her culture." Do not assume you know anything about the client. Each client is a unique individual with a unique history.

Taking over

Taking over the encounter is a common risk for untrained interpreters and especially for bilingual employees, who are often accustomed to playing a dominant role in encounters with LEP clients. Yet freelance interpreters may make the same errors. Community interpreters who take over an encounter often:

1. Mediate too long.
2. Get involved in side conversations.
3. Give advice.
4. Give inaccurate information about culture.
5. Become emotionally involved and lose impartiality.
6. Allow the provider and client start speaking to the interpreter, not each other.
7. Speak to clients after the encounter (when they are not caseworkers).
8. Become de facto social workers.

Non-equivalent concepts

Whether for cultural or linguistic reasons, interpreters who try to render a word or phrase in the target language can sometimes feel like lost because there is no exact equivalent.

> **Examples of difficult words:**
>
> Hooponopono: (Hawaiian) Solving a problem by talking it out.
> Uffda: (Swedish) Word of sympathy, used when someone else is in pain.
>
> - Rheingold, Howard (2000)

Solutions for non-equivalent concepts

- Give a brief paraphrase of the term or phrase.(one sentene or shorter).
- If you do not know a concise equivalent, mediate by saying, "Excuse me, as the interpreter I'm not aware of an equivalent concept in [language X] for case manager. Could you please explain it?" (Then interpret this question for the client.)

But remember, time is limited. Don't get distracted or spend too much time on difficult words or concepts.

STEREOTYPES AND BIAS

OBJECTIVE 3.2 (d) Show awareness of stereotypes and bias

> **Stereotyping**
>
> Characterizing or labeling social or ethnic groups on the basis of preconceived, usually negative, over-generalizations without regard to accuracy, individuality or humanity.

> **Bias**
>
> An opinion or perspective that is neither fair nor impartial.

> **Discrimination**
>
> Any words or acts that may injure the dignity or undermine the legal or social rights of an individual or group.

Stereotypes are socially established overgeneralizations. In individuals, the perspectives embodied in stereotypes may cause feelings and attitudes of bias about individuals or groups. These feelings of bias can, in turn, lead to acts of discrimination. (Thoughts→feelings→acts.)

Stereotypes are thoughts and images that tend to paint everyone with the same brush, as if there were no exceptions. Stereotypes are not based on facts and tend to be negative, e.g., "Muslims are terrorists." But positive stereotypes also exist, for example, "Asian kids are smart." Even positive stereotypes are negative in their impact: Asian children often report feeling stressed by such stereotypes.

Stereotypes are based on opinions. Generalizations, in contrast, can be neutral and are usually educational in intent. They are based on facts, research or knowledge (e.g., "Vietnamese children score higher than white children on standardized tests in math"). Stereotypes are based on opinions.

Advocacy and Discrimination

Advocacy

Advocacy is one of the nine principles of the NCIHC Code of Ethics. It is also one of the most hotly contested responsibilities of community interpreters anywhere in the world.

> **ADVOCACY**
>
> Advocacy: Any action taken by an interpreter on behalf of a client when the client's safety, well being, dignity or equal access to a public service are compromised or at risk.

In the U.S., community interpreters are permitted to advocate on behalf of clients. In some countries, they are not permitted to advocate at all. In other countries, the community interpreting profession (if it exists formally) has not even grappled with the question of advocacy.

Examples of discrimination

Here are some real-life examples of situations that have left community interpreters wondering if they should advocate:

- Providers say discriminatory things about clients, even during the session (because they don't believe the interpreter will interpret them).
- Providers may act in insulting ways toward LEP clients, intentionally or accidentally, e.g., behave coldly and speak abruptly.
- Institutions do things that are discriminatory and even illegal, e.g., ask LEP clients to come back with an interpreter.
- Providers do not check adequately for understanding, leaving the client confused.
- Providers sometimes make LEP clients wait much longer than English-speaking clients.
- Providers offer inferior services to LEP clients.

> **THE PRESSURE**
>
> Interpreters are seen as important intermediaries between a powerful system ... and the community. So, the community puts pressure on the interpreter to stay true to the norms and beliefs of the culture and not jeopardize the survival of that culture, while at the same time asking the interpreter to make possible access to the desired benefits of that powerful system. —Beltran Avery (20001:11)

Confusion about advocacy

At the heart of the problem of advocacy is the question about what, if anything, you should do as an interpreter when you witness acts of discrimination. Yet almost no one agrees on what advocacy is. There are so many different definitions and understandings about advocacy that it is often difficult in community interpreting to tell the difference between cultural mediation, advocacy and simply reporting a critical incident. Even referring or accompanying clients to another service may be called advocacy or "referral advocacy" (Beltran Avery, 2011:8).

Advocacy: The Riskiest Form of Mediation

> NCIHC proposes the following definition: "Advocacy is understood as action taken on behalf of an individual that goes beyond facilitating communication, with the intention of supporting good health outcomes. In general, advocacy means that a third party (in this case, the interpreter) speaks for or pleads the cause of another party, thereby departing from an impartial role."

Should you advocate?

In the U.S., advocacy is an ethical requirement for community interpreters under certain circumstances. However, advocacy is also a highly advanced and specialized professional skill—perhaps the riskiest activity in the field. So the first rule is: when in doubt, do not advocate.

The second rule is: keep it simple. In most cases, treat discrimination and other disturbing acts that you may witness as critical incidents. Report them as such to the appropriate supervisor and let that supervisor take action. This is the simplest way to prevent harm.

Basic advocacy

When performing advocacy, the interpreter will have to juggle many different considerations: possible outcomes, risks to the client, agency and/or the interpreter (some interpreters have lost their job for advocating), any legal implications, and the interpreter's knowledge of the service, the institution and the system. Advocacy is complex. That's why it is important for most community interpreters to treat advocacy as the responsibility to report an action rather than to engage in action. You are not trained, professional advocates. You are interpreters.

UNIT 3

A real-life example of advocacy as "reporting"

> A French-speaking interpreter was sent by a nonprofit community interpreter service to a doctor's appointment set up by a refugee resettlement agency. The patient was an educated woman from Africa. The doctor was brusque, rude and insulting. Appalled at his behavior, the patient felt hurt and humiliated but said nothing about this to the doctor. Instead, on the way out, she expressed her distress to the interpreter.
>
> After the appointment, the interpreter had to make a decision about what action to take. Without violating patient confidentiality, she reported the doctor's behavior to the community interpreting service that sent her. The supervisor then reported this information to the refugee resettlement agency that made the appointment, so that the resettlemtn could reconsider its policy of referring refugee clients to that doctor.

Why advocate?

Advocacy is such a high-risk activity that some interpreters have lost their jobs for advocating.

However, clients who do not speak the language of service or know its culture well are marginalized in many ways. If community interpreters do not engage in advocacy when a client's health, safety, well being or access to the service is at risk, perhaps no one will help the client. That risk is a sobering responsibility for the interpreter

Appropriate interpreter advocacy can:

- Protect equal access to a service.
- Reduce errors.
- Ensure correct follow-up.
- Shield a client from discrimination.
- Protect an agency from legal liability.
- Ensure correct, effective service delivery.
- Protect a marginalized population.
- Ensure that clients understand their legal rights and responsibilities.
- Help clients successfully navigate a complex system.
- Reduce injuries or loss of services or benefits.
- Prevent disastrous outcomes such as illness, eviction, foreclosure and or death.

UNIT 3

Advocate when:
- The health, well-being or safety of the client is at risk.
- Equal access to the service is compromised.
- You witness acts of bigotry, racism or discrimination.
- The agency could be legally liable if you do not act.

Advocate *only* if you have already tried clarification, checking for understanding, culture mediation and/or other appropriate mediation without success.

Final Considerations About Interpreter Roles

The quotations below were written in 2001. These observations are still true today, and every community interpreter should give them careful consideration.

> Notwithstanding all these complexities, the working group eventually arrived at some cautious agreements on basic aspects of the role of health care interpreter. These agreements are as follows.
>
> - The basic function of the health care interpreter, as in other interpreter-mediated settings, is to provide a linguistic conversion from one language system into another in such a way that the original meaning is maintained.
>
> - Accuracy and completeness are professional standards that underscore the practice of interpreting. In the health care setting, however, fidelity to meaning may require the use of metaphors as well as negotiated explanations of concepts that do not necessarily have matching referents in the other language.
>
> - In providing this linguistic conversion, the interpreter also functions to facilitate understanding and communication between people who speak different languages. The interpreter acts in the interest of the shared goal of achieving the well being of the patient.
>
> - In the health care setting, in which shared meaning is so critical to the successful achievement of the goal of the encounter, the interpreter cannot remain a passive, uninvolved party. There are times when, because of the cultural distance between the parties, the interpreter may have to serve as a cultural bridge.
>
> - Transparency in the actions of the interpreter is paramount whenever the interpreter steps out of the core function of providing a linguistic conversion. That is, the interpreter has an obligation, whenever she speaks in her own voice, to make sure that the both parties understand what she has said.
>
> - Interpreters do not speak for either the patient or provider during the interpreter-mediated encounter.
>
> Beltran Avery 2001:12-13

UNIT 3

Closing Words for Unit 3

Here are some helpful words from a well-known researcher on interpreting in Spain, Carmen Valero-Garcés (2005).

> A large percentage of IPS [interpreters in public services] admit that the tasks that are requested of them usually go beyond the simple transfer of information. They are frequently seen as "catalysts" and cultural consultants. They are asked to master the same abilities (cognitive and linguistic abilities as well as observing a code of ethics) as other types of interpreters (conference, court, medical), but they also need to incorporate other abilities related to the specific atmosphere they work in (e.g. social, cultural and sometimes religious settings; situations involving asymmetry of knowledge; and even power and gender differences). In this context, the IPS often have to explain cultural habits or beliefs in order to balance these inequalities in an effort to make communication effective. They also very often must serve as a bridge in conversations about specific aspects of community life, the distribution of functions and responsibilities in the family, and stories of misfortune, honor, religion, and faith. To cope with this active involvement, the IPS must possess tremendous emotional stability in order to successfully undertake certain aspects present in the nature of their work.

UNIT 3

REVIEW

UNIT 3 REVIEW EXERCISES

Steps for mediation

List the five steps for mediation.
1. _____
2. _____
3. _____
4. _____
5. _____

Name three things that interpreters often forget to do when they mediate:
_____
_____
_____

Why is transparency important when mediating?
_____
_____
_____

Why should you mentally rehearse examples of things that you might say during a mediation?
_____
_____
_____
_____

UNIT 3

Strategic Mediation

Write down what you might say to both parties when you perform mediation in the following cases:

1. The provider is speaking at a very high register.
What would you say to the provider?
_____
_____
_____

What would you say to the client?
_____
_____
_____

2. You don't understand a regional phrase that the client has just used.
What would you say to the provider?
_____
_____
_____

What would you say to the client?
_____
_____
_____

3. The client does not appear to understand the provider.
What would you say to the provider?
_____
_____
_____

What would you say to the client?
_____
_____
_____

UNIT 3

4. The client is a woman. The provider is a man. The client is not answering the provider at all, and you strongly suspect it's because in the culture and/or religion of the woman, she may feel she that should not speak to a male without family members present.

What would you say to the provider?
_____
_____
_____
_____

What would you say to the client?
_____
_____
_____
_____

UNIT 3

Three Interpreter Responsibilities

Add labels to the following diagram to show three basic interpreter responsibilities.

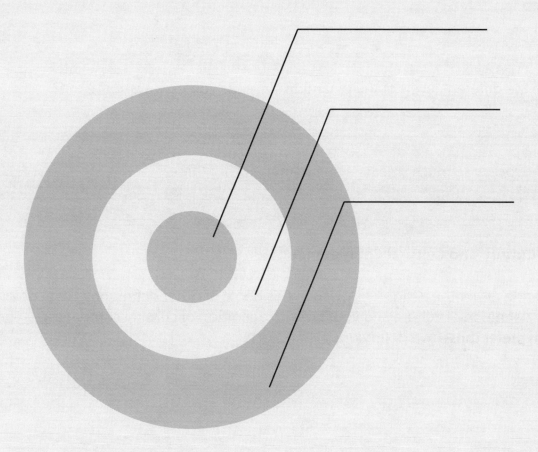

In an ideal world, which responsibility would involve the most time from the interpreter?

_____

Which responsibility is more common for adjunct interpreters than contract interpreters?

_____

UNIT 3

Incremental Intervention

Put the following four roles of the Roat model of "incremental intervention" in the correct order (use the order of the pyramid):

Culture Broker _____
Advocate   _____
Conduit   _____
Clarifier   _____

Why are the different levels of the pyramid smaller as you go toward the top?
_____
_____

Why is advocacy so much smaller a role than the other three?
_____
_____

Define Culture and Cultural Competence

Considering either the definitions given in this book, or other definitions, write down your favorite definition of culture and your favorite definition of cultural competence. Then state why you prefer those two definitions over others:

1. Culture
_____
_____
_____
_____

2. Cultural competence:
_____
_____
_____
_____

UNIT 3

Components of Culture

Strike out those details in the list below that are not a part of culture

- Language.
- Clothing.
- Values and beliefs.
- Customs and traditions.
- Gender and family roles.
- Folk dances.
- Education.
- Books.
- Music.
- Socioeconomic status.
- Tools.
- Religion.
- Laws.
- Occupation.
- Concepts of health.
- Taboos.

Intervention Skills

Put the following intervention skills in the correct order in the table below:

Mediate; interrupt the session; identify the problem; return to basic interpreting; assess the situation; make a decision.

1.
2.
3.
4.
5.
6.

UNIT 3

Non-intrusive Cultural Mediation

Fill in the blanks below using the following words or terms:

all parties, interpreting, cultural barrier, implicitly, basic, explore.

1. Follow all steps for _____ mediation.
2. Identify the _____.
3. Alert _____ to the nature of the cultural barrier.
4. Invite them (_____ or explicitly) to _____ the issue.
5. Return to basic _____.

Stereotyping, Bias and Discrimination

Circle one answer.

1. Stereotypes are usually:
(a) Positive.
(b) Negative.
(c) Neutral.
(d) None of the above.

2. A problem with stereotypes is that providers with stereotypes:
(a) Treat some groups more positively than others.
(b) Treat certain groups of people as if they shared certain characteristics when they may not do so.
(c) Fail to consider an individual as a complex human being.
(d) Any or all of the above.

3. Bias usually involves:
(a) Underlying attitudes that are not always conscious.
(b) An honest, open examination of one's motives.
(c) Careful treatment of other human beings in an effort to be fair.
(d) Any or all of the above.

4. The result of bias may be:
(a) Discrimination.
(b) Favoritism.
(c) Violations of Title VI of the Civil Rights Act.
(d) Any or all of the above.

UNIT 4
COMMUNITY SERVICES

Unit 4 Objective

OBJECTIVE 4.1
Develop skills sets in specific sectors of community interpreting.
4.1 (a) Contrast and compare legal and community interpreting.
4.1 (b) Discuss systems in health care, education and/or human and social services and their impact on interpreters.
4.1 (c) Develop strategies to enhance competence in terminology.

OBJECTIVE 4.1

Develop skills sets in specific sectors of community interpreting.

Introduction

Many and perhaps most community interpreters around the world are foreign born or have foreign-born parents. Even those who are born in the country where they reside are often unfamiliar with the complex institutions and services for which they interpret.

4.1 (a) Contrast and compare legal and community interpreting

4.1 (b) Discuss systems in health care, education and/or human and social services and their impact on interpreters.

4.1 (c) Develop strategies to enhance competence in terminology (medical, educational and/or human and social services).

UNIT 4

While bilingual employees have an advantage in this regard, for they generally know their institutions (and often the terminology of those institutions) quite well, contract interpreters typically work across a broad range of services. The latter face special challenges, for community services are often complex, and many systemic barriers face immigrant clients who access those services. Systemic barriers are often as important as the language or cultural barriers faced by the clients.

In order to interpret effectively, it is important to understand the organizational culture of the service for which you interpret. In addition, due to widespread confusion about legal interpreting as a practice and a profession, community interpreters need to be particularly careful if they perform legal interpreting, which in the U.S. is a different profession from community interpreting. Even in those countries where legal interpreting falls under the larger umbrella of community interpreting, legal interpreting poses a special set of challenges for community interpreters, who often do not understand the special nature of legal interpreting.

Unit 4 therefore looks at the global service system in which the community interpreter works. First, we look at legal interpreting in an effort to make clear what community interpreters should do if they are asked to perform legal interpreting. The remainder of Unit 4 looks at other challenges that may arise in specific settings, including the daunting challenge of mastering the jargon and technical terminology in hundreds of different service settings.

Broadly speaking, this unit provides guidance in four areas of service where community interpreters often work: legal services; health care; social and human services; and education.

Legal Interpreting

OBJECTIVE 4.1 Contrast and compare legal and community interpreting.

What is legal interpreting?

Legal interpreting is a profession that encompasses interpreting in *any legal process or proceeding*. As an independent profession, it has its own ethics, standards and professional skills. While legal interpreting began in the U.S. in the early 1800's, it was formally established as a profession in 1978 with the passage of the federal Court Interpreters Act. That same year, the National Association of Judiciary Interpreters and Translators (NAJIT) was founded. Today, NAJIT has nearly 1,200 members.

Isn't legal interpreting part of community interpreting?

No. Though many people believe so, community interpreting in the U.S. is *a separate profession* from legal interpreting. This confusion is widespread. While legal and community interpreters share many professional skills, and their work often overlaps, the ethics, standards of practices, skills, requirements, protocols and professional culture of legal interpreting are very different from those for community interpreting, at least in the U.S. For example, in this country, legal interpreters are not permitted to perform cultural mediation or advocacy. Even in those countries where legal interpreting falls under the umbrella of community interpreting, legal interpreting practices may differ from those for general community interpreting.

> **Legal Interpreting**
>
> Interpreting related to legal processes and proceedings, including but not limited to lawyer-client representation, prosecutor-victim/witness interviews, and law enforcement communications.
> Framer *et al* (2009:xi)

What do legal interpreters do?

Many people think that legal interpreting takes place in the courtroom. In fact, most legal interpreting takes place outside the courts. Legal interpreters work in many settings that may include:
- Attorney-client meetings
- Bail reviews
- Depositions
- Detention (jail, prison, holding cells, juvenile detention, etc)
- Law enforcement
- Legal clinics
- Immigration services
- Mediation and arbitration
- Offices of human rights
- School Board hearings (e.g., about student suspensions or expulsions)

Community and Legal Interpreting

Community interpreters are often asked to perform legal interpreting. In many cases, they should not accept legal interpreting assignments because they lack adequate training and skills in legal interpreting ethics, protocols, requirements and terminology.

In addition, many community interpreter do not realize when they have "crossed the line" into legal interpreting. For example, in the same day, a community interpreter may interpret for a counselor at a domestic violence center, which is clearly a community interpreting encounter, and then interpret across the hall for the same client and an attorney who wants to determine if the client is eligible for legal permanent residency. The same interpreter is now performing legal interpreting.

DIFFERENCES BETWEEN LEGAL AND COMMUNITY INTERPRETING

Legal Interpreters	Community Interpreters	The Challenges
Legal interpreters interpret for any legal process or proceeding, including attorney-client interviews.	Community interpreters work in a wide array of community settings.	Many community interpreters do not know whether they are performing legal or community interpreting.
Most of them adhere to a court code of ethics or the NAJIT code (in the U.S.).	Most (if they are trained) adhere to a code of ethics from NCIHC, ATA and/or another professional association.	Some significant differences exist between the ethics, protocols and requirements for legal and community interpreters.
Their professional skills evolved largely from the formal setting of the courtroom.	The professional skills of community interpreters evolved largely from the medical setting.	Most court situations are *adversarial*. Most community service interviews are *collaborative*.
Errors in legal interpreting have grave consequences that may jeopardize a case.	Errors in community interpreting have consequences that can jeopardize a patient's health, safety or access to quality care.	Many community interpreters fail to see the possible legal consequences of their errors.
Many legal interpreters become skilled at simultaneous mode and often prefer it.	Community interpreters are supposed to use consecutive mode in most settings.	Many community interpreters lack the skill and terminology to perform legal interpreting safely and appropriately.

UNIT 4

Legal Interpreting Ethics

You must adhere to the appropriate ethics and standards for community or legal interpreting. Many of the ethical principles are the same. Some are different. The table below compares principles from several widely followed codes of ethics. The two legal codes addressed are the Model Code of Professional Responsibility for Interpreters in the Judiciary, developed by the National Center for State Courts, and the NAJIT Code of Professional Responsibility, of NAJIT, a professional association.

UNIT 4

Differences Between Ethical Codes for Legal and Community Interpreters

Legal Interpreter Ethical Requirements NCSC and NAJIT [1]	Community Interpreter Ethical Requirements NCIHC, IMIA, CHIA
Accuracy: Legal interpreters must interpret everything without interjecting their own words or paraphrasing and should not address or interpret body language.	**Accuracy:** Interpreters are permitted to interpret with paraphrases or explanations. Community interpreters are not prohibited from addressing body language if significant meaning would otherwise be missed.
Representation of qualifications: Interpreters must accurately represent their credentials	**Representation of qualifications:** No such ethical standard exists in NCIHC, IMIA or CHIA ethics.
Impartiality: An interpreter should not accept an assignment if also interpreting for an opposing party. Interpreters may not interpret for a friend, associate, relative or counsel or speak to clients outside the proceedings.	**Impartiality:** An interpreter should not accept an assignment if also interpreting for an opposing party. Interpreters may not interpret for a friend, associate, relative or counsel or speak to clients outside the proceedings. If a past experience is similar to the case, e.g., sexual assault, interpreters should consider recusing themselves (declining).
Confidentiality: May be required to report knowledge of a crime revealed by client.	**Confidentiality:** Not obligated to report crimes except in cases of imminent danger or if required by law.
Scope of practice: Interpreters may not perform other services such as explaining forms or case management.	**Scope of practice:** Community interpreters often provide services outside encounter, although parameters are not clearly specified.
Duty to report ethical violations: Interpreters must report ethical violations.	**Duty to report ethical violations:** No comparable ethical requirement is stated in NCIHC, IMIA or CHIA ethics.
Professional development: Interpreters must stay abreast of relevant statutes, rules and policies of the judiciary.	**Professional development:** No requirement to know laws and legal policies is made of community interpreters
Cultural mediation/brokering: Not stated in the codes and not permitted.	**Cultural mediation/brokering:** There is an ethical requirement to consider cultural barriers to communication.
Advocacy: Not permitted.	**Advocacy:** Interpreters may advocate if the client's safety, health or dignity are at risk.

---

1 These two codes are available respectively at: www.ncsconline.org/wc/publications/Res_CtInte_ModelGuideChapter9Pub.pdf and www.najit.org.

UNIT 4

Community and Legal Interpreting

Grateful acknowledgement is made to Ana Stover for her collaboration and her contributions to this section.

A community interpreter should be informed about legal interpreting because at any moment a community interpreting assignment might turn into a legal encounter. Here are a few examples.

A doctor's visit

Injuries or disabilities may turn a medical appointment into legal interpreting. Medical appointments and examinations that can be used as evidence in court or for legal determinations include:
- Workers Compensation
- Insurance liability
- Disability determination (for Social Security Disability Income)

A medical exam

Certain types of cases could include or involve forensic evidence and/or victim statements that may become part of a police report and can be used in court in criminal cases or for psychiatric assessments. Such cases may include:
- Hospital Emergency Room visits by domestic violence victims
- Emergency hearing/petition for psychiatric evaluation (e.g., for involuntary commitment to a psychiatric hospital)
- Exams performed by Sexual Assault Forensic Examiners (usually at hospitals)
- Competency evaluations, to determine if someone is fit to stand trial

A Department of Social Services (DSS) home visit

A visit by DSS investigator could lead to the separation of a family. Issues that emerge during the visit of a caseworker, social worker or investigator, especially from Child Protective Services or Adult Protective Services, could include:
- Child custody
- Child abuse or neglect
- Vulnerable adult abuse or neglect
- Determination of compliance with court orders

UNIT 4

An Office of Human Rights investigation

A routine appointment to interpret for a discrimination complaint could turn into a situation where:
- An attorney (or attorneys) is present.
- The interview is a taped deposition.
- The investigator provides several long, legal documents for sight translation.
- A tape or transcript of the interview may be used in court.

In all these cases, everything is memorialized and may be presented in court, including errors by the interpreter.

How to know if the appointment is legal interpreting

In the U.S., community interpreters should find out ahead of time if an assignment is *community* or *legal* interpreting. If you know the session will be legal interpreting, and you have had no training in legal interpreting, you should probably decline the assignment if you can.

First, when making that decision, it is important to realize that there is no hard and fast line between community and legal interpreting. So the easiest rule is: when in doubt, *assume that the encounter is, or may become, legal interpreting, and adhere to the ethics and practices of legal interpreting*. The reason for doing so is that the rules for legal interpreting are stricter and safer in legal situations than those for community interpreting. It is almost always therefore advisable (for the interpreter as well as for everyone else involved) to follow the rules for legal interpreting whenever the slightest doubt exists.

In the following situations, always assume that you are performing legal interpreting:

- Nonprofit legal services
- If an attorney is present in any official capacity
- If a police officer or detective is asking questions
- When any legal documents are involved—including consent forms, financial qualification forms, advance directives, Special Education forms, and almost any document that the client signs
- Discrimination complaints, e.g., for offices of human rights
- School Board hearings about student suspensions or expulsions.
- Immigration services and counseling
- Legal clinics
- Domestic violence hearings or paperwork
- Health department inspections of restaurants
- Formal meetings about Special Education services

UNIT 4

If you are not certain whether an upcoming assignment is legal or community interpreting, you may contact:
- A local nonprofit legal services provider, such as a legal aid bureau.
- Your local Administrative Office of the Courts
- NAJIT (www.najit.org)

But remember: when in doubt, decline the assignment or interpret according to legal ethics and standards.

Training and Credentials for Legal Interpreting

There are no shortcuts in any area of interpreting. As with any other profession, before engaging in legal interpreting seek professional training and qualifications.

Court Certification

1. **Federal court certification**: This rigorous exam is currently offered only in Spanish. Only about 4% of candidates pass the exam.

2. **State certification**: Currently, 41 states belong to the consortium on language access that offers this exam to member states. Certification is currently offered in up to 18 languages, with testing for other languages under development. To find out if your state offers a certification program, contact your state's Administrative Office of the Courts. The state certification exam, like the federal exam, is rigorous and has a low passing rate. It often includes a language proficiency test component. A typical certification exam centers on consecutive interpreting, simultaneous interpreting and sight translation.

3. **NAJIT certification**: NAJIT offers certification for judiciary interpreters in interpreting and translation in Spanish only.

Training

A number of state courts offer a two-day orientation for court interpreters who speak any language, and some offer formal training for Spanish interpreters. Legal interpreter training is available at conferences hosted by interpreter associations and at some two- and four-year colleges such as the University of Arizona, the Monterey Institute of International Studies and University of Charleston, South Carolina. Online training for legal interpreters includes U.S. based programs such as those by de la Mora Interpreter Training, Bromberg & Associates and the UK-based program DPSI Online. Cross-Cultural Communications offers the only national program designed for legal interpreting in community settings, *The Language of Justice*.

COMMUNITY SERVICES

OBJECTIVE 4.2 Discuss systems in health care, education and/or human and social services and their impact on interpreters.

The next section offers a broad overview of three key sectors in community interpreting: health care, education (including public and private schools, preschool, Head Start, community colleges and universities) and government and nonprofit human and social services.

Each sector is considered from the perspective of what a community interpreter should know about this system to interpret effectively within it. Even if the interpreter works primarily in one area, such as health care or a public school, it is *very helpful to know about the other sectors,* because they often interconnect. For example, at a hospital the interpreter might have meetings with social workers, teachers, Department of Social Services staff and police officers, all about one case. In a school setting, the interpreter might interpret for a school nurse or for a phone call to Child Protective Services.

Community interpreter, including bilingual staff, may be called on to interpret in almost any sector of community interpreting at any time.

UNIT 4

THE U.S. HEALTH CARE SYSTEM

Overview of Health Care in the United States

> *The health care system in the United States (US) is a decentralized, market-based system without universal access. The system is a shifting mixture of public, private, and voluntary sector programs. The role of the federal government includes that of a major payor for care through large programs such as Medicaid and Medicare, a provider of health services to special populations, and a supporter of the education and training of many types of health care providers.*
>
> Gutzler & Kuta (2003)

The health care system in the United States is one of the most complex medical systems in the world. It is often difficult for even a highly educated immigrant to understand it. Many educated native-born Americans struggle with the complexities of the U.S. health care system.

Medical care in many other countries, including industrialized countries, offers more consistent access to care than the American system. Healthcare access in the U.S. is a complex patchwork system.

Interpreting in health care is a particular challenge for contract interpreters who interpret in many different types of healthcare settings, including hospitals, community health centers, health departments, free clinics, school nurse offices, domestic violence shelters and substance abuse programs, among other services.

UNIT 4

Health Insurance: A Crisis in Care

> "The first myth is that it's only the poor who are uninsured. In fact, half of the uninsured are over the poverty level and one in three adults under 65 in the middle income range--defined arbitrarily here between $44,000 and $65,000 a year for a family of four--were uninsured at some point in the year." Thomas Frieden, Director of CDC, speaking at a news conference in November 2010

According to the U.S. Centers for Disease Control (CDC), in 2010 about *59 million* U.S. residents had no health insurance for at least part of the year.

The cost of insurance is high. The Kaiser Family Foundation reports the 2010 cost of average annual premiums as $5,049 for coverage of one individual and $13,770 for family coverage. For most Americans, this cost is unaffordable unless subsidized by an employer, but an increasing number of employers no longer offer health insurance.

In addition, this monthly premium does not usually include deductibles or the co-payments required each time a person visits a doctor or Emergency Room or for prescriptions. Each co-payment for a doctor's visit or prescription may cost from $10 to $30 or more, depending on the insurance plan and type of service. These co-payments can add up quickly when a family member is ill. In addition, some family members may be excluded from coverage or charged more per month if they have a pre-existing health condition such as diabetes, heart disease or asthma.

> **WHO IS UNINSURED IN THE U.S.?**
>
> In the U.S., although many of the very poor are covered by Medicaid, in general the "working poor" have no insurance. In addition, many middle-class individuals and families now lack health insurance.

Many of the uninsured in this country are immigrants, most of whom hold paid jobs. Immigrants are disproportionately affected: according to U.S. Census Bureau data, in any given year, up to half of low-income non-citizens may lack health insurance.

How health insurance works

Health care in the U.S. is primarily provided at the workplace to employees. Such insurance may be part of the worker's compensation package, although for jobs that pay less well it is difficult to get health insurance benefits.

This employment-based financing system started decades ago during World War II when wage and price controls were enacted in the U.S. Employers were not permitted to increase wages, but they were permitted to increase fringe benefits like medical coverage. Because of

UNIT 4

government programs like Medicare and Medicaid, the government's portion of the nation's healthcare cost has increased over the decades, but the majority of health care funding still comes from the private sector.

Employment remains the single most common way that American families access health insurance. However, due to rising health care costs, a growing number of employers now offer health insurance (if at all)it only for employees who pay most or all of the cost of premiums. As a result, many immigrants are hit hard because they fall into a difficult demographic category where they earn too much money to qualify for government health care programs, but not enough to pay for private health insurance.

Children's Health Insurance Program (CHIP)

The State Children's Health Insurance Program (S-CHIP) is a program for low to low-moderate income families that offers government health insurance to children. Many immigrant families qualify for this program. S-CHIP is designed to let states insure children from working families whose incomes are too high to qualify them for Medicaid but too low for them to afford private health insurance. Federal funding, state programs and Medicaid expansions, or a combination of these, support CHIP programs. In general, only residents with legal status may participate, and in some states only citizens are eligible.

Each state with an approved plan receives enhanced Federal matching payments for its S-CHIP expenditures. For many immigrant families, S-CHIP programs have become an invaluable resource to obtain health insurance for children. In some states, families earning up to 150% or even 200% of federal poverty levels may qualify. Unfortunately, cutbacks to this program are currently underway in a number of states.

Managed Care

Managed care is a controversial topic in the U.S. It is a form of health care delivery that seeks to control the rapid growth of health care costs through strict oversight of the types of services and health providers that a participant in the program may visit or use.

On the one hand, managed care has helped to control some costs. It has also enrolled a growing number of patients in programs where physicians or managers try to see the "big picture" for each patient and watch over important health issues for each plan member. On the other hand, patients may not be able to see the doctor or specialist of their choice or may have to pay much more to do so.

Membership in managed care groups such as Health Maintenance Organizations (HMOs), Preferred Provider Organizations (PPOs) and Independent Practice Associations (IPAs) has steadily increased. About a third of Americans are now enrolled in such programs, while in some states enrollment is as high as 50%. Typically, for one monthly fee and co-payments of $10 to $30 or more for doctor visits (in addition to other co-payments for medication, medical tests, emergency room visits and hospital stays), all remaining health care costs are covered by the managed care organization. A significant portion of the monthly fee is paid for by the employer, with the employee paying a smaller portion.

HMOs and other managed care organizations control costs by requiring patients to use a network of approved doctors and hospitals and by reviewing the reasons for referring patients for tests, procedures and specialists. In many cases, patients must ask for the insurer's approval before undergoing operations, seeing a specialist or even going for emergency care. Many managed care groups have employed other complex methods to control costs, including a system of "capitation" that financially rewards physicians who reduce the number of medical services used by patients.

Fee-for-Service Plans

The more traditional "fee-for-service" health insurance plans cost about the same per month as managed care programs but may involve higher deductibles (the amount that patients must pay themselves each year before the insurance begins to pay for health care). However, the patient may choose almost any doctor and receive any type of treatment covered by the plan whenever the patient or doctor chooses. Then the insurance company is billed for that service.

Today, in most fee-for-service plans the patient usually has to pay a significant annual deductible before the insurance company pays. The patient also typically must pay a co-payment and/or a certain percentage of the total bill for each health care visit. This system provides more freedom of choice for patients. On the other hand, many government officials and others in the insurance industry feel that this structure, especially with physicians' fear of lawsuits, has encouraged physicians to refer patients for medically unnecessary tests, services and specialists.

> **Disturbing Statistics**
>
> - 79 million: *Number of Americans who report medical debt or problems paying medical bills in 2008*
> - 49%: *Proportion of people in foreclosure who said medical bills were a cause of their financial problem*
> - 25%: *Proportion of people studied reporting medical debt of $5,000 or more.*
>
> *The Washington Post,* January 13, 2009, quoting sources: Commonwealth Fund; C.T. Robertson of Harvard University; and Center for Studying Health System Change

Aging Americans

The federal Office on Aging provides funding for many public health and human services for older adults, who are served through state services and county agencies on aging.

UNIT 4

Medicare, Medicaid and the Safety Net

To support U.S. residents without health insurance, in 1965, federal Medicaid and Medicare programs were established.

Medicaid

Medicaid is a joint federal-state program that funds medical care for the very poor, although the eligibility requirements vary from state to state. Health services and private physicians who take Medicaid patients are, at least in theory, expected to provide interpreters at no cost to LEP patients. In reality, many and perhaps most private physicians who accept Medicaid patients do not provide interpreters for LEP patients, and it is unclear whether they will ever be compelled to do so. The obligations of physicians to provide interpreters under Title VI of the Civil Rights Act are complicated and unclear to the public and to many physicians. There is little enforcement.

> **Lack of Insurance Can Be Deadly**
>
> In 2009, researchers at Harvard Medical School linked 45,000 deaths annually in the U.S. to lack of coverage. "Tragically, we know that the new [Census Bureau] figures of uninsured mean a preventable annual death toll of about 51,000 people - that's about one death every 11 minutes."
>
> *Dr. Quentin Young, Physicians for a National Health Program*

Medicare

Medicare is a type of federal health insurance program that does not require a person to be in poverty to qualify, since the program is funded through employees' and employers' contributions to the Social Security system. Medicare pays a significant portion of the medical bills of those who are 65 and older and those who are legally determined to be disabled. In general, a U.S. resident who receives Social Security payments is covered by Medicare.

Medicare is divided into parts, and there is no cost for basic coverage under Part A. However, Medicare does not cover all health care costs. Participants in Medicare Part B must pay a relatively modest monthly premium once they are covered to supplement their Part A coverage. Part D addresses coverage for certain types of prescription medicines, but this is a complex voluntary program with fees and deductibles. Private physicians who accept Medicare Part B only (and not Medicaid patients) may not be required to provide interpreters for LEP patients.

Qualifying U.S. residents who are very low income may receive supplements from Medicaid to pay the monthly Part B premiums of Medicare and to cover health care out-of-pocket expenses.

The Safety Net

Medicaid and Medicare are not enough. With 59 million uninsured residents in 2010 (and another up to 25 million who are underinsured), sometimes other services must provide assistance. Resources for the uninsured include community health centers, health departments, free clinics, mobile clinics, clinics for immigrants or ethnic groups run by local government or nonprofits, faith-based health organizations and other community services.

UNIT 4

How Does the Health Care System Work?

There is no single delivery system for health services in the U.S. Instead, there are many complex models for delivering care to different populations. These models have varying levels of complexity and are funded through different types of health insurance. The United States health system has more specialists, expensive medical technology, equipment, and trained personnel per capita than any other country in the world. This is one reason why medical care costs more in the U.S. than in other countries.

Primary care may takes place in the office of a health care provider, a Health Maintenance Organization (a coordinated group of health care providers working under the umbrella of one health insurance program), a community health center, a free clinic migrant health clinic or other types of health centers.

Primary care physicians refer patients to specialists as needed. Care for chronic conditions such as heart disease and diabetes is usually managed by physicians and nurse-practitioners. Long-term care for the aging or those with major disabilities often takes place in nursing homes, hospitals, group homes, certain types of "assisted living" facilities (communities for older adults where medical help may be available on site for those who do not need it on a daily basis) or through home visits from various types of medical and other caretaking personnel.

Language barriers in all these settings have emerged as a critical problem across the U.S. The Department of Health and Human Services (often called HHS or DHHS) is the United States government's principal agency for overseeing public health activities at the national level. Each state has an equivalent department, or more than one department, that corresponds to the national HHS. For example, in Maryland there is both a Department of Human Resources (which covers social services) and a

The Process

```
THE PRIMARY CARE PROVIDER or PCP
(may order tests as needed)
            │
            ▼
REFERRAL PROCESS (PCP acts as the
            "gatekeeper")
            │
            ▼
        SPECIALIST
            │
            ▼
         TESTING
           ╱ ╲
          ╱   ╲
BACK TO THE    MORE
 PRIMARY     SPECIALISTS
   CARE
 PROVIDER
```

UNIT 4

Department of Health and Mental Hygiene (which covers health care). Some federal and state money is funneled into local health departments and other local health care services.

At the federal level, HHS offers hundreds of programs that cover a spectrum of activities. State and local governments have created health departments to deliver and oversee their public health programs, and in many areas immigrants seek care from health departments and community health centers that offer free or low-cost primary care services for common conditions.

Immigrants bring important public health issues with them, including tuberculosis and sexually transmitted diseases (STDs).

Addressing language barriers

A growing number of hospitals, clinics and health departments offer their bilingual employees professional interpreter training. They also contract with for-profit and community-based interpreter services. Some health care organizations also offer training to health providers about how to work effectively with interpreters.

Certain health organizations try to get their employees to take Spanish courses so that these providers can bypass interpreters or reduce the number of interpreters needed, although experts point out that this solution is not usually adequate or safe. They are concerned that providers who take one or two language courses lack the necessary language proficiency to safely deliver health care services in that language.

UNIT 4

Laws and Legal Requirements

Numerous laws govern the health care system. A number of these laws require that language assistance be offered to LEP patients.

Title VI of the Civil Rights Act of 1964

Title VI is the article of law that pushed the profession of health care interpreting onto a higher platform. Title VI is so important that it was discussed in Unit 1 of this manual

The key contribution of Title VI to the field of medical interpreting is that this law requires the provision of interpreters for health care programs, services and agencies that receive federal financial assistance. In recent years, large health care institutions have become more aware of their legal obligations under Title VI than educational or human service institutions. It is quite common today that large healthcare institutions work with staff interpreters, contract interpreters, telephone and video interpreters, and bilingual staff who are trained to interpret.

Because the consequences of a failure to provide interpreters in health care are so serious, and often more visible than the consequences of failing to provide interpreters in other community services, Title VI has often been invoked to investigate hospitals. Sometimes lawsuits are brought by the federal government or private attorneys against large health care institutions. Investigations by the HHS Office for Civil Rights and other lawsuits, large and small, have had a ripple effect throughout the entire nation, changing the way that health care institutions serve LEP patients in their communities.

Other federal, state and local language access laws were discussed in Unit 1 of this manual.

HIPAA

In 1996, the Health Insurance Portability and Accountability Act (HIPAA) was signed into law. This act requires important privacy protection for patients in U.S. health care settings. Those individuals who have preexisting medical conditions might suffer discrimination in health coverage based on health.

A patient's record is private. Providers must obtain consent before showing the records to anyone not involved in the patient's care. Federal regulations require that all persons who have access to confidential patient information receive training in confidentiality rules and regulations, including HIPAA legislation. This requirement applies to interpreters, yet many medical interpreters receive no HIPAA training. Although HIPAA includes provisions to

UNIT 4

standardize electronic health care transactions to ensure consistency across the U.S., the law strictly requires the adoption of privacy and security standards in order to protect individually identifiable health information.

Across the U.S. many bilingual staff members are asked to translate or sight translate long HIPAA documents (written in legal language) even when they are not qualified to do so. Unless they are trained, qualified legal translators, bilingual employees should not translate or sight translate legal documents, particularly in health care. Instead, ask the provider to read aloud, explain or summarize the document, and the interpreter may interpret what is said.

For more information about HIPAA and interpreters, a helpful document called *HIPAA and Language Services in Health Care* ITALICIZE THE TITLE published in 2005 by the National Health Law Program (NHeLP) is available online at the NHeLP website at: http://www.healthlaw.org.

Private lawsuits

Most medical lawsuits brought against hospitals and other healthcare institutions for failure to provide adequate interpreting services are settled out of court, so we do not hear about them. A growing number of these cases have become public, many ranging from settlements or awards of several hundred thousand dollars up to $71 million dollars (a famous case settled out of court that involved the misinterpretation of a single Spanish word: *intoxicado*).

Anecdotal reports from lawyers and physicians in the field attest to the number of "hush-hush" settlements related to inadequate or incompetent interpreting. While these cases and the silence that surrounds them are unfortunate, at least they are leading hospitals and other healthcare institutions to pay more attention to the importance of trained, qualified professional interpreters.

Liability

Liability for interpreters in the medical field is a growing concern. Medicine in the United States is a litigious field. Patients are prone to file major lawsuits when they believe they were not served appropriately. Will interpreters be included in such lawsuits? Already this is the case, and no one knows for certain if this trend will continue. Many interpreters have been deposed to testify in court, either as witnesses or expert witnesses in cases related to medical (and also legal) interpreting. This uncertainty has left some interpreters nervous for the future. Information about interpreter insurance is discussed later in Unit 4.

UNIT 4

Signing as the interpreter or as witness

More and more interpreters in health care are being required to sign patient charts or other documents identifying the interpreter. This significant trend signals the legal responsibility of interpreters. In general, interpreters are asked to sign either as interpreters or as witnesses.

Interpreters may sign a patient chart as the interpreter, but they should not sign the chart or any other document as the witness when they are acting as the interpreter, because doing so may be a conflict of interest. Industry (ASTM) standards for interpreters advise interpreters not to sign as witnesses, and national standards for community interpreting in Canada published in 2007 also explicitly state that the interpreter should refrain from signing as a witness. Yet it is common for health care staff to ask medical interpreters to sign documents as witnesses.

UNIT 4

The Evolution of Medical Interpreting

The professionalization of medical interpreting

In general, professional boundaries are tighter and stricter in medical interpreting than in other areas of community interpreting, but less restrictive than the formal requirements of legal interpreting. Three driving forces have played a key role in the professionalization of this field in the U.S.: medical interpreter associations; a training program called *Bridging the Gap*; and NCIHC.

Medical interpreter associations

The U.S. is home to the largest association of medical interpreters in the world. The International Medical Interpreters Association, IMIA (formerly the Massachusetts Medical Interpreters Association) has about 2,000 members in the U.S. and in countries around the world. IMIA has proved a powerful force for the professionalization of the field. California Healthcare Interpreting Association (CHIA), the second largest such association in the country, has also proved influential, in addition to a significant number of regional, state and local professional associations, including those specific to healthcare interpreting (e.g., the Texas Association of Healthcare Interpreters and Translators, TAHIT) or associations that address general interpreting, such as chapters of the American Translators Association. These associations have contributed to the development of the medical interpreting profession in many ways, including hosting conferences, trainings, workshops and other forms of continuing education. Many also provide listservs, resources and credentialing programs.

Bridging the Gap

In 1995, Cross Cultural Health Care Program, a nonprofit organization in Seattle, developed the widely known 40-hour training program for medical interpreters, *Bridging the Gap*. This training was created in response to the lack of resources available to train interpreters in health care. Training in conference or legal interpreting did not prepare interpreters well for working in health care. The shortage of trained medical interpreters, together with the demands of Title VI and need for equal access to health care for LEP patients, made it imperative for institutions and interpreters to train medical interpreters.

Nearly 15 years later, *Bridging the Gap* is still taught throughout the United States and has in some respects transformed the profession of medical interpreting. It helped to establish common standards across the country, mobilize support for the profession and foster a common understanding of appropriate roles for a professional medical interpreter. Today, to one degree or another, most interpreter training programs for healthcare interpreters reflect some or many of the standards, concerns and perspectives established in *Bridging the Gap*.

UNIT 4

NCIHC

The National Council on Interpreting in Health Care (NCIHC) is a national multidisciplinary nonprofit organization founded in 1996 that supports quality interpreting in health care settings. NCIHC developed the national ethics and standards for interpreters in health care discussed in Units 1 and 5 of this manual. NCHIC has published many other documents, mobilized interpreter associations across the U.S. and fostered important research in the field. It has had enormous influence on the professionalization of healthcare interpreting.

UNIT 4

HUMAN AND SOCIAL SERVICES IN THE U.S: A Brief Overview

What are Human and Social Service Agencies?

> Human and social services are publicly or privately funded agencies in the U.S. whose purpose or mission is to support individuals and/or families (typically with low to moderate income) who need assistance with activities of daily life.

Traditionally in America, helping the poor was a matter for private charity or local government. Arriving immigrants depended mainly on predecessors from their homeland to help them start a new life. In the late 19th and early 20th centuries, several European nations instituted public-welfare programs. But such a movement was slow to take hold in the United States because the rapid pace of industrialization and the ready availability of farmland seemed to confirm the belief that anyone who was willing to work could find a job.

The Great Depression, which began in 1929, shattered that belief. For the first time in history, substantial numbers of Americans were out of work because of the widespread failures of banks and businesses.

U.S. Department of State, Portrait of the USA

UNIT 4

The Birth of Social Welfare Programs

Public assistance

In 1932, during the Great Depression, President Roosevelt proposed a recovery plan that created jobs for hundreds of thousands of people. They were soon employed in a variety of public works projects like road repair, renovating buildings and building dams. Most of these measures were temporary, but one of them has become an important institution in the U.S.: Social Security. This program provides a modest monthly income for retirees. It also offers disability payments and other forms of assistance.

> **Americans Help Each Other**
>
> It is estimated that almost 50 percent of Americans over age 18 do volunteer work, and nearly 75 percent of U.S. households contribute money to charity.
> U.S. Department of State,
> Portrait of the USA

In the years since the great Depression, legislation by Congress, along with the policies of several presidents, has established or expanded vital public assistance programs. These include Medicaid/Medicare, supplemental nutrition assistance (food stamps), public housing, WIC (a program for Women, Infants and Children), services for persons with disabilities, and many other programs.

Volunteerism

Perhaps no other country of the world counts as many volunteers as the United States. With their help, an astonishing array of social and human services support the needy. The legal structure of nonprofit organizations also requires a volunteer board of directors.

While organizations that support the needy include nonprofits, volunteers in the U.S. also assist government-funded services such as area agencies on aging, Community Action agencies or public hospitals. A number of faith-based organizations, including those that resettle refugees, also offer services to the needy with volunteers.

Many organizations in these services provide volunteer interpreters.

UNIT 4

The Evolution of "Welfare" Programs

Cash assistance for the poor

Although many nonprofit and government agencies assist those in poverty, individuals and families below the poverty line may need additional help. They are eligible to receive what used to be called "welfare," that is, temporary cash assistance paid by federal and state governments. Such programs are typically administered by local departments of social services.

Culturally, "welfare" is a touchy topic in the U.S. Many interpreters have noted that it can provoke debates and harsh accusations by native-born American against those people who "sponge" off the system. A number of Americans feel that social assistance programs are used too heavily by healthy people—including minorities and immigrants—who do not need the assistance and are too lazy to work. In fact, a number of immigrants share these views and some immigrants refuse to accept public assistance, including health programs.

Public assistance programs have an interesting history. For many years, payments to families in poverty were made through a program called Aid to Families with Dependent Children (AFDC). Historically, this program assisted children whose fathers had died. However, many families became so dependent on AFDC that it was perceived creating generations of welfare-dependent families. In addition, many Americans believe welfare services lead to social problems such as violence and drugs. In the end, Congress responded to these and other concerns and passed large-scale welfare and immigration reform in 1996. This act had a tremendous impact on both native-born and foreign-born residents.

The Welfare and Immigration Reform Act

As a result of this law:
- A program called Temporary Assistance for Needy Families (TANF) replaced AFDC.
- Lifetime welfare assistance was limited to five years.
- Most able-bodied adults were required to work after two years on welfare.

The law directly affected immigrants as follows:
- Most traditional welfare benefits were eliminated for those immigrants who obtained legal residency status after August 22, 1996 and were not yet citizens.
- Affected programs include cash programs, , supplemental nutrition assistance (food stamps), Medicaid, and Supplemental Security Income (SSI), among others.
- Refugees and asylees who do not become citizens within 9 years of obtaining legal residency may risk of losing their public benefits.

UNIT 4

Social Services

A broad array of services

Many of the social services offered in the United States are accessed through private and public social service agencies. All government-funded services require an eligibility process. This section of Unit 4 addresses what these services are, who funds them, and what interpreters need to know about them.

> **Eligibility**
>
> Many of the welfare services in the United States are accessed through private and public social service agencies. All government-funded services require an eligibility process. This often means that providers must ask questions that many immigrants and refugees may find disturbing or intrusive.

Social Security

Social Security offices administer federal programs that are paid for by taxpayers and the federal government. These vital programs include Social Security for workers who have reached official retirement age. (Formerly 65, this age now varies according to one's year of birth: the retirement may be 66, 67 or older, because the younger you are the more likely you are to have a delayed retirement age.)

Other programs administered by Social Security include Social Security Disability Insurance (SSDI) for taxpayers who cannot work because of disabilities, and Supplemental Security Income (SSI), a program for seniors and residents with disabilities who are not eligible for Social Security or SSDI because they have not worked long enough to pay into the system at an adequate level.

Social security programs are *not* considered welfare because, with the exception of SSI, they are usually available only to those who have worked at least 40 quarters in the U.S. and paid into the Social Security system through payroll deductions or self-employment contributions.

Departments of Social Services

Departments of Social Services (DSSs) are not managed by the federal government. Individual states may set up DSSs in their counties and cities. DSSs use federal funding, combine it with state and other funding, and use the funds to administer programs such as cash assistance (TANF), supplemental nutrition assistance (formerly known as food stamps), Medical Assistance, job training and other vital services.

UNIT 4

Local public services

Local government agencies and school systems offer many services to low-income residents. Some are provided through county or municipal Social Services, while others are offered through a number of other agencies and funded through a combination of federal, state and local tax dollars and other funding streams, including money from foundations, corporations and private donors.

These public services include housing programs, transportation, libraries, child care, landlord and tenant offices, and services to the aging. Some local Health Departments also provide human services, including the federally funded WIC program (Women, Infants and Children).

Increasingly, as family units in America grow smaller, U.S. residents and immigrants rely on these public services because families lack the support that extended family members once provided. For example, a family member with a disability may need special transportation services for a medical appointment. An elderly person may seek an English class at a senior center, or need subsidized senior housing. Local communities assist with many such cases. And often, an interpreter is needed.

Community Action Agencies

Community Action agencies are an unusual U.S. creation. Essentially they operate as a national "chain" of social service agencies that are government funded, structured like nonprofits but closely tied to (and often physically located within) local government agencies. Most often they are called Community Action Agencies, Community Action Councils or by some other name that includes the words "Community Action."
One may think of Community Action organizations as a hybrid of government and nonprofit services. Historically, they have relied heavily on volunteers (including past or current clients) to carry out their mission. They typically offer a number of important services for those in poverty such as emergency assistance for eviction notices and gas-and-electric cut-offs, emergency shelter for the homeless, first month rent programs, food banks and other services.

Private nonprofit organizations

All the services described above are important, but the U.S. is a nation with a large divide between rich and poor. Those in poverty and those who face hard economic times due to unemployment, large medical bills or a recession may need additional services.

UNIT 4

Private nonprofit organizations fill the gaps. Local nonprofit agencies that provide community services are often referred to as community-based organizations (CBOs). Nonprofit organizations are independent private organizations. They may receive some funding from federal, state and/or local government agencies through grants and contracts. However, they are required by the federal laws that govern the nonprofit sector to seek funding other than government grants, for example, through annual appeals, donations from individuals and businesses, support from foundations, and fees charged to clients, their membership or the public for services the nonprofit organizations provide (known as "fee for service" programs).

Many nonprofit agencies serve as intermediaries or case managers for clients who are applying for public benefits. Some nonprofit agencies have a charitable mission, while others support an "empowerment" mission that promotes the self-sufficiency of clients. Nonprofit agencies offer a wide array of such human and social services. Some of them include:

- Domestic violence shelters
- Sexual assault centers
- Homeless shelters
- Subsidized housing
- Crisis hotlines
- Special or low-cost transportation
- Immigration counseling
- Refugee resettlement
- Senior centers
- Community interpreter services

These are only a few examples from the vast array of human and social services provided by nonprofit agencies in the U.S.

Faith-based organizations

Historically, congregations in churches, mosques, temples and other faith-based organizations (FBOs) constitute a special form of nonprofit organization. In the U.S., many FBOs have been active in supporting families and individuals in poverty. Whether faith volunteers are making food or holiday baskets, taking in homeless families or resettling refugees, they offer many of the same services as other private nonprofit organizations. FBOs may rely even more heavily than other nonprofits on the work of volunteers.

UNIT 4

Despite the legal separation in the U.S. between "church and state," FBO's are sometimes able to obtain government funding to help provide these services to the poor. Some faith-based organizations are particularly sensitive to the discrimination encountered by immigrants and refugees in poverty. They, too, seek interpreters and translators to serve LEP individuals.

Refugee resettlement agencies and services to immigrants

Most services to immigrants are administered by private nonprofit organizations and local government agencies. Refugee resettlement is a special case. Unlike other immigrants, refugees and asylees are entitled to federal assistance and special benefits because they are fleeing persecution in their homeland and cannot safely return. Refugees obtain refugee status before coming to the U.S.; political asylees apply for their asylee status after their arrival in the U.S. Otherwise, the legal status of refugees and asylees and their benefits are comparable.

Refugee and asylee services are federally funded. Each state has its own office for refugee resettlement and may contribute state funding to the federal funds. Funding to provide direct services to refugees, however, is typically given in the form of grants to nonprofit organizations that specialize in refugee resettlement. Some of the larger ones are called VOLAGs (short for "voluntary agency"). These refugee agencies then carry out the work on the ground, such as helping refugee families register their children at school, find jobs and obtain health care.

In addition to refugee resettlement agencies, a broad spectrum of nonprofits across the U.S. specialize in services to immigrants and refugees. They include:

- Agencies that support survivors of torture and trauma.
- Job counseling services for immigrants and refugees.
- Nonprofit legal services that serve immigrants
- Social services nonprofits for immigrants.
- Broad-spectrum agencies, e.g. agencies that provide assistance with jobs, domestic violence, crisis intervention, consumer issues, housing and other services.
- Agencies that specialize in a particular regional population, such Latinos, Africans or Southeast Asian women.
- Faith-based organizations that serve foreign-born members such as Muslims or Jews.
- Nonprofits that serve clients from a particular country, such as Ethiopia or Korea.

Special needs of elderly immigrants

Older immigrants were once able to provide for themselves by settling into a supportive

UNIT 4

community. However, in recent years many older immigrants are finding it more difficult to receive extensive support from their families. Often, their grown children are more acculturated than they are to the western lifestyle and lead hectic lives.

In a country like the U.S. with a high level of industrialization and fast-paced progress, aging immigrants may feel confused and lost. They may arrive expecting that they will be well cared for, as they might be in many traditional societies. Many aging immigrants have a small pension or none at all. Perhaps more than any other age group, aging LEP immigrants find themselves in need of services from social service agencies, nonprofits and faith-based organizations.

The elderly often need interpreters. Because it is difficult for older immigrants to learn a new language, they tend to rely on their family members and friends to interpret. But these informal interpreters are rarely trained to interpret. They may not know both languages well, do not typically interpret accurately and often withhold information, either from embarrassment about their aging relatives or because they do not wish service providers to know what is being said. In some cases, the family interpreter may be covering up elder abuse or neglect.

It is vital that aging LEP immigrants receive the services of trained, qualified interpreters, just like any other client of human services who needs an interpreter.

The legal right to an interpreter

Often when people think of Title VI, they think this law applies to health care, or perhaps the courts. In fact, however, any organization that receives funding from the U.S. government is required through Title VI of the Civil Rights Act to take reasonable steps to ensure equal access to its services. In practical terms, this requirement means that the organization must offer interpreters for most of their services at no cost to clients. (See Unit 1 for details.)

Title VI therefore typically applies to most state services, local government agencies and a large number of human and social services nonprofit organizations—and also some faith-based organizations—in health and human services. Most of them do receive federal financial assistance either directly (in federal grants) or indirectly (in federal funds channeled through state agencies, local governments, or subcontracts from larger nonprofits that receive federal funding). Title VI covers any vital or important service, such as health care. It may not always apply to discretionary activities such as an aging LEP resident who takes a crocheting class or an LEP child listening to storytime at a public library. Title VI, however, certainly applies to basic human and social services. (When in doubt about whether Title VI does or doesn't cover a particular type of service, ask a specialized attorney or your regional

UNIT 4

Office for Civil Rights for Health and Human Services.)

The difficulty with Title VI and other state and local language access laws is *that most LEP immigrants and many human and social services do not know about the legal rights of LEP clients*. This is also a problem in other countries with language access laws. In the U.S., while many hospitals and large health care organizations understand their Title VI obligations, this is far less often the case in human and social services. As a result, sometimes the interpreter is the only one present who is familiar with language access laws.

A surge in volunteer interpreting

As a result of the surge in immigration since 1970, there has been an increase in the number of requests for volunteer interpreters and translators at community service agencies across the nation.

Community-based organizations may operate on a shoe-string. Such agencies often depend on the good will of volunteer interpreters, many of whom are immigrants who have been through difficulties themselves. However, most volunteer interpreters have not been trained to interpret and have not even attended a basic workshop or orientation about interpreting.

The need for interpreters is growing urgent in many community services. Unfortunately, agencies who request volunteer interpreters typically have no idea about the importance of interpreter training. Most do not even check to see if the interpreter speaks both languages proficiently or is qualified to interpret.

UNIT 4

Community Interpreters in Human and Social Services

Within the broader field of community interpreting, the field of human and social services may be the environment with the least structure for interpreters. In part, this is because agencies in this field are only now starting to use qualified interpreters. Interpreting is still barely recognized as a separate occupation and has little recognition outside health care. Outside a few urban areas, bilingual employees who interpret in human and social services rarely receive training or recognition.

> **Client Autonomy**
>
> Community interpreters often know the client and family well and want to help them out. When the interpreter takes charge, however, it works against a client's ability to function independently in U.S. culture and undermines the client's right to self determination.
>
> Remember: never make a decision for a client, never give the client your opinion—and never do for the client something that the client can do for himself.

When an LEP person needs to access community services, he or she requires the aid of a trained, qualified interpreter and in many cases has a legal right to one. But in an environment where community interpreting is not a formal profession, volunteer interpreters and bilingual staff still try their best to "help out" the client. Many times, untrained interpreters believe that the best way to help is by taking charge of clients' lives. But when interpreters take over the encounter, they may inadvertently create dependent behaviors.

The interpreter should never answer for the client, give advice, make decisions or otherwise interfere with the client's autonomy. Yet such behavior is common among untrained interpreters.

Client: (to the interpreter) I'm scared this will hurt me later when I try to become a citizen. What do you think I should do?
Untrained interpreter: Go ahead! Apply for the food stamps. What do you have to lose?

Client: (to the interpreter) I'm scared this will hurt me later when I try to become a citizen. What do you think I should do?
Trained interpreter: [interprets the question into English]
Income support specialist/caseworker: Oh, sure, a lot of immigrants worry about that. But let me explain.

Client: (to the interpreter, outside the session) What do you think I should do?
Trained interpreter: The Income Support Specialist should be here any moment. I'm only the interpreter, so I can't advise you, but she'll be happy to answer your questions.

THE COMMUNITY INTERPRETER

UNIT 4

Challenges in Social and Human Services

The adjunct interpreter who works as a bilingual employee in public or private social service agencies faces many challenges and dilemmas, for example:

• What are your roles?

• What is your "real" job?

• What can you do about interpreting assignments you aren't qualified to perform (or aren't ready for) when your boss expects you to do them?

As a staff member, you may have access to client records and other information that a contract interpreter does not have. How should you use this information? This is a question for supervisors to address.

When serving a client, bilingual employees in public or private social service agencies often spend long periods of time alone with the client—up to several hours. The relationship with one client may extend for months or even years. While there is usually a professional code of ethics for providers that they are familiar with, this is not always the case for untrained adjunct interpreters (who may not be aware that interpreter ethics even exist). You may therefore have untrained colleagues who interpret incorrectly, but your other co-workers may find their unethical behavior acceptable and even preferable to your ethical behavior, further complicating your work. Indeed, this problem affects both adjunct and contract interpreters in the often chaotic environment of community services.

UNIT 4

Language Banks

Language banks are an affordable resource for community services in the U.S. who need access to free or low-cost interpreters. By setting up a list or database of volunteer or community interpreters, organizations in human and social services (and also education and healthcare) can more easily serve clients who speak other languages.

> **Language Banks**
>
> A language bank is a group of volunteers, bilingual employees or low-cost interpreters who perform community interpreting.

How do language banks start?

An organization, typically a nonprofit agency, a health department, a community, a school district, or a hospital, assembles a group of bilingual employees and/or volunteers to assist clients or patients who speak little English. The group may start out as a simple list or database of names with contact information, organized by language. This type of entity is called a language bank. A trend in some urban areas is to pay language bank interpreters $15 to $20 per hour or more. Sometimes a language bank may develop over time into a professional interpreter service (usually nonprofit) that works only with trained, qualified interpreters.

Whom do they serve?

Language banks may serve a particular organization, such as a refugee resettlement agency or a domestic violence center, or a community, such as a county government or a network of local agencies.

How do language banks work?

If the "bank" is simply a list or database of names with contact information, organized by language, then the person who needs the interpreter will consult the list, calling up several interpreters until one interpreter is available. Some language banks have a paid or volunteer coordinator who will locate an interpreter on the list when one is needed and book the appointment.

Are language bank interpreters trained?

While some interpreters in language banks receive training, the majority do not. Many receive an orientation or workshop that may last from a half day to a day. This situation is slowly changing across the U.S. as more language bank interpreters attend professional training.

UNIT 4

The Education System in the U.S.

A state-run system

Contrary to popular belief, the United States does not have a national school system. Although it manages military academies, the federal government does not run public schools. Instead, it lays down legislation and offers funding, standards and guidance to the states, who oversee public and private schools.

Community interpreters come from around the world. Each nation has its own system for education, and that system may be very different from the education system in the U.S., which is often confusing (and daunting) for immigrant parents.

The basic system

Most public school systems in the U.S. include free elementary, middle school and high school education. Some preschool services are free, and some higher education studies in community and four-year colleges, may be subsidized through grants and scholarships. But only elementary, middle and high school education is available to every U.S. child at no cost—even if that child is undocumented.

Historically, elementary school included kindergarten and often extended through the eighth grade (or even, especially in some rural areas, through high school). Today, the local school system usually divides schools into elementary (kindergarten through fifth or sixth grade), middle school (often sixth, seventh and eighth grades, which may be called junior high school), and high school, which often runs from eighth through twelfth grades. Middle schools (or junior high schools) and high schools are collectively known as secondary education.

Public elementary and secondary schools do not charge tuition but rely on local and state taxes for funding. These school systems, however, can and do impose a number of fees for materials, field trips and other events. Many low-income families find these fees a burden, including many immigrant families. Sometimes funds are available through private fundraising to help waive these fees for low-income families.

A number of children attend private schools for which their families pay tuition ranging from little or nothing to $45,000 a year or more. Most private schools in the U.S. are run by religious organizations so that they can include religious instruction in their curriculum, which is not permitted in public schools.

Finally, a growing number of parents educate their own children outside of schools in a practice known as home schooling which is supervised by the state.

UNIT 4

Historical Background on the U.S. Education System

American public education differs from that of many other nations in that it is primarily the responsibility of the states and individual school districts. Jefferson was the first American leader to suggest creating a public school system. His ideas formed the basis of education systems developed in the 19th century. Until the 1840s, the education system was highly localized and available only to wealthy people. Reformers who wanted all children to gain the benefits of education opposed this. The common-school reformers argued for the case based on their belief that common schooling could create good citizens, unite society and prevent crime and poverty. As a result of their efforts, free public education at the elementary level was available for all American children by the end of the 19th century.

The rise in American high school attendance was one of the most striking developments in U.S. education during the 20th century. From 1900 to 1996, the percentage of teenagers who graduated from high school increased from about 6% to about 85%. As the 20th century progressed, most states enacted legislation extending compulsory education laws to the age of 16.

Individual states have primary authority over public education in the United States. Local districts oversee the administration of schools, with the exception of licensing requirements and general rules concerning health and safety. Public schools have also relied heavily on local property taxes to meet the vast majority of school expenses. American schools have thus tended to reflect the educational values and financial capabilities of the communities in which they are located. This aspect of the U.S. education system strikes many as unfair, because quality schools are found in wealthier districts.

The U.S. federal government does not have any direct authority over education in the United States. There is no national ministry of education and no education framework-law or set of such laws in the United States.

K-12 Education

Currently, most community interpreters in education work in "K-12" schools: that is, schools for kindergarten through Grade 12. Bilingual employees at K-12 schools are soaring in number due to a simple statistic from the U.S. Census Bureau: one child in four in the U.S. is an immigrant or an immigrant's child.

As a result, the need to train more community interpreters for K-12 schools is urgent. In most cases, bilingual employees such as parent-teacher liaisons or interpreters for a school language bank interpret for LEP parents. (They also interpret for LEP children, but most LEP

UNIT 4

children receive special classes in English and quickly become bilingual.) For example, in one county in Virginia with a large foreign-born population, it is estimated that there are more than 500 bilingual employees in the school system who could be called on to interpret in any of the county's K-12 schools.

The greatest interpreting demand is for elementary schools, parent-teacher conferences and Special Education services. Elementary schools hire immigrants to work as parent-teacher liaisons, clerical staff, counselors and teaching assistants. In addition, schools often create language banks of community interpreters and pay them an hourly fee to interpret for parent-teacher conferences, Back to School Nights, school fairs, Board disciplinary hearings, or Special Education meetings such as Admission, Review and Dismissal meetings.

Attendance

Each of the 50 states has its own laws regulating education. From state to state, laws vary. In all states, children in the U.S. are required to attend school. However, the age limit varies:

- Most states require attendance up to age 16.
- In some states, children must attend school until 18.
- All children are required to attend at least 11 years of education.
- Elementary and secondary education is required regardless of sex, race, religion, learning problems, disabilities, fluency in English, citizenship or immigration status.

While there is no national school system, certain subjects are taught everywhere. They include:

- Mathematics.
- Language arts.
- Science.
- Social studies (including history, geography, citizenship, and economics).
- Physical education.

Working with computers is now becoming a common school subject. In addition to required courses, students at secondary schools can choose electives such as drama, foreign languages (which are sometimes required), home economics and "tech ed" (technical education).

UNIT 4

U.S. Colleges

Community College

A community college is a two-year institution of higher learning that is often considered preparation for studying at a four-year college. However, a community college offers a valuable educational service in its own right. It confers certificates that require one or two semesters of study and two-year degrees such as Associate in Arts (AA degree) and Associate in Science (AS degree).

Community colleges cover a number of vital professional areas, e.g., nursing, physical therapy and radiology. In some states, more than half of in-state undergraduate students may be enrolled in community colleges, in great part because of lower cost (often half the cost of tuition at four-year colleges). Due to higher standards and performance as well as the lower cost, community colleges appear to be gaining in popularity, and many of their student bodies are increasing.

A growing number of community colleges across the U.S. offer certificates in medical, legal or community interpreting. However, such programs are still rare.

Universities

A university or college is a four-year institution of higher learning that awards degrees, most often in the arts or sciences. A bachelor's degree usually requires four years of full-time study to obtain a Bachelor of Arts (BA) degree or a Bachelor of Science (BS) degree, among others. A four-year college may also offer graduate degrees such as Master of Arts (MA), Master of Fine Arts (MFA), Master of Science (MS) and Doctor of Philosophy (PhD). Some professional schools may offer a law degree (Juris Doctor, JD) or a medical degree (Doctor of Medicine, MD). Four-year colleges may be independent, private, religious, state-run or components of universities. A large university may have several colleges.

Few four-year colleges offer degrees in interpreting (usually for "Translation and Interpreting" programs). Yet a growing number are discussing such programs. A few graduate programs also exist. Those of the graduate school of Translation and Interpretation at Monterey Institute of International Studies, for example, are considered some of the world's most prestigious education programs for interpreters.

UNIT 4

The Impact of Federal Laws of Education

The Education for the Handicapped Act (EHA) (P.L. 94-142)

Passed in 1975, the Education for all Handicapped Children Act is more commonly known as the EHA It guarantees a Free and Appropriate Public Education (FAPE) for all children with disabilities, ages 5-21.

Appropriate education is the provision of regular and Special Education and related services designed to meet students' individual educational needs. Special Education and related services must be free, provided by the public agency at no cost to the parents. To the extent possible, all children and youth with disabilities will be educated in the least restrictive education (LRE) environment. Parents have the right to participate in every decision related to the identification, evaluation, and placement of their child. Parents must give consent for any initial evaluation, assessment or placement decision.

The Rehabilitation Act of 1973 (P.L. 93-112) Section 504

As part of the Rehabilitation Act of 1973, Section 504 became the first federal civil rights law to protect the rights of individuals with disabilities. Section 504 states that "no otherwise qualified handicapped individual in the United States shall, solely by reason of his/her handicap, be excluded from participation in, be denied the benefits of, or be subjected to discrimination under any program or activity receiving federal financial assistance." Under this law, students who have a physical or mental impairment that substantially limits one or more of their major life activities are protected; those who have disabilities such as orthopedic impairments or conditions such as hepatitis but do not qualify for Special Education services are included. A student 504 plan describes all reasonable accommodations for the student's education that may include a change in educational routine, method or approach.

Individuals with Disabilities ACT- IDEA (1990)
Individuals with Disabilities Education Improvement Act-IDEIA (2004)

In 1990 the EHA was renamed as the Individuals with Disabilities Education Act (IDEA). The amendment replaced the phrase "handicapped child" with "child with a disability." Part of the intent behind IDEA was to provide Transition Services for students by age 16, to extend eligibility to children with autism and traumatic brain injury, to define Assistive Technology Devices and Services for children with disabilities for inclusion in the Individualized Education Plan for each student with disabilities, and to extend the Least Restrictive Environment (LRE) to require the child be educated with children without disabilities, as much as possible.

In 1997, this law was amended to include more provisions to make the environment as minimally restrictive as possible for the student. Then in 2004, President Bush signed into law The Individuals with Disabilities Education Improvement Act, stating the intent to " help children learn better by promoting accountability for results, enhancing parent involvement, using proven practices and materials, providing more flexibility, and reducing paperwork burdens for teachers, states and local school districts."

No Child Left Behind

The No Child Left Behind Act of 2001, also known as "NCLB," is a U.S. federal law that was originally proposed by President George W. Bush in 2001. The legislation funds a number of federal programs aimed at improving the performance of U.S. schools by increasing the standards of accountability for states, school districts, and schools, as well as providing parents more flexibility in choosing which schools their children will attend.

Additionally, No Child Left Behind promotes an increased focus on reading and math. Under this law, which addresses all children including those with disadvantages, disabilities and limited English, children must achieve academic proficiency as regulated by standardized testing known by different names in various states. (For example, in Virginia these tests are called SOL, short for Standards of Learning.) Immigrant students who speak limited English are not exempt from the requirement of this law.

This act caused controversy by setting standards that many educators feel are impossible for schools in impoverished areas to achieve. They feel that many LEP children may not be given sufficient time to learn English. Schools also complain that funding to support the act and student achievement has been inadequate.

The current administration says it is necessary to provide the funding that was promised and give states the resources they need in order for teachers to maintain high academic standards and expectations. Additionally, President Obama suggested two fundamental reforms to NCLB:

- Improvements to Assessments to evaluate higher-order skills, including students' abilities to use technology, conduct research, engage in scientific investigation, solve problems, and present and defend their ideas.

- Improvements to the Accountability System to help schools to improve, rather than one that focuses on punishments. In this view, schools should assess all children appropriately, including English language learners and special needs students. The system would evaluate continuous progress for students and also for schools along the learning continuum and would consider measures beyond reading and math tests.

UNIT 4

Title VI, ADA and Schools

Schools are legally required to provide important information to families in other languages and through interpreters in order to comply with Title VI of the Civil Rights Act of 1964, ADA and IDEA, among other laws. According to a Memorandum issued in 1991 by the Office for Civil Rights of the U.S. Department of Education:

"Schools districts have the responsibility to adequately notify national origin minority group parents of activities which are called to the attention of other parents. Such notice in order to be adequate may have to be provided in language other than English, especially for language groups that represent 5% or more of the student population and as needed during the Special Education eligibility process."

Immigrant Children in American schools

Because of recent immigration trends, children with immigrant parents—whether the parents legal or undocumented—are now the fastest growing segment of the nation's child population. The well-being of these children is influenced not only by the legal status of their parents but by family income and structure; parental work patterns, educational attainment and English proficiency; health insurance coverage; and access to work supports such as tax credits, food assistance and child care.

The U.S. Census Bureau has identified the following concerns among immigrant populations as issues that have greatly impacted the US school system.

- The number of children with immigrant parents is rising. More than 15 million immigrants entered the United States during the 1990s alone. The number of foreign-born residents in 2009 was 38.5 million, and their children number over 15 million.

- Immigrants comprise over 12% of the U.S. population. Children of immigrants represent a quarter of all U.S. children.

- Four-fifths of children of immigrants were born in the United States and are therefore citizens. Most children of immigrants—61% in 2003—live in families where one or more children are citizens but one or more parents are non-citizens. In these "mixed-status" families, the well-being of children can be greatly affected by their parents' lack of citizenship or legal status.

- There are over 5 million children living with unauthorized parents. Even in families where parents are undocumented, two-thirds of the children are U.S.-born citizens. Children who are citizens are entitled to public benefits, but their unauthorized parents may be reluctant to approach public institutions for services because they fear deportation. Unauthorized parents also often work at low-paying, unstable jobs and lack access to bank accounts and other financial services.

With successive new waves of immigrants, American schools have had to cope with the arrival of large numbers of children who speak little or no English. The K-12 curriculum is supposed to reflect the cultures of all these children but has not yet caught up with the diversity in schools today. Schools must also make sure that these students pass graduation exams and state tests designed for native speakers of English. However, these tests pose cultural as well as linguistic obstacles for LEP students.

Barriers to Education for LEP Students

Family participation

Schools are well aware that state tests are among the most serious barriers to success and graduation for LEP students. This is currently a serious topic in national educational circles. Schools therefore want more LEP parents to participate in the education of their children, both for the family's sake and because research shows that when parents participate in children's education, their children perform better academically at school.

Many school systems have engaged a number of teachers of English for Speakers of Other Languages (ESOL), found tutors for LEP children and launched after-school homework clubs. They also hire parent liaisons and use more and more interpreters.

To make multicultural families feel included, school systems are also beginning to embrace diverse cultures through international festivals at schools, dances, cultural displays in hallways, cultural competence conferences and events, cultural concerts, ethnic speakers (including parents), multicultural holiday celebrations and other activities. Many schools are sensitized to the importance of making parents feel included and part of their children's education

Legal status

Public schools should not request formal documentation of immigration status to assess whether a child should attend school. If a school demands such documentation from foreign-born parents—and many schools have done so—the client should see an immigration attorney immediately.

UNIT 4

In a few cases, parents have kept their children out of school when immigration documents were requested by public schools for fear that the whole family would be deported.

Universities and private schools may request such documentation. Public schools should not. They have a right to verify local residency, not immigration status. Yet a number of public schools have tried to exclude undocumented students when they had no legal grounds to do so. Interpreters should be aware that such activities are illegal.

Interpreting in the School Setting

The challenges of diversity and poverty

As the number of LEP students and parents grows in the United States, schools have an additional responsibility to provide a broad array of services to these students and their parents. In general, schools are often expected to compensate for the social problems associated with poverty to help assure that children of all backgrounds succeed at school and have a fair opportunity to go on to higher education.

Schools feel the pressure of those expectations. Now that the diversity of the cultures and languages has increased dramatically over the last decades, it puts an additional burden on schools to address linguistic and cultural differences.

Most students who are new arrivals in the U.S. have attended formal schooling, but many have not. This leaves school systems with the additional challenge of educating these children and meeting the national academic standards in non-traditional ways.

Linguistic challenges

LEP students register in their local jurisdiction. Their parents may speak limited English, but most schools still have relatively few bilingual personnel (and in some jurisdictions, the bilingual employees they have employed feel overwhelmed by the heavy demands placed on them). Due to the recession, some bilingual personnel such as parent-teacher liaisons are losing their jobs after cuts in funding, though they perform very valuable work—including interpreting for LEP families.

The most common language other than English spoken in schools is Spanish, but many students come from countries in Asia, the Middle East, Africa and other parts of the world. Some of the languages that these students speak are written languages and some are not. A single school system may be dealing with more than 100 languages.

UNIT 4

The need for interpreters

Schools are legally required to provide an interpreter and/or translator for parent-teacher conferences, administrative level conferences with parents, Special Education processes, information regarding disciplinary actions, suspensions or expulsions and retentions, medical appointments at school and any other matter affecting the student's academic program. As a result, more and more school systems are hiring bilingual staff to "solve the problem" of interpreters.

Some bilingual employees who interpret are screened for language skills. Most are not. This may be a particular problem for heritage speakers, who grow up speaking two languages in a home setting but who may feel lost when faced with technical vocabulary and the higher register often involved in interpreting for schools and sight translating education documents. A school disciplinary hearing or a Special Education process for a student can be intimidating to interpreters who do not know both languages very well.

> **Confidentiality**
>
> Federal regulations require that all persons who have access to confidential student information receive training in confidentiality rules and regulations. The federal regulations state: "All persons collecting or using personally identifiable information in public education institutions must receive training on confidentiality requirements."* This requirement would apply to interpreters in school settings.
>
> *The Family Rights and Privacy Act and Individuals with Disabilities Education Act

School systems tend to assume that interpreting in schools is easy. It is not. Bilingual employees who interpret in educational settings need professional interpreter training, like any other interpreter.

As an interpreter in education you should be familiar with appropriate educational terms, forms, procedures, techniques, and tests utilized by the institution. You should also know the culture of the school and the culture of the student

The interpreter is not the only one with requirements: school professionals should be familiar with the skills needed by interpreters and the skills that they themselves need to work successfully with interpreters.

UNIT 4

Special Education Eligibility Process

Special Education is instruction that is specially designed to meet the unique needs of children who have disabilities. This is done at no cost to the parents. Special education can include special instruction in the classroom, home, hospital, institution or any other setting.

IDEA P.L. 105-17

Special Education

One of the greatest challenges that interpreters face in educational settings is interpreting for Special Education programs for children with disabilities.

Trained interpreters may be needed in various situations that involve services to children with disabilities. (In fact, Special Education meetings are among the most common situations where interpreters are requested in school settings.) Some of these assignments include parent-teacher conferences, the referral process (for children to be tested), evaluation, assessments and social history, admissions, reviews, eligibility meetings, dismissal meetings, placement meetings, meetings about the Individualized Education Plan (IEP) and triennial reviews.

A student's records are private. With some exceptions, schools must obtain parental consent before showing the records to anyone not involved in the student's education, such as the interpreter.

An interpreter should be ready and able to handle complex documents and vocabulary. An IEP, an academic decision, a placement, a disciplinary action and so forth are all legal processes or, at a minimum, processes with serious legal implications. Parents have the right to information concerning their child's education and the right to appeal any decision made by the school system. Inadequate or inaccurate interpreting can lead to misunderstandings, conflicts, and miscommunication that could have a negative impact on a child, up to and including legal actions taken by the school or parents that were at least partly the result of poor interpreting. (For example, suspensions and expulsions—whether or not the outcomes were influenced by inaccurate interpreting—can affect the child's success when applying to colleges.)

Finally, by failing to address language barriers in Special Education services—for example, by not providing interpreters when they are needed—the school may expose itself to the threat of a lawsuit from parents or from the Office for Civil Rights. Such lawsuits have already taken place.

UNIT 4

Impact of Individuals with Disabilities Educational Act (IDEA)

The United States provides an exceptional array of services at no cost to students with disabilities to ensure their equal access to education. Indeed, so many legal safeguards, processes, documents and meetings surround these Special Education services that it is truly necessary to have qualified interpreters present at relevant meetings to ensure that LEP parents grasp the issues at stake for their children's future. It is therefore also important that interpreters understand the complex process involved.

This subject is all the more sensitive because many immigrant parents believe that their children are incorrectly assigned to Special Education services. In some cases, they believe that their child may simply need more help with English and have no disabilities at all (and they may be quite correct). In other cases, they may feel that their child has been misunderstood due to differences of culture, the bias of the system or prejudice by individuals. Sometimes such feelings lead to conflicts with school staff. In still other cases, parents are so confused by the system that instead of advocating for their child they allow school staff (and even interpreters) to make important decisions on their behalf. This passive approach is also inappropriate, and the interpreter can play a key role in make sure that the process is well understood by the parent.

In addition, the terminology of Special Education can be intimidating both for LEP parents and their interpreters. Indeed, such terminology is intimidating to many native-born parents of Special Education students as well.

Referral Process

Students who may need Special Education services come to the attention of school officials in a number of ways.

- Parents may contact their child's teacher or another professional.
- A school professional asks that a child be evaluated.
- A community agency sometimes intervenes to suggest testing.
- An individual or group working with the student may recommend a referral for testing.

The request that a child be assessed for learning delays or disabilities may be a verbal request or may be made in writing. This request initiates a referral process for the child to be considered for Special Education and related services. A team of professionals will then gather information and decide if the child needs to be formally evaluated. If the school decides to test the child, they notify the parent or guardian in advance, in writing, about the evaluation process. They obtain written consent from parents or guardians before the evaluation starts.

Notice and Consent

The parents or guardian must be given written notice each time the school proposes to initiate or change the identification, evaluation, or educational placement of the child or the provision of a free and appropriate public education (FAPE) to the child. This notice consists of two parts:

- Notice of Procedural Safeguards
- Specific notice for that activity

School personnel must give notice about proposed actions before they:

- Make decisions about whether the child has a disability.
- Change his disability category.
- Conduct an evaluation.
- Change the current education program.
- Change the placement.
- Consider transition.

School administrators must give specific written notice if the parent asks them to make any of these changes and they refuse. For any actions described above, the parent must be told in writing about:
- The action the school wants to take and the reason for that action.
- Options the school considered, and why other options were considered inappropriate.
- Evaluation, tests and other information supporting the school's position.
- Sources for parents to contact for help in understanding the relevant laws.

The school must notify the parent or guardian, obtain written parental consent before testing, complete the evaluation and have a written report within 60 calendar days of the date the school district receives written consent for the full individual and initial evaluation signed by the student's parent or legal guardian. The school may not start the referral process if the parents have not signed the appropriate consent and notification forms.

UNIT 4

Evaluation

The evaluation must cover all areas of suspected disability and may consist of printed tests, observations, parent input and other forms of information. This evaluation is performed by trained professionals authorized by the school. It provides information regarding the child's abilities and disabilities. It also offers information about the child's educational needs.

The parent receives a written report with all the findings of the evaluation. With input from the parents or guardians, the school decides on the need for Special Education services or accommodations. The report will include recommendations for managing the child's education. These recommendations will be considered as the Admission, Review, and Dismissal (ARD) Committee develops the child's Individualized Education Program (IEP).

Eligibility

The ARD Committee, of which the parent is an important member, decides if the child is eligible for special services under the law. In order to receive special services, the law has established specific guidelines that the committee must follow.

As a parent and member of the ARD committee, the parent has a right to be an equal participant in developing the child's IEP. The school must give written notice at least five school days before the eligibility meeting. The notice should include the purpose, time and place of the meeting and a list of the people attending.

The Individualized Education Program/Plan (IEP)

An IEP is an agreement between the school and parents on the educational plan for the student. It describes the frequency and type of service the student will receive. It also establishes the goals and persons involved. Specially designed for each student found eligible, the IEP states what services the school will provide, when and where those services will be provided, and how progress will be measured.

The members of the IEP meeting are the same as the ARD committee. An older child can be a member of the committee and be involved in designing goals and objectives. (If so, the older children may be free to offer an opinion about whether he or she still needs services or not.) Federal laws and regulations require that the committee develop an IEP before a student receives Special Education and related services. This IEP could be one that was in effect at the end of the previous school year, as long as the committee meets at least once a year to review the IEP. For new students, a temporary IEP can be developed while the evaluation is being completed.

UNIT 4

In the case of a child with Limited English Proficiency, the committee must consider the language needs of the child as these needs relate to the child's IEP.

If a student is placed in a non-public school by the public school district, an IEP is also required, and the public school is responsible both for protecting the student's rights and paying the private school's tuition fees.

Placement

Federal law requires school districts to educate students with disabilities in the Least Restrictive Environment (LRE). This means the student must be placed in the setting that puts the fewest limits on his opportunities to be educated alongside students who do not have disabilities. If the ARD committee places the child somewhere other than the general education classroom, they must specify in the IEP why a more restrictive placement is needed.

In order to determine the final placement for a child, the committee needs to discuss the alternatives and possibilities the child has in regular classes with modifications, aides and adaptations. If placement in a regular classroom is not possible, the committee must document why the placement, even with the use of modifications and supplementary aids and services, is not appropriate.

Many students placed in Special Education programs also need related services in order to benefit from Special Education. The most common related services are:

- Physical therapy
- Speech therapy
- Occupational therapy
- Psychological services
- Special transportation
- Counseling
- Orientation and mobility training
- Audiology services

Instruction

Once the child is placed in Special Education services, parents and teacher work on the academic goals and objectives of the IEP. Parents and teacher must work as a team and remain in constant communication. A bilingual employee may be asked to interpret when communicating with the parents on a regular basis.

Annual Review

The committee must meet every year to determine the progress the child has made and changes in the placement if needed. Every three years, the child must be tested again to update the information regarding skills and weaknesses. Each time the committee meets, they must assess the child's progress and services and make recommendations accordingly.

Interpreting in Special Education

The Special Education process is one of the most confusing processes for many LEP parents (and for interpreters). Special Education programs in the United States differ a great deal from Special Education services in many other countries.

Parents should express any of their concerns to school officials. The school needs to explain to the parents what this process involves. The interpreter may also have to explain to school staff outside the session how and why the process of Special Education placement is confusing for families from other cultures, who may never have heard about speech therapy, cognitive delays or occupational therapy.

In addition, a number of immigrant parents have believed that "Special Education" means a gifted and talented program and have been horrified and shocked when they eventually realized that their child has a learning delay or a disability that has led to placement in Special Education.

The community interpreter will frequently be called upon to interpret and assist with legal documents such as consent and release forms. Typically, the interpreter will also have to attend to the emotional dimensions of an encounter. Parents tend to be emotionally invested in their children, and this is often what makes education meetings in general, and Special Education meetings in particular, a challenge for interpreters (although terminology may be a greater challenge).

An interpreter might be called to interpret for some of the professionals gathering the information, and in some cases to interpret in some of the assessments. Interpreting is needed in assessment when the child in question uses a language for which there are no bilingual professionals able to administer the test in the child's language.

UNIT 4

Logistic challenges

Interpreting for Special Education can involve logistic challenges as well. These include:

- Often, a Special Education meeting involves several people.
- Sometimes several people may be speaking quickly all at once.
- Finding an effective position can be difficult at meetings that involve numerous participants. Wherever the interpreter chooses to sit will have an impact on the proceedings.
- Documents for sight translation are often very long, high register and legal in nature.

Interpreters should, in advance, ask for any relevant documents to study, such as reports and the IEP, so that they may prepare themselves, research unfamiliar terminology and ensure accurate interpreting.

What happens at meetings

If a school team is working with a child of an LEP family, an interpreter must be present at the eligibility meeting. This meeting is a confusing process for anyone not familiar with the rules and regulations, including an interpreter new to educational interpreting. All persons present at the meeting will ask questions and hold discussions that involve technical language as they try to determine the child's eligibility for services.

It is common for a parent to try to ask community interpreters for their opinion regarding the choices and decisions they need to make for their children, not only during an eligibility meeting but at any point throughout the Special Education process. Many parents feel that the knowledge the interpreter has will help them make culturally sound decisions. In many cases, parents are more concerned about culturally sound decisions than they are about academic decisions.

The risk of getting involved

Bilingual employees in the school setting are more prone to offer advice than contract interpreters and they may even make decisions for the child. This is a disservice to the family and the child. It disempowers them and takes away their right to self determination.

The role of the community interpreter in Special Education and other school-based services is to facilitate communication clearly so that parents will be able to gather the information they need to help them make an informed decision for their child.

Risk and Liability

Have there been lawsuits about interpreting?

Yes. There are a growing number of lawsuits in healthcare, though it appears the majority of them are settled out of court and do not become public. So far, such lawsuits in the U.S. are rare in education or human services. Also, without a recording of the interpreted session (such recordings are rare except in legal interpreting and telephone or video interpreting), it is difficult for a court of law prove that an interpreter made significant errors. The interpreter is usually the only person in the encounter who knows both languages. A case might hinge on the credibility, training and professionalism of the interpreter. As a result, some interpreters feel that insurance for interpreters is overpriced and not ultimately good protection.

Should I carry special interpreting insurance?

There is no simple answer to this question. The short answer is that if you are a contract interpreter, then yes, you should consider purchasing insurance. If you are a bilingual employee, or a language service employee[1], perhaps not, because you are probably covered by professional liability insurance of some kind, though perhaps not by errors and omissions insurance (see below).

Contract interpreters are sometimes covered by the organizational insurance of an interpreter agency that uses their services, but not always. Find out. Whether you are a contract interpreter for a language service provider, a staff interpreter, a language company employee or a bilingual employee (adjunct interpreter), ask questions about insurance. Be specific: ask, "What would happen if someone sued me for interpreting incorrectly? Would your insurance policies cover me?" If the answer is no, consider purchasing insurance.

What type of insurance do I need?

> 1) Liability insurance. If you are a contract interpreter, you are self employed. Liability insurance covers liability in general, and any self-employed individual should have it.

---

[1] Some large language companies are switching to an employee model. As a result, both their in-person and remote (telephone and video) interpreters are now legally employees, not contractors. The future of this trend is unclear, but it may continue.

2) **Errors and omissions insurance.** This is the type of policy that covers the errors you make as an interpreter (or translator) that may result in a lawsuit. If you are a bilingual employee who interprets, ask your employer if you are covered by errors and omissions insurance. By initiating this dialogue, you may stimulate them to purchase the insurance. A number of hospitals now do so for their staff interpreters and bilingual staff.

What does insurance cost?

Insurance for interpreters varies greatly. In the U.S., liability insurance for a self-employed interpreter can cost less than $200 but it is possible to pay much more: you may wish to "shop around." The typical recommendation is to have at least $1 million in liability coverage. For errors and omissions insurance, the cost in the U.S. one can range from a few hundred dollars to more than $1,000 a year. Many freelance interpreters take out policies offered through the American Translators Association.

Terminology

OBJECTIVE 4.3 Develop strategies to enhance competence in terminology.

Why terminology is a challenge

One of the most common challenges in all areas of community interpreting is terminology. As one interpreter reported, "It's all about vocabulary. Vocabulary. Vocabulary."

In some respects, terminology is less of a challenge for adjunct interpreters who interpret in a specific area where they also work. For example, a teacher who works Special Education and also interprets is very familiar with Special Education terminology. A refugee resettlement caseworker who interprets quickly gets to know the terminology of those services. Adjunct interpreters know the culture of the organization and services so well that they pick up its new terms quickly.

However, this is not always true for bilingual employees in a large organization who may be called to interpret in areas outside their usual work. Even so, that terminology may still be easier for them to master than it is for contract interpreters who work in a broad array of settings. One contract interpreter may work in dozens or even hundreds of different services. Each service setting has its own terminology.

How to expand your knowledge of terminology

An interpreter can develop or research appropriate terminology in many ways. Note that there is a special part of the Resources section of this manual devoted to resources for terminology. In general, the interpreter should consider any or all of the following.

- Obtain the following dictionaries, if possible:
  - A comprehensive monolingual dictionary for each working language, more extensive than a "collegiate" dictionary.
  - A bilingual general dictionary.
  - Bilingual dictionaries or glossaries in areas in which you work often, e.g., medical terminology dictionaries or education glossaries.

- Purchase specialized software for your computer or for your portable electronic devices.

- In your smartphone, do a search for "dictionary apps." Depending on your phone, you may find dozens or hundreds of bilingual, multilingual and specialized (e.g., medical) dictionaries.

- Collect or create mini-glossaries of a few pages or longer for specific services where you may interpret (e.g., food stamps, domestic violence, Child Protective Services investigations, OB-GYN, Special Education services, etc).

- Memorize 5 (or any number of) new terms per day from your glossaries.

- Carry a small notebook to note down new terms that arise.

- Use self-study resources.

- Watch TV shows (e.g., medical shows), news and general talk shows in all your working languages, writing down new terms as you listen to look up later.

- Practice simultaneous interpreting while listening to such shows or to the radio to become more comfortable interpreting in simultaneous mode.

- Ask other interpreters what strategies work for them.

- Use websites such as www.wordreference.com to find words that are not available in your dictionary (see the Resources section of this manual for other online dictionary and glossary sites).

- Join a translators forum such as www.proz.com or a language forum such as http://forum.wordreference.com and post questions.

- Join listservs of interpreter associations such as NCIHC, IMIA and NAJIT and ask questions about where to find specific glossaries in your language.

Preparing for assignments

Before an assignment, obtain as much information you can about the encounter, including the client's country of origin, preferred language/dialect/regional variation, the type of service involved and the nature of the session. You can ask if any specific terminology might be required.

In addition, try to:

- Obtain sample brochures from the organization and study that terminology.
- Ask for any documents you will sight translate and then practice with those documents.
- Check for online glossaries with terminology specific to that service.
- Study the area of service in articles in Wikipedia, now available in more than 260 languages. Write down key terms that you think you may have to interpret and make sure you know them in both languages.
- Read articles online relevant to a particular area of service and note down any new terms.
- Build a bilingual glossary for a particular area by adding from various sources, then creating a Word or Excel file (or any other format) to save that glossary and keep adding to it as you learn knew words. Study it each time you get an assignment in that area.
- Call another interpreter who has interpreted for that service and ask for advice and guidance about terminology issues.
- Ask the interpreter service that sends you out whether they have an in-house terminology resource for any of these areas of service.
- SELF-TEST: before the assignment, take your mini-glossary for that service, print an extra copy, cover up the column that has the terms in your weaker language and check to see which terms you already know well in both languages. Cross out those terms. Now try again with those terms you did not know so well, and strike them out once you feel certain you know them. Keep doing so until you have crossed out all the terms for that glossary and feel confident about them.
- Have a friend test you by asking you terms at random from any of your lists for you to interpret into the target language.

Web resources

It's a new world out there. For many of us who occupy the "graying" sector of the profession, watching what younger interpreters do to prepare for research assignments today is exciting—and perhaps intimidating or bewildering.

Here are just a few examples from Katharine Allen of California, who has helped many interpreters navigate this new world of "Web 2.0." Today, instead of just passively reading content online, you can collaborate interactively to help each other with terminology and other interpreting challenges. Here are a few examples:

- *Dropbox.* By sharing folders across computer desktops with other interpreters, you can share resources, build glossaries, or prepare for assignments together. For example, if one interpreter in a group makes an addition to a bilingual glossary of Special Education terms in English and Burmese, that change is automatically updated to the same glossary file on the desktops of the other interpreters in that group. No more emailing multiple revisions of the same document, and you always know where to find the most current version.
- *Wiki sites, Google docs and other group editing formats.* The phrase "Wiki site" is almost becoming a generic term for a website that can be edited by multiple users. Google and others offer ways of creating similar projects among groups who work together in a specific area or on a specific topic, such as terminology.
- *Blogs.* By subscribing to specialized blogs, you can keep up with developments and terminology in a particular field or research the specific areas where you interpret most often. You can also search run searches of blog sites for specific content, just as you would run a search on Google.
- *Social networking sites.* These are online groups where you can build a profile, share information about yourself and link to others within the network. Examples include LinkedIn, Facebook, and Twitter. Social networking sites are not used only by individuals, but by media outlets, companies, non-profits and just about any kind of entity you can imagine. You can network with other interpreters and professionals or target specific fields or groups, such as Academia.edu, AsianAvenue or WiserEarth. They can be used as research tools for interpreting in general or interpreting in specialized sectors. You can put in a search, for example, about gestational diabetes or school Board hearings to get a glimpse of the terminology involved or ask questions.

- *Podcasting, Vodcasting and Youtube.* You can now find quality audio and visual content for just about any subject in dozens of languages online, through iTunes or by searching video sharing sites such as Youtube or Vimeo. Need to familiarize yourself with a specific Chinese health practice, learn more about diabetes in Spanish or even start studying a third language? Chances are it's all online.

For those of us who remember plunking away on manual typewriters, this is a brave new world. Nowadays, many interpreters text-message each other on site with questions about terminology. They check regularly for new online glossaries for their phones and use hand-held dictionaries or phones during a session (instead of a big dictionary) to look up unfamiliar terms. In these and in many other ways, interpreters are bringing the technology of interpreting into the 21st century.

Imagine what lies ahead.

Professional Networks

There are several ways to pursue professional development in general or for terminology in particular. For example:

- Join the listerv of a professional association. First, become a member of (for example) NCIHC, IMIA, ATA or NAJIT, and/or state or regional translator and interpreter associations, then join their listservs or discussion groups. Interpreter listservs often discuss terminology and related issues. You may also pose queries to the listserv if a particular term is not found in your dictionaries and glossaries.

- Such associations also offer seminars, conferences and meetings all across the country, including language-specific peer groups, medical terminology "bootcamps" and other valuable workshops that will help you expand your knowledge of specialized terminology.

- Read newsletters from these associations. In addition to relevant articles, these publications often features news about workshops and trainings to enhance terminology or other skills being offered by prestigious universities with well-established programs such as Monterey Institute of International Studies and University of

Arizona's Agnes Haury Institute for Court Interpretation (which runs the longest running intensive Spanish/English interpreter training program in the United States). Interpreting or terminology-focused programs are also offered by some community colleges, Area Health Education Centers or other organizations.

Maintain your languages

All interpreters should keep up with their working languages. Television and radio programs in hundreds of languages are now widely available through satellite dish services and Internet sites. Local libraries increasingly carry books, magazines and CDs in other languages. Countless books around the world can be ordered via the Internet, either in print or, increasingly, in e-book format.

If you are a foreign-born interpreter who wants to shore up your English, community colleges often offer courses of all kinds that may help you, and these include not only English language classes but (for example) medical terminology for allied health professionals, courses in social work and other professional areas. Taking almost any community or four-year college class with native speakers of English will help you increase your command of general English vocabulary.

In addition, interpreters can play word games to hone their general word skills. The Resources section of this manual offers examples.

These are only a few sample strategies. Every interpreter can create others. See the Resources section of this manual for details and examples. Terminology is vital. No community interpreters can become truly accomplished without making special efforts to master the terminology of the areas in which they interpret.

Medical Terminology

At a minimum, a medical interpreter should be familiar with:

- Anatomy and physiology
- Latin/Greek roots and affixes in medical terminology
- Medical specialties
- Body parts
- Body systems (e.g., the gastrointestinal system, the cardiovascular system, etc)
- Diseases and disorders
- Terms for symptoms
- Medical abbreviations
- Health care/insurance forms
- Medical procedures and surgery in the relevant areas of care.
- Medical tests
- Medications

Regarding medical terms, it is highly recommended that interpreters who work extensively in health care purchase or download:

- A medical resource in English such as the Merck Manual of Diagnosis and Therapy.
- A medical dictionary for both languages (e.g., English-Spanish).
- A medical interpreter training manual that explains body systems, specialties, etc.
- A bilingual medical glossary.
- Smaller specialized bilingual glossaries with terminology relevant to specific types of medical services, as needed.

UNIT 4

Community Services and Agencies

In order to give a representative idea about the terminology challenges that face contract interpreters in community service settings, and the diversity of topics and issues they encounter—each with its own set of terminology—here is a *partial* list of community services and agencies available in *one* county in Maryland:

Adult abuse and neglect
Affordable Dwelling Unit Program (ADU)
Affordable health insurance
AIDS drug assistance
Alcohol counseling
Alcohol treatment
Ambulatory care
Area agencies on aging
Assessments and taxation
Babysitting
Bankruptcy
Bereavement counseling
Board of Education
Burial/funeral assistance
Bus services
Child care
Child Protective Services
Consumer protection
Correction and rehabilitation
County Attorney
Courts
Custody issues
Disability resources
Drug assistance
Drug therapy
Emergency financial assistance
Employment and training services
Fair housing
Family services
Family well-being
Financial assistance
Fire and Rescue
Food banks
Food stamps
Foster care
Handicapped parking
Health and Human Services
Health care assistance
Home-based services
Home healthcare
Home modifications for people with disabilities
Home ownership programs
Home repairs for the elderly
Homeless programs/shelters
Hospice
Hospitals and health care facilities
Hotlines
Housing assistance
Human rights
Job seeker services/job training
Immigration courts/hearings
Landlord/tenant issues
Legal services (low income)
Libraries
Licenses and Permits
Long-term care
Marriage licenses
Medicaid referral
Medical care coordination
Medical referrals
Mental health services
Mental retardation services
Motor Vehicle assistance
Nursing/assisted living homes
Nutritional services
Occupational therapy
Parenting classes
Permits and licenses
Physical therapy
Police
Psychological/counseling services
Public assistance
Public safety
Public schools
Public works
Recreation centers
Recreation services
Rental housing programs
Rental rehabilitation programs
Senior centers
Senior housing
Services for at-risk youth
Sheriff's Office
Speech therapy
SSDI referral (Social Security Disability Income)
SSI referral (Supplemental Security Income)
State's Attorney
Tax deferrals for persons with disabilities
Teen centers
Teen pregnancy program
Therapeutic recreation
Transportation
Vocational rehabilitation
Women, Infants and Children (WIC) programs

UNIT 4

UNIT 4

REVIEW

UNIT 4 REVIEW EXERCISES

Legal interpreting

Give a definition of legal interpreting.
_____
_____

In most countries, legal interpreting is part of community interpreting. Is that true in the U.S.? Why or why not?
_____
_____
_____
_____

Name four key differences in the ethics of legal and community interpreters:
_____
_____
_____
_____
_____

Why do community interpreters need to know about legal interpreting?
_____
_____
_____
_____
_____

Give two examples of acts that a community interpreter may perform during an interpreted session and which a legal interpreter should not perform.
_____
_____
_____
_____

UNIT 4

What are some risks inherent in legal interpreting if it is performed by community interpreters who have not been trained to perform legal interpreting?

_____
_____
_____
_____
_____

Health Care
Give definitions for the following terms:

HMO: _____
_____
_____

Medicaid: _____
_____
_____

Medicare: _____
_____
_____

SCHIP: _____
_____
_____

HIPAA: _____
_____
_____

UNIT 4

Name three or more organizations that support medical interpreters.
_____
_____
_____

What should an interpreter do if asked to sign as a witness?
_____
_____
_____

UNIT 4

Human and Social Services

Give definitions for the following terms.

DSS: _____
_____
_____

TANF: _____
_____
_____

SSI: _____
_____
_____

CBO: _____
_____
_____

Refugee: _____
_____
_____

Community action agency: _____
_____
_____

Language bank: _____
_____
_____

UNIT 4

True or false

Write "true" or "false" beside each statement

1. The Welfare and Immigration Reform Act of 1996 had a small impact on immigrants. _____

2. Refugees who do not become citizens within 7 years of obtaining legal residency are at risk of losing their public benefits. _____

3. Social Security Disability Insurance is a form of welfare (public assistance). _____

4. Interpreters rarely interpret for faith-based organizations. _____

5. Interpreters who speak up about Title VI are protecting their agencies from legal liability and supporting clients' legal rights to an interpreter. _____

6. Interpreters should not interpret for their own family members, e.g., in a hospital or school. _____

Are the following programs and services administered by federal, state, local or private agencies, or a combination thereof? List the type(s) of agency (federal, state or local government and/or private) that may be involved in funding each type of service below.

Social Security: _____

Community Action councils: _____

Prenatal services (Health Department): _____

Emergency Medical Assistance: _____

Domestic violence shelters: _____

Low income housing: _____

UNIT 4

Education

Give definitions for the following terms.

IDEA: _____
_____
_____

ADA: _____
_____
_____

Special Education: _____
_____
_____

No Child Left Behind: _____
_____
_____

IEP: _____
_____
_____

Where might a school interpreting appointment be a case of legal (not community) interpreting? Give at least two examples.
_____
_____
_____
_____

UNIT 4

True or False

1. Interpreters in school settings are required to receive special training on confidentiality.   T   F

2. Special Education services are high quality services that must be paid for by parents.   T   F

3. Terminology is one of the great challenges of interpreting for Special Education services.   T   F

4. You should always sit beside and a little behind the client at school meetings.   T   F

5. One role of the educational interpreter is to guide parents to make the right decisions for their child.   T   F

Terminology

Write your six favorite strategies (from the examples given in section 4.3 of this unit) for preparing for an assignment in a sector with terminology you do not know well.
_____
_____
_____

What resources should a medical interpreter purchase or obtain?
_____
_____

Give some examples of new electronic and web-based tools that can help interpreters with terminology.
_____
_____
_____

Liability

As an interpreter, do you think you need errors and omission insurance? Why or why not?
_____
_____

296   THE COMMUNITY INTERPRETER

UNIT 5
STANDARDS OF PRACTICE

Unit 5 Objective

OBJECTIVE 5.1
Develop a working knowledge of national standards of practice.
5.1 (a) Review the 32 principles of the NCIHC national standards of practice.
5.1 (b) Discuss strategies for promoting and practicing standards.
5.1 (c) Act out standards of practice in challenging situations from real life.

OBJECTIVE 5.2
Apply national standards of practice to interpreting.
5.2 (a) Demonstrate the application of standards of practice in community service settings.
5.2 (b) Relate ethics and standards to professional development for interpreters.

OBJECTIVE 5.1

Develop a working knowledge of national standards of practice.

Introduction

It is often a challenge to respect professional ethics and standards in community services, in part because these services are complex and those who work in them typically know little about interpreting. This means that providers in these services often expect interpreters to behave in ways that violate professional ethics and standards of practice.

5.1 (a) Review the 32 principles of the NCIHC national standards of practice.

5.1 (b) Discuss strategies for promoting and practicing standards.

5.1 (c) Act out standards of practice in challenging situations from real life.

UNIT 5

For example, you may be requested to:

- Interpret beyond your level of skill.
- Answer questions during the session.
- Summarize.
- "Help out" the client.
- Take—or drive—the client somewhere.
- Interpret and perform another task at the same time.
- Perform sight translations of long, complex or legal documents.
- Perform written translation (without training or qualifications).

These are only a few random examples of common requests made to community interpreters.

When community interpreters first receive training in interpreting and learn about the ethics and standards, they are often surprised by what they learn. Sometimes they find the requirements for professional interpreting too rigid for their workplace or the daily realities in community services. Often, after training, when they try to apply professional ethics and standards in their daily work, this training conflicts with the culture or habits of the workplace or community service settings. Providers' expectations and the confusing or chaotic situations that often arise in community interpreting add to the challenges.

In many cases these problems come down to issues of boundaries: the interpreter's ability to assess the situation and say "no," firmly, respectfully and appropriately. On many occasions, whether during a pre-conference or outside the session, the interpreter will also need to educate providers, colleagues and agencies about professional interpreting requirements and why they matter.

Here is the bottom line: It is not enough to learn the ethics, skills and standards of community interpreting. You must also learn how to apply them in real life. This means learning how to think quickly, on your feet.

Unit 5 explores this fundamental dilemma of the community interpreter and offers practical solutions that will help you maintain professionalism and promote quality interpreting.

Standards of Practice

OBJECTIVE 5.1(a) Review the 32 principles from NCIHC National Standards of Practice.

What Standards Are

Standards of practice are formal guidelines that show those who practice a certain occupation how to perform their work well and conduct themselves professionally. Standards of practice were discussed briefly in Unit 1, where the following definition from NCIHC was mentioned:

> A clear set of guidelines that delineate expectations for the interpreter's conduct and practice.
>
> NCIHC (2005)

Why Standards Are Important

Community interpreters need to know professional ethics and standards:
- To perform at a professional level.
- To support equal access to public services.
- To support legal and professional requirements.

As we discussed in Unit 1, standards of practice for interpreters in various sectors of interpreting are often organized under the rubrics (headings or titles) taken from the principles in codes of ethics. For example, in the NCIHC standards of practice, standard number 6 for *Transparency* can be found under ethical rubric, *Accuracy,* because transparency supports accuracy. This idea of grouping standards under the titles of relevant ethical principles helps to make both ethics and standards easier to remember. Also, grouping standards of practice under ethical principles reinforces the importance of ethics.

Remember: ethics are the rules of the profession. They show the interpreter what to do. (And what not to do.) Standards are the guidelines. They show interpreters how to do the job. (And do it well.) Ethics are strict and rigid while standards are more flexible.

Violating ethics may carry penalties. Violating standards may have consequences, but these consequences tend to be less serious than the penalties for violating ethics. Standards support ethics and give the interpreter specific guidance on how to respect ethics in practical situations. Finally, standards of practice promote quality interpreting.

UNIT 5

ETHICS AND STANDARDS

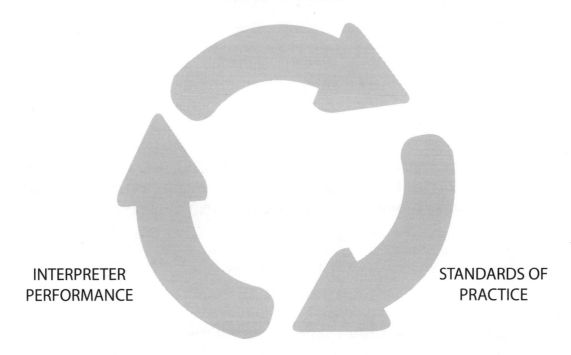

A Continuum

CODES OF ETHICS

STANDARDS OF PRACTICE

INTERPRETER PERFORMANCE

Ethics influence standards of practice.

Ethics and standards taken together promote ethical conduct, high levels of performance and equal access to services.

UNIT 5

Standards for Community Interpreting

No national standards of practice currently exist in the U.S. for community interpreters in general, although such standards do exist in Canada (Healthcare Interpretation Network, 2007). Standards of practice also exist in the U.S. within one important area of community interpreting: health care.

Published in 2005, the NCIHC national standards of practice for interpreters in health care are a historic achievement. In fact, these may be the first such national guidelines for health care interpreters in the world. Unit 5 proposes to use these national standards as the model for standards of practice in all areas of community interpreting in the U.S.

However, two other sets of influential standards of practice discussed in Unit 1, the IMIA and CHIA standards, as well as the Canadian standards for community interpreting services, are extremely influential. They inform the discussion throughout this manual and specifically here in Unit 5.

Community interpreters in other countries may wish to consider all three sets of standards of practice, together with the Canadian standards. Of these four sets of standards, however, IMIA are the only international standards. They deserve particular attention not only because they are international but because they appear to be the most detailed and sophisticated standards of practice for any area of community interpreting in the world.

For purposes of this unit, the NCIHC national code of ethics and national standards of practice constitute an excellent foundation for the profession of community interpreting because they are clear and concise. With this guidance, it is possible for community interpreters, whether they are contract interpreters, bilingual staff or volunteers, to interpret according to the same guidelines.

Overview of the NCIHC Standards of Practice

Interpreters should consult a copy of the complete document, the NCIHC National Standards of Practice for Interpreters in Health Care (available at www.ncihc.org). The 32 standards are summarized below for purposes of review and in-class activities.

1. Do not add, omit or substitute.
2. Conserve register, style, and tone.
3. Advise that everything will be interpreted.
4. Manage the flow of communication.
5. Correct errors.
6. Maintain transparency.
7. Maintain confidentiality.
8. Protect written patient information.
9. Do not let personal judgments influence objectivity.
10. Disclose conflicts of interest.
11. Show respect.
12. Promote direct communication.
13. Promote client autonomy.
14. Try to understand cultures.
15. Alert parties to cultural misunderstandings.
16. Limit personal involvement.
17. Limit activities to interpreting.
18. Bilingual employees must respect all standards.
19. Be honest and ethical.
20. Prepare for all assignments.
21. Disclose skill limitations.
22. Avoid complex sight translation.
23. Be accountable for performance.
24. Advocate for quality working conditions.
25. Show respect for professionals.
26. Uphold the dignity of the profession.
27. Develop knowledge and skills.
28. Seek feedback to improve.
29. Support fellow interpreters.
30. Participate in organizations and activities.
31. Protect individuals from harm.
32. Correct mistreatment or abuse.

Strategies for Promoting and Practicing Standards

5.2(b) Develop strategies for promoting and practicing standards.

Overview

The following standards of practice are taken from the NCIHC national standards of practice at www.ncihc.org.

The examples and discussion below each standard constitute commentary by the authors (not by NCIHC). These comments are intended to illustrate how to support each standard. They also reflect the authors' understanding of the CHIA and IMIA standards of practice in addition to the Canadian standards of practice for community interpreting services (Healthcare Interpretation Network, 2009). However, responsibility for the content of the following discussion of standards of practice rests solely with the authors.[1]

Accuracy and completeness
NCIHC Standards of Practice

> ETHICAL PRINCIPLE: The interpreter strives to render the message accurately, conveying the content and spirit of the original message, taking into consideration its cultural context.

The following six NCIHC standards of practice support the ethical requirement of accuracy.

1. The interpreter renders all messages accurately and completely, without adding, omitting, or substituting.

For example, an interpreter repeats all that is said, even if it seems redundant, irrelevant, or rude.

---

[1] The astute reader will note some overlap with the commentary on ethics in Unit 1. Any apparent overlap constitutes intentional redundancy. These two key sections of the manual, taken together, are intended to drive home the most critical points that are often difficult for interpreters to remember in the field, particularly those who have never studied interpreting and those who cannot attend training or education programs and therefore rely on this manual as a study reference.

To support accuracy:

- Use first person wherever appropriate.

- Interpret everything, even if it seems long, irrelevant or rambling or makes no sense.

- Interpret offensive, rude and obscene language.

- Paraphrase only briefly (e.g. a sentence) and only when linguistic equivalents do not exist in the target language for a word, phrase or concept.

- If a paraphrase would be longer than a sentence, mediate to clarify instead.

- Do not summarize, except in emergencies, or situations when even simultaneous mode is impossible, e.g., when too many people speak at once (and refuse to stop); when a client speaks too quickly and will not be interrupted; when a client speaks rapidly and incoherently; or when dementia, mental illness or substance abuse make accurate interpreting impossible.

- If a word is used that you do not understand, interrupt the session to ask for the meaning and then interpret the answer (do not explain it).

2. The interpreter replicates the register, style, and tone of the speaker.

For example, unless there is no equivalent in the patient's language, an interpreter does not substitute simpler explanations for medical terms a provider uses, but may ask the speaker to re-express themselves in language more easily understood by the other party.

You may not change the register (level of language), even if the other party does not understand what is said. Instead, mediate to suggest that the speaker change the register and/or have the provider check for understanding. Additionally:

- Do not simplify technical terms.

- Interpret even casual remarks.

- Interpret body language (using words or equivalent gestures) only if it has meaning that the other party would otherwise miss. (Do not do so for legal interpreting.)

- Avoid literal interpretation: interpret for meaning.

- Do not maintain a neutral tone of voice: use voice to reflect the tone and spirit of the speaker and the message.

- Interpret the spirit, intention and tone of voice to the extent possible, taking the cultural context into account. Check for understanding if body language or other cues indicate that the message is not accurately understood.

Note that interpreting the tone and spirit will vary somewhat according to the culture. For example, expressivity in Asian languages may be less pronounced than in English, so you could raise the volume in English to indicate intensity. Expressivity in Spanish might at times be more voluble or intense than in English, and in such cases you could lower the volume in English.

Regarding body language, the appropriate response by an interpreter may vary. Consider the following situations and possible responses by the interpreter:

- *Client nods, but in his culture a nod means "no."* You could shake your head or simply say, "No."

- *When the provider asks, "So you understand what you need to do next?" the client nods and says yes but does not appear to understand.* (The interpreter is aware that in the culture of the client, saying "yes" can mean many different things, not always assent.) In this case you can mediate to suggest that you are afraid what you are interpreting may not be clear so that the provider can check for understanding.

- *Client does not meet provider's eyes. Provider is clearly puzzled, offended or concerned*. You could mediate to have the client offer a cultural explanation for avoiding eye contact (e.g., showing respect). Alternatively, outside the session, the interpreter can educate providers about the possible meaning that avoiding eye contact has in different cultures.

- Body language of the client shows distress and alarm, but the provider does not perceive this. The interpreter can intervene to have the provider check for understanding, or wait until the end of the session to discuss some of the cultural issues around body language.

You do not need to interpret any body language that is clear and obvious to the other party. You are also not obligated to interpret body language. The purpose of community interpreting is, however, to facilitate communication, and sometimes the interpreter's cultural knowledge of body language will help to promote accuracy and completeness. You may even mediate to address a cultural issue regarding body language, for example, "Excuse me, as the interpreter I wanted to point out that in parts of the Middle East such as Jordan, a sharp nod actually means no, not yes. You may wish to ask the client about this." (Then interpret your mediation for the client.)

Regarding vulgar language: if you are uncomfortable because the message includes obscenity, do not reveal your discomfort (either through facial expressions or body language) but simply interpret the words accurately. You will need to find approximate cultural equivalents, since rude language often will not make sense if you interpret it literally.

If a party uses language that shows discrimination (providers, for example, may insult a client's ethnic origin in the client's presence) or says things that are deeply offensive to the other party, as discussed in Unit 3, interpreters differ as to whether the interpreter should simply interpret what is said or mediate to educate the offending party. Please refer to Unit 3 for that discussion. However, keep in mind as discussed in Unit 3 that the interpreter is expected to interpret deliberately offensive language. If you elect to give the offending party "another chance" by mediating to explain the offensive nature of the message, and the offending party does not wish to change the comments, you *must* interpret exactly what is said.

3. The interpreter advises parties that everything said will be interpreted.

For example, an interpreter may explain the interpreting process to a provider by saying "everything you say will be repeated to the patient."

During introductions, after a greeting and name, it is important to state clearly that everything said will be interpreted. This is a point that interpreters often forget to mention, yet it is the most important part of the introduction and you should emphasize it. In addition:

> • If necessary, remind one or all parties of this disclaimer during the session.
>
> • Do not apologize for interpreting everything: if one party tries to "shoot the messenger," (e.g., by saying, "I didn't want you to interpret that!"), remind that person of what was said during your introduction and your ethical obligation to interpret everything said.
>
> • During introductions, explain the proper use of first person if this is helpful.

Very often, clients or providers say things during a session that they do not expect the interpreter to interpret. If this is a recurring problem, it is acceptable to add to your introduction: "Please do not mention anything during this session that you do not wish to be interpreted, because I am ethically required to interpret everything."

One interpreter tells the story of a defendant in court who disagreed with a judge's remarks. Turning to the interpreter, he said: "Is this judge some kind of nut?" The interpreter dutifully repeated in English: "Is this judge some kind of nut?" This comment in open court probably did not help the defendant's case.

Remember: often the situation is so rushed that it is difficult for you to perform your introduction. If you have time to say only one thing, say that you will interpret everything that is said.

4. The interpreter manages the flow of communication.

For example, an interpreter may ask a speaker to pause or slow down.

Most interpreters know their memory limits. In general, beginning interpreters find it to difficult to render more than two or three sentences accurately. Therefore the interpreter should:

- Practice memory skills to enhance memory.
- Interrupt as needed.
- If new to the field, ask providers and clients to speak slowly and use simple language.
- Request that excited parties slow down.

To be accurate, the interpreter must manage the pace of the session. Some interpreters build up experience more slowly (for example, those who speak less common languages) because they are called on to interpret less frequently than Spanish interpreters, and this can make it more difficult to become proficient. Less experienced interpreters may also be hesitant to interrupt the speakers for cultural reasons, but they must do so if either party speaks too fast or too long. Even very experienced interpreters must interrupt at times.

5. The interpreter corrects errors in interpretation.

For example, an interpreter who has omitted an important word corrects the mistake as soon as possible.

As soon as you realize you have made an error, set the record straight. Doing so is a sign of interpreter professionalism.

6. The interpreter maintains transparency.

For example, when asking for clarification, an interpreter says to all parties, "I, the interpreter, did not understand, so I am going to ask for an explanation."

Transparency means that everyone present knows what the interpreter is doing at all times. To respect transparency:

- Interpret everything that is said, even when someone speaks to you.
- Always interpret your mediations.
- Avoids side conversations.
- Introduce a mediation clearly and in a way that shows you are speaking for yourself, e.g., "Excuse me, as the interpreter I need to clarify a term that the provider just used."
- Interpret what is mediated to both parties.
- Keeps mediations brief and simple.

Confidentiality

> ETHICAL PRINCIPLE: The interpreter treats as confidential, within the treating [professional] team, all information learned in the performance of professional duties, while observing relevant requirements regarding disclosure.

7. The interpreter maintains confidentiality and does not disclose information outside the treating team, except with the patient's consent or if required by law.

For example, an interpreter does not discuss a patient's case with family or community members without the patient's consent.

Confidentiality is the single principle that appears in virtually all codes of ethics and standards of practice for interpreters around the world, in any field of interpreting.

There are many factors that interpreters need to consider when making decisions about how to respect confidentiality. For example:

- Many experts believe that you may consult with members of a team who work with the same client if they are all bound by confidentiality. This means sharing something you heard from a client outside the session with members of that team is not considered a violation of confidentiality. However, professional opinions on this issue vary. Consult your supervisor. If you are a contract interpreter, ask the language service provider that sent you on the assignment about its rules or professional guidelines regarding this issue.

- If you are an adjunct interpreter, do not reveal details of a session to a colleague who does not work with the same client (such as a receptionist or clerical worker) because that would be a clear violation of confidentiality.

- Confidentiality extends indefinitely, even after employment ends (or a volunteer assignment).

- Confidentiality must be broken if required by law. Laws vary by state: typical examples include reporting to the authorities any suspicion of child abuse or elder abuse or cases when the client is considered an imminent danger to others (risk of homicide) or himself (risk of suicide). See Unit 1 for details.

- You may be subpoenaed to testify at a deposition or in court but remember: you are not legally required to respond to all subpoenas and should consult with an attorney before going to court to testify about an interpreted encounter.

- You may not share information about the client with family members except by client consent, in person or in writing.

Stories about clients may be shared in professional settings such as interpreter trainings and in-services if any details that could identify the client are removed.

Sharing stories with a colleague, spouse, family member, or friend is permissible only in the most general terms, with all identifying details removed. The greatest risk of violating confidentiality tends to occur in casual conversations.

8. The interpreter protects written patient information in his or her possession.

For example, an interpreter does not leave notes on an interpreting session in public view.

Notes are important in all areas of interpreting. Remember:

- Confidentiality is intended to protect the client. Therefore, any details that could identify that client should not be shared outside the agency, including your notes.
- Destroy notes before leaving the session, if possible, and certainly before leaving the building. (Legal interpreters may need to leave notes with an attorney.)
- A professional team that is treating or case managing a client may be privy to written information about the client. If so, ask for the policies regarding confidentiality and written information.

Impartiality
9. The interpreter does not allow personal judgments or cultural values to influence objectivity.

> ETHICAL PRINCIPLE: The interpreter strives to maintain impartiality and refrains from counseling, advising or projecting personal biases or beliefs.

For example, an interpreter does not reveal personal feelings through words, tone of voice, or body language.

The goal of the encounter in community services is to provide a service, promote equal access to services and ensure client well-being.

For the interpreter, this goal is not met by siding with either the client or provider. Your loyalty is to the outcome of the session, not to either party. Both client and provider are seeking a positive outcome. The best way for you to support them is to adhere to the ethics and standards of interpreting.

This means that you may not have neutral feelings but must strive to master those feelings by exhibiting neutral behavior at all times, allowing the client and provider to communicate directly with each other. Do not let them be distracted by your frowning, muttering, shuffling papers, rolling eyes or any other behavior that might indicate your personal feelings during the session. Even if you are interpreting for a domestic violence victim or a torture survivor, try very hard not to cry, as this will cause an unfortunate distraction and may make the client more reluctant to open up.

Avoiding the influence of personal judgments is not easy, however. Ideally you will:

- Become aware how your personal and cultural values distort objectivity.
- Use a tone of voice and body language that reflect the feelings of all parties speaking, not your feelings.
- Remain objective, impartial, neutral and calm, even if a quarrel erupts. (Your voice may reflect the angry feelings of the parties quarreling, not your own anger.)
- Insert no opinions, even if asked.
- Offer no advice.
- Maintain a neutral facial expression except to interpret the speaker's emotions.
- Allow no influence of personal beliefs to distort the content of the message.
- Allow parties to speak for themselves, without interfering, even if they disagree.
- Never give advice.

The temptation to offer advice is particularly risky for adjunct interpreters. However, bilingual employees are often allowed, and sometimes encouraged, to refer clients to other community services. Referrals are not considered "advice" if they are approved in advance by providers or supervisors.

Contract interpreters should not provide referrals without the explicit knowledge and consent of both the client's organization and the agency that sent the interpreter.

10. The interpreter discloses potential conflicts of interest, withdrawing from assignments if necessary.

For example, an interpreter avoids interpreting for a family member or close friend.

To avoid any real or apparent conflicts of interest:

- Disclose immediately if the client is a family member, friend or acquaintance.

- Decline any assignment for which you have a strong bias. For example, if you are a survivor of sexual assault, carefully consider whether you should interpret for a rape survivor.

- Declare any conflict of interest, including potential conflicts or the appearance of a conflict.

- After disclosing the conflict, decline the assignment or withdraw at once, or allow all parties present to decide whether or not to retain your services despite the conflict—and then only remain if you are completely sure you can be impartial.

- Decline or withdraw from any assignment that could compromise your impartiality by creating intense emotion. For example, interpreting for a survivor of torture or war trauma is often an overwhelming experience for refugee interpreters. If you are a refugee, especially a recent arrival, perhaps you should consider not interpreting in such cases.

Respect

11. The interpreter uses professional, culturally appropriate ways of showing respect.

> ETHICAL PRINCIPLE: The interpreter treats all parties with respect.

For example, in greetings, an interpreter uses appropriate titles for both patient and provider.

Respect for all parties is fundamental. Even if you do not feel respect, display it nonetheless. Make every effort to:

- Exercise cultural sensitivity (for example, regarding gender, age, family roles, relationship to authority, etc.).

- Avoid the more intimate form of pronouns. Use the formal form except for children, e.g., say *Ud.* in Spanish and *vous* in French (not *tu*).

- Use an appropriate title or formal level of language as needed.

- Offer cultural mediation in a respectful manner.

- Promote transparency so that everyone present understands what you are doing and feels included, not excluded.

- Avoid side conversations.

- Provide information that may be needed to promote mutual respect.

- Never share cultural information that the client can provide.

In addition, the interpreter may wish to monitor the situation for potential areas of discomfort for the client, including the age, gender, religion or refugee ethnic group of the interpreter, which can sometimes cause a client to withdraw or feel intimidated. For example, sometimes a male interpreter may not be culturally appropriate for a female client, and the provider may not know this.

An interpreter from an ethnic group that persecuted the client's group or geographical area may arouse visceral memories of fear and even flashbacks of torture or trauma. In such cases, during introductions you may wish to verify that your presence is welcome, emphasize your impartiality and confidentiality and, if appropriate, reassure the client about your commitment to professionalism. If you ascertain that the client feels uncomfortable with your presence, withdraw.

12. The interpreter promotes direct communication among all parties in the encounter.

For example, an interpreter may tell the patient and provider to address each other, rather than the interpreter.

In order to promote direct communication:

- During your introduction, ask the client and provider to speak directly to each other.

- Adopt an unobtrusive role.

- Avoid direct eye contact with all parties while interpreting.

- Use effective positioning to promote direct client-provider communication.

- If the client and provider speak to you, gently redirect them to each other.

- If reminders fail, use a hand gesture to redirect the speakers to each other.

Note that physical positioning will vary according to the setting. Try to remember that the goal of effective positioning is to promote the most direct possible dialogue between the client and provider.

In many cases, interpreter introductions offer an important opportunity help to promote client-provider communication. Therefore the introduction should also be used to:

- Establish the interpreter's role.
- Build rapport.
- Set the stage for successful communication.
- Lay down parameters that promote direct communication.

13. The interpreter promotes patient [client] autonomy.

For example, an interpreter directs a patient who asks him or her for a ride home to appropriate resources within the institution.

While contract interpreters often have stronger boundaries, adjunct interpreters (especially bilingual staff who are also case workers or case managers) are at risk for promoting client dependence on the interpreters.

Supervisors are often unaware how often clients seek out bilingual staff after the interpreted encounter and ask for help. Client autonomy benefits everyone: the interpreter, the agency and most of all the client. Success in U.S. culture stems from self-sufficiency. To minimize client dependency and promote autonomy:

- Do not perform any service for a client that the client can perform for him- or herself.
- During the session, use mediation skills with care: intervene appropriately, and only when necessary.
- Respect role boundaries.
- Refer clients to other services instead of becoming a de facto social worker.
- Even if clients approach you for special services, resist the temptation to solve the client's problems.

- When a client requests you to come back, assure the client that other trained interpreters are also competent and caring.

Note, however, that in some cases, such as counseling for survivors of sexual assault, torture and trauma, or in therapy for mental health, it may be seen as beneficial to use the same interpreter for ongoing sessions.

In addition to modeling respect for all parties in your conduct, strive to:

- Respect the autonomy of the provider.
- Interpret racist, bigoted and prejudiced remarks— do not cover them up or soften them.
- Never make decisions on behalf of a client or provider.
- Promote the client's self-sufficiency by actively discouraging dependence on the system.
- Treat all parties with dignity.
- Notify supervisors as appropriate if a provider engages in culturally insensitive or offensive behavior.
- Report unresolved cases of racism, discrimination or obvious bias by providers. (Warning: such reporting may not be possible in legal interpreting sessions with lawyers, due to the risk of breaching attorney-client privilege. When in doubt, ask to speak to the attorney's supervising attorney, if possible.)

Cultural Awareness

> ETHICAL PRINCIPLE The interpreter continuously strives to develop awareness of his/her own and other (including biomedical) cultures encountered in the performance of their professional duties.

14. The interpreter strives to understand the cultures associated with the languages he or she interprets, including biomedical culture.

For example, an interpreter learns about the traditional remedies some patients may use.

Culture is complex. No one, including an interpreter, is culturally static. Interpreters need to develop knowledge and awareness about many different aspects of culture, including their own. The interpreter should try to study and become familiar with:

- The culture of clients' native countries, regions, religions and ethnic groups.
- Cultural body language, including facial expressions.
- Clients' literacy and education levels.
- Degrees of client cultural assimilation and acculturation.
- Your own process of cultural assimilation and acculturation.
- Cultural gender differences.
- Cultural health remedies (for health care interpreters).
- The culture of the service provided (e.g., a health department, transportation services, the local school system or subsidized housing services).
- The organizational culture of the agency or system providing the service, e.g., biomedical culture.
- The cultures of bureaucracy.
- Cultures of the region where the service is provided (e.g., rural, urban, Midwest).
- Other cultural issues that may be relevant to the session.

15. The interpreter alerts all parties to any significant cultural misunderstanding that arises.

For example, if a provider asks a patient who is fasting for religious reasons to take an oral medication, an interpreter may call attention to the potential conflict.

Cultural mediation and advocacy are probably the two most demanding skills for community interpreters. When performing cultural mediation, the interpreter should:

- Remember transparency.
- Wait to be sure a cultural barrier is present—do not "jump the gun" by acting too quickly on assumptions.
- Refrain from explaining anything that the provider or client can explain.
- Try to have the client perform his or her own cultural mediation.

(Remember: every client is unique, and it is easy to make incorrect assumptions about a client.)

- Provide cultural context only if no one present can provide it.
- Avoid detailed cultural "explanations."
- Do not tell the provider one thing and the client another: make the same mediation to both parties.
- Avoid discussing gender differences or family roles during a session. Instead, let the client elaborate.
- Have the provider check for understanding if it appears that the client is not grasping the message.
- Sensitize providers to the risks of asking clients for "yes/no" responses to questions, since many clients respond "yes" when they do not mean assent.

Role Boundaries

> ETHICAL CODE The interpreter maintains the boundaries of the professional role, refraining from personal involvement.

16. The interpreter limits personal involvement with all parties during the interpreting assignment.

For example, an interpreter does not share or elicit overly personal information in conversations with a patient.

As difficult as it may be, the interpreter will try to avoid personal or social contact with clients—which means not being alone with the client if possible. Avoiding post-session client contact can be challenging, especially for some interpreters who speak languages of limited diffusion, either because the local language community is so small that most or many speakers of that language know each other well or because the adjunct interpreter is a caseworker who may spend extended periods alone with the client.

There are other challenges to maintaining role boundaries. For example, it is not unusual for some clients and interpreters to attend the same religious congregation or marketplace.

Personal involvement with clients is a slippery slope, and this can also be true with some providers. (For example, an intimidating provider may make it difficult for the interpreter to uphold interpreter ethics for fear of getting fired or creating a problematic relationship.)

To avoid blurring boundaries with clients:

- Avoid being alone with the client, wherever possible.
- Engage in no personal or professional side conversations with clients.
- Avoid disclosing personal information to the client during or outside the session.
- Refuse to provide personal contact information to clients, even when asked, unless the employer requires it.
- Avoid conversations with clients when leaving a session.
- Do not drive clients anywhere, if possible.
- Recommend an agency policy of having the interpreter walk out of a session each time the provider leaves. Being alone with clients is perhaps the major cause of erosion of professional boundaries between interpreters and clients.
- Refrain from socializing with clients.
- Engage in no sexual contact with clients or their families.
- Explain your roles to a client if he or she tries to offer you a gift, invites you to dinner or otherwise try to make you a friend.
- Where reasonable and possible, avoid venues where you are likely to run into clients off hours.
- Refrain from offering services to clients that are not part of your job description or professional role.
- Refer clients who need extra services to public or private organizations that offer them, if appropriate.

To avoid blurring boundaries with providers:

- Work with supervisors to develop a set of policies and procedures for staff on how to work with interpreters.
- Recommend that all staff at the agency receive cultural competence training.

- Ensure that staff members are trained in how to work with an interpreter.

17. The interpreter limits his or her professional activity to interpreting within an encounter.

For example, an interpreter never advises a patient on health care questions, but redirects the patient to ask the provider.

Interpreters should not perform a variety of tasks during a session. If you are interpreting, then interpret. During the session:

- Clearly establish your role as interpreter.
- Refrain from offering advice, even if a colleague or client asks for it.
- Let the provider and client maintain control.
- Redirect any questions to you back to the provider or client.
- Do not case manage the client.
- *Do not perform sight translation or assist a client filling out forms unless the provider remains in the room to answer client questions.*

18. The interpreter with an additional role adheres to all interpreting standards of practice while interpreting.

For example, an interpreter who is also a nurse does not confer with another provider in the patient's presence, without reporting what is said.

In general, even interpreters who are bilingual employees and who therefore may be expected to perform their job while they interpret should not do so. They must do one task (their job) or the other (interpret), but not both at the same time.

Whether the bilingual employee is a teacher's aide, a physician, a social worker or an administrative assistant, the employee should still not perform that job while interpreting. Keep the following recommendations in mind:

- Refrain from taking over another provider's role while interpreting, even if the provider leaves the room.
- Avoid consulting with another provider while the client is there and instead limit your activity to interpreting.
- Consider mediation carefully before performing it to decide if it is truly necessary.

- Engage in no mediation outside the session or perform client support tasks without the employer's knowledge, permission and approval.

It must be recognized that it is a great challenge for many interpreters to maintain professional boundaries when they are greeted by clients with affectionate hugs and kisses and left alone with clients, sometimes for extended periods, e.g., in labor and delivery. Some interpreters may spend months or years working with the same client, both as a bilingual employee and as an interpreter. In addition, many adjunct interpreters provide direct services to the same clients for whom they interpret.

Professionalism

19. The interpreter is honest and ethical in all business practices.

> ETHICAL PRINCIPLE: The interpreter must at all times act in a professional and ethical manner.

For example, an interpreter accurately represents his or her credentials.

Around the world, in codes of ethics and standards of practice, professional competence is emphasized for interpreters. Community interpreting is still a young profession, and it is vital that interpreters help to create a strong reputation for the field. To support this standard:

- Obtain proof of language proficiency if possible (see Unit 1) to ensure that you are linguistically qualified to call yourself an interpreter.

- Refrain from exaggerating your qualifications.

- Do not claim to be a "certified interpreter" after graduating from a training program or being "certified" by a language company, a school system, a local government agency or any other group. (See Unit 1 for clarification about certification.)

- Represent all your credentials accurately.

- Report critical incidents.

- Refrain from seeking additional business from either clients or providers on site. (External marketing of one's services is permissible.)

THE COMMUNITY INTERPRETER

Needless to say, you should be clear about your rates, invoice appropriately without inflating the time spent on assignments and otherwise uphold the highest standards of professional integrity in every aspect of your work.

20. The interpreter is prepared for all assignments.

For example, an interpreter asks about the nature of the assignment and reviews relevant terminology.

There can be no adequate interpreting if you arrive unprepared. As discussed in Unit 2, be carefully informed about:

- The date, time and location of the encounter.
- The language, dialect and/or region of the client, to ensure that you are a good linguistic match for the client.
- The nature of the appointment, so that you can assess whether you are qualified to interpret it.
- The nature of the service, so that you can research terminology.
- Any special or sensitive concerns or challenges.

However, for adjunct interpreters who have another job in the same agency where they interpret and may be called in to interpret at a moment's notice, it will not always be possible to prepare adequately.

21. The interpreter discloses skill limitations with respect to particular assignments.

For example, an interpreter who is unfamiliar with a highly technical medical term asks for an explanation before continuing to interpret.

The interpreter must ensure that he or she can manage an assignment. This means that you should:

- Accept no assignments unless you are qualified.
- Withdraw from an assignment if too many terms or concepts are unfamiliar.
- Notify parties immediately if you make an error.
- Always ask for clarification or repetition, as needed.

22. The interpreter avoids sight translation, especially of complex or critical documents, if he or she lacks sight translation skills.

For example, when asked to sight translate a surgery consent form, an interpreter instead asks the provider to explain its content and then interprets the explanation.

Sight translation is an extremely controversial area of interpreting. Some experts feel that community interpreters are not qualified to perform it and should not sight translate at all. Others in the field emphasize that interpreters should sight translate only documents of a page or two in length. When sight translation is necessary, remember the guidelines discussed in Unit 2:

- Perform sight translation only for brief, simple documents.
- Make sure that the provider remains to answer questions.

- Read the document carefully first.
- Scan it for problematic language, grammar, terms or acronyms.
- Ask the provider for clarification as needed.
- Render the entire document in the target language.
- Keep the pace and maintain the flow.
- Respect the register.

If the document is a long, difficult or a legal document, do not perform the sight translation. Instead, ask the provider to explain or summarize the content and orally interpret what is said.

23. The interpreter is accountable for professional performance.

For example, an interpreter does not blame others for his or her interpreting errors.

You alone are responsible for your performance.

24. The interpreter advocates for working conditions that support quality interpreting.

For example, an interpreter on a lengthy assignment indicates when fatigue might compromise interpreting accuracy.

It is important to recognize your limitations. Most providers do not understand the intense concentration required to interpret, nor the high level of skill that is needed to perform well. Try to:

- Advocate for decent working conditions, including appropriate light and freedom from interfering noise.

- Request a break after no longer than two hours of consecutive interpreting and no longer than half an hour of simultaneous interpreting.

- Educate all parties that fatigue compromises accuracy.

- If you are an adjunct interpreter, make sure that you receive sufficient time to perform your "official" job if you are often asked to interpret.

- Avoid overly long assignments without breaks.

- Try to have interpreting tasks written into your job description (for adjunct employees), including specifications about time spent on interpreting, working conditions and interpreter fatigue.

- Educate providers about interpreting ethics and standards.

25. The interpreter shows respect for professionals with whom he or she works.

For example, an interpreter does not spread rumors that would discredit another interpreter.

Interpreters should support colleagues in the field, including both providers and other interpreters. Therefore:

- Show respect for providers.
- Share resources with all.
- Avoid saying anything malicious or negative about other interpreters or the profession.
- Help beginners.
- Avoid fighting with other interpreters in front of clients.
- Avoid inappropriate advertising of your services.

26. The interpreter acts in a manner befitting the dignity of the profession and appropriate to the setting.

For example, an interpreter dresses appropriately and arrives on time for appointments.

Interpreters are responsible for behaving in a manner that credits the profession of community interpreting. Remember to:

- Promote national interpreter ethics and standards.
- Be punctual or early: plan to arrive 15 minute early where possible.
- Dress appropriately, in business dress or "business casual."
- Show courtesy.
- Cancel with proper notice and only if truly necessary.
- Respect all appropriate codes of ethics and conducts (for one's workplace as well as for the interpreting profession).
- Refrain from chewing gum.
- Silence cell phones and non-emergency pagers while interpreting.
- Bring no friends or family members to the assignment.

Regarding gifts: in no case should you accept money from any party but only from the organization itself, either for interpreting or as salary or wages for work performed. Gift policies should be dictated by the employer, but you should make the employer aware that most professional interpreter ethics either prohibit or strongly discourage accepting gifts.

Gifts to the interpreter (especially of food) may sometimes be shared with colleagues if institutional policy states that this permissible. Remember that interpreters who accept gifts may inadvertently:

- Erode impartiality.
- Imply that all clients should bring gifts for interpreters.
- Create an expectation of bigger gifts from a client for longer sessions or more vital services.
- Strain a client's resources.
- Set a poor precedent for other interpreters and make it difficult for them to refuse gifts.
- Create a quid pro quo expectation so that the client expects better or extra services in exchange for a gift.
- Create interpreter bias in favor of clients that bring gifts.

To discourage gift-giving, thank the client profusely and emphasize that you are already reimbursed for interpreting. Suggest that the greatest gift is seeing the client well served. If a client is offended by the refusal of a gift, suggest alternatives such as writing a thank you note to the agency; giving a gift in kind or a donation to an organization that serves the needy; or spreading the word about the agency's multilingual services.

Professional development

> ETHICAL PRINCIPLE: The interpreter strives to continually further his/her knowledge and skills.

27. The interpreter continues to develop language and cultural knowledge and interpreting skills.

For example, an interpreter stays up to date on changes in medical terminology or regional slang.

The profession of community interpreting is not static. Just as it continues to evolve, so, too, must the interpreter. Both linguistic knowledge and cultural knowledge are critical fields, and you will need to stay up-to-date with the interpreting profession itself. That will mean continuing to develop your skills and also keeping abreast of changes in the field. There are many ways to do so:

- Develop your memory skills
- Research/update your knowledge of terminology.
- Take advanced language or translation courses.
- Purchase specialized dictionaries and glossaries, for example, those that include "bad words."
- Read books and articles about culture in general and about the specific cultures involved in your work.
- Read about the field of interpreting, including the websites and publications of professional associations.
- Purchase reference manuals about relevant community services.
- Read online information, watching media and listening to music in one or more of your working languages.
- Practice word games to hone your language skills.

Professional development is discussed later in this unit. You may also refer to the Resources section of this manual for examples of resources that support your professional development.

28. The interpreter seeks feedback to improve his or her performance.

For example, an interpreter consults with colleagues about a challenging assignment.

No improvement comes in a void. You should look for feedback on your performance. There are several ways to do so:

- Attend professional in-services.
- Offer educational feedback in a positive, supportive manner to other interpreters, and ask them to do the same for you.
- Ask supervisors to monitor your performance and offer feedback.
- Try to shadow professional interpreters to compare their performance to your own.
- Have regular meetings with a supervisor to discuss challenging aspects of interpreting and review specific or recurring situations.

29. The interpreter supports the professional development of fellow interpreters.

For example, an experienced interpreter mentors novice interpreters.

In general it is helpful to:

- Help beginners.
- Mentor younger or newer interpreters.
- Share resources with all.
- Support other interpreters.
- Provide colleagues with support, resources, encouragement and feedback.

30. The interpreter participates in organizations and activities that contribute to the development of the profession.

For example, an interpreter attends professional workshops and conferences.

Because the field of interpreting changes constantly, and no interpreter knows everything, you are expected to continue your professional education in various ways that may include:

- Courses and seminars in specialized areas of interpreting.
- Language classes in literature, grammar or linguistics.
- In-services for interpreters.
- Conferences.
- Books, periodicals and other literature in the field.
- Books, periodicals and other literature in both languages (to maintain language skills).
- Courses on related subjects such as intercultural communication, sociolinguistics or language access laws.
- Listening to media in both languages (radio, television, movies).
- Self-help materials such as interpreting manuals with accompanying practice cassette tapes.
- Videotapes on subjects related to interpreting.

Advocacy

> ETHICAL PRINCIPLE: When the patient's health, well-being, or dignity is at risk, the interpreter may be justified in acting as an advocate. Advocacy is understood as an action taken on behalf of an individual that goes beyond facilitating communication, with the intention of supporting good health outcomes [or client safety and well being in other community services]. Advocacy must only be undertaken after careful and thoughtful analysis of the situation and if other less intrusive actions have not resolved the problem.

When or if to perform advocacy or mediation is often a difficult judgment call for interpreters. NCIHC writes on this issue in their national code of ethics:

> *On the surface, advocacy appears to be a contradiction of the ethical principle of impartiality – the obligation not to judge, take sides, or express personal opinions and biases with respect to the content of the communication in the clinical encounter. But these proscribed actions are clearly not examples of advocacy. The act of advocacy should derive from clear and/or consistent observations that something is not right and that action needs to be taken to right the wrong. On a deep level, advocacy goes to the heart of ethical behavior for all those*

involved in health care – to uphold the health and wellbeing (social, emotional and physical) of patients and ensure that no harm is done.
   NCIHC National Code of Ethics for Interpreters in Health Care
   www.ncihc.org, p. 20

31. The interpreter may speak out to protect an individual from serious harm.

For example, an interpreter may intervene on behalf of a patient with a life-threatening allergy, if the condition has been overlooked.

Advocacy is the professional skill that is perhaps the most difficult in all areas of community interpreting, and perhaps the riskiest activity in the field. However, there may be many instances of potential harm which the interpreter may have to address through advocacy.

Mediation and advocacy are complex skills that the interpreter will strive to exercise with due diligence. Situations that may require advocacy or mediation fall into several categories. They include: linguistic, institutional and cultural mediation; mediation to address unequal access to a service or biased treatment by a provider (discrimination); and advocacy outside the encounter.

Any act performed by the interpreter that is not interpreting and is intended to promote the success of the encounter, equal access to the service and/or the client's safety, health and well being is a form of mediation. Such mediation may or may not ultimately constitute advocacy. There is no widespread agreement on what advocacy really is and there is also a great deal of confusion about this topic. What is often called advocacy lies at the riskier end of the continuum of mediation.

When in doubt, report a critical incident to an appropriate supervisor. If you are not a trained advocate, do not engage in advocacy unless you are an experienced interpreter, know the institution well, feel certain that you are doing the right thing and are prepared to accept the consequences of advocating, up to and including losing an interpreting contract or your job, or facing a lawsuit.

32. The interpreter may advocate on behalf of a party or group to correct mistreatment or abuse.

For example, an interpreter may alert his or her supervisor to patterns of disrespect towards patients.

It is not unusual to hear stories of discrimination and even abuse by providers. An interpreter may have to advocate if:

- The client's ability to access a community service differs from that of native English speakers.
- A provider insults a client.
- A provider makes racist, discriminatory or insensitive comments about clients during or after an interpreted encounter.
- A client is asked to bring an interpreter to a public service.
- A child is asked to interpret.

UNIT 5

5.1 (c) STANDARDS IN REAL LIFE

OBJECTIVE 5.1(c) Act out standards in challenging situations from real life.

The Challenge

Community interpreting is a profession in its infancy. Most employers, supervisors and colleagues of interpreters do not understand interpreting well.

What should a bilingual employee or community interpreter do if professional ethics or standards seem to get in the way of normal workday routines?

The next section looks closely at these problems. Many typical challenges are listed in this unit. With each challenge comes a set of solutions: ideas, strategies and "tools" for making appropriate changes in the workplace. These are provided as suggestions only: the interpreter alone will know which suggestions are most appropriate for a particular situation or workplace.

UNIT 5

Red Light, Green Light, Yellow Light

Often , contract interpreters find it easier to respect ethics and standards than adjunct interpreters do. Sometimes the opposite is true. But how do standards impact the daily lives of interpreters, whether they are bilingual staff or contract interpreters?

Consider the analogy of traffic lights. Think of the red light as representing any forbidden practice. For example, if a client offers the interpreter money, you must refuse, whether you are a bilingual employee, a contract interpreter, a volunteer, or a zookeeper who interprets.

Another clear example is telling a friend the name of a client. That is forbidden—a "red light." Similarly, if you are offered an assignment for which you are not qualified (e.g. a school interpreter is sent to interpret for brain surgery, without training or preparation), you must decline.

The "green light" refers to basic *requirements* in interpreting. These practices are often clear as well. For example, you must be accurate and faithful to the spirit the message. You must exhibit *professionalism*, use *cultural knowledge* to overcome communication barriers and show *no bias* for or against either party. These are ethical requirements. According to standards of practice, you should also promote direct communication among the parties and respect transparency.

But what does a yellow light mean in English? Often, it refers to the idea of being careful, slowing down, being ready to stop. So with interpreting, a "yellow light" in this sense refers an area where the situation is not clear-cut.

When bilingual staff and community interpreters try to apply ethics in real life, many of them complain persistently, and at times with a great deal of emotion, that they cannot respect professional ethics and standards. But respecting ethics is not as difficult as you think: you must simply recognize the reality of "yellow light" situations and exert caution when something is not immediately clear. You will often have to make decisions on the spot.

Ethics help interpreters to understand the red and green lights of interpreting. But there are a great number of yellow lights in the field. Standards of practice give you guidance about how to act professionally in "yellow light" situations. When in doubt about what to do, standards of practice help you decide.

In this portion of the curriculum you will be very focused on practice, including role plays that bring together all your previous knowledge that you have gained so far that you can apply it to some of the interesting challenges that will face you in real life.

UNIT 5

Examples from the Field

Examples of green lights

- Maintain accuracy at all times.
- Interpret everything that is said.
- Maintain confidentiality unless required by law to break it.

Examples of red lights

- Avoid giving advice.
- Share no opinions, even if the client asks for one.
- Never take money from a client as a gift.
- Do not change register.
- Never cut short the ramblings of a client. (The provider may cut the client short—not the interpreter.)

Yellow lights…

- Are you required to interpret everything that is said? Yes. However, in life-or-death emergencies, or cases where too many people speak at once, you may summarize.

- Should you always prepare for assignments? Yes, but if you are sent in with no time to prepare, in reality that will not be possible.

- Should you use first person? Yes. But you may not be able to do so with small children, persons with dementia or severe mental illness, or in cases where using first person might cause serious confusion.

- May you disclose information shared privately outside the session by a client to your colleagues? Perhaps—but only to those colleagues who work as part of a team with that same client. You may not share the information with the receptionist or the person in medical records. This decision should be part of organizational policies and procedures for interpreters at your institution.

- If you must cancel at the last minute, may you send in another interpreter? Only if the organization or language agency agrees and the other interpreter is qualified to interpret for that session.

UNIT 5

- Should body language be interpreted? Under some circumstances it may be, e.g., when body language adds critical information to the message that the other party would miss.

- Should personal values guide your work? Yes, if that means ethical and professional values; no, if it means personal bias. This is a distinction that sometimes hard to make in real life.

- Should you plan to arrive on time? No! Plan to arrive early (at least 15 minutes early)—to allow for any unexpected delay. Some interpreter services will pay you for that time.

OBJECTIVE 5.2

Apply national standards of practice to interpreting.

Applying Standards

OBJECTIVE 5.2 (a) Demonstrate the application of standards of practice in community service settings.

5.2 (a) Demonstrate the application of standards of practice in community service settings.

5.2 (b) Relate ethics and standards to professional development for interpreters.

UNIT 5

Challenge # 1: Decline inappropriate assignments

The interpreter is asked by a supervisor or agency to perform a task for which the interpreter is not qualified.
Relevant NCIHC standards: 19, 20, 21, 22, 23

Examples of inappropriate tasks:

Translating complex documents that the interpreter is not qualified to translate; sight translating long, complex and/or legal documents; interpreting in a secondary language which you does not speak well enough to interpret accurately; explaining a health procedure or a Special Education document.

The supervisor says:

- "Oh, no one will know. It won't make a difference."
- "Sorry, but we don't have the money to hire a translator."
- "But that's why we hired you, remember? To do all these things."
- "Come on. Spanish is Spanish. You can do it."

SOLUTIONS

Try holding "brown-bag" lunches to educate colleagues about interpreting and standards. Look for external resources such as associations, NCIHC, listservs and advocacy groups.	Photocopy pages from this training manual or other resources and offer the documents respectfully to the supervisor or agency—or your organization's attorney. Offer to sit down and explain the documents.	Advocate for staff training on how to work with interpreters (that discusses which tasks are appropriate for interpreters). Mention that the federal government highly recommends such training.

Ask for a written job description that specifies interpreting duties. Use a resume to show those duties for which you are qualified. If you meet with a supervisor on this issue, bring with you any documents (articles and research) that support your arguments. Mention federal guidance on Title VI of the Civil Rights Act.

UNIT 5

Challenge # 2: Advocate for professional working conditions.

The interpreter feels too ill at ease to establish professional parameters or procedures for interpreting.
Relevant NCIHC standards: 23, 24, 26.

Examples:

You don't perform according to professional ethics and standards because you're afraid of:
- Losing job or the assignment.
- Offending a colleague.
- Upsetting a provider or supervisor or a contact at the language service provider.
- Creating stress and tension.
- Creating a backlash against clients.
- Causing trouble for an interpreter agency.
- Increasing costs.
- Reducing the time given to immigrant clients (because often doing something right requires extra time and/or resources).
- Causing LEP clients to lose access to a service.

SOLUTIONS

Are any of these barriers cultural? You may wish to explore your own culture and how it interrelates with American culture. Depending on your degree of acculturation, perhaps you could be more willing to confront authority assertively.

Sometimes these problems are tied to a need for diversity training in the workplace, which helps workers from different backgrounds work together more effectively. Advocate for such training.

Seek support from colleagues. With supervisors, discuss risk management and Title. Document the time spent interpreting, and use it to justify professional conduct.

Each agency that receives federal funding must establish clear, written policies and procedures for interpreting (as part of the larger federal requirement to have an LEP plan). Staff should be trained on these policies and procedures. Solicit support from a supervisor, the agency's lawyer, or the interpreter agency. Emphasize the legal liability involved in unprofessional interpreting.

UNIT 5

Challenge # 3: Respect role boundaries.

The interpreter is often expected to perform the work of a provider, during or outside the session, even when he or she has received no training in that field.
Relevant NCIHC standards: 16, 17, 18

Examples:

You are asked to:
- Perform another job while interpreting.
- Explain things such as prescriptions or procedures that you do not understand well due to lack of training and qualifications.
- Help a client fill out forms when the provider is not there.
- Consult with the provider during the encounter (side conversation).
- Summarize educational videos for the client, who becomes distressed while watching (in the case of birth videos, for example) or feels confused (e.g., in videos about parenting, job training, diet/health, the educational system, etc. when the provider is not there to answer questions.
- Sight translate a consent form after the provider leaves. The client then asks questions the interpreter cannot answer.

SOLUTIONS

| Ask for a clarification of your roles, in the form of a detailed job description, to determine expectations in writing. Then request the exact qualifications that the organization finds necessary to execute particular tasks with clients. | If appropriate, request that the workplace send you for training to gain credentials for a particular service. This would enhance your qualifications and increase employment options later while reducing tension now. | Make clear that it could be considered discrimination to ask an unqualified person to provide services for LEP clients and not for English-speaking clients. Invite the supervisor to offer suggestions to solve this problem, given the limitations of time and resources. |

Clarify exactly why you are being asked to perform tasks for which you are not qualified. For requests outside the session, ask the employer if other employees who lack training and qualifications are expected to step in to fill a provider's role. Contract interpreters should discuss the problem with the interpreter agency.

UNIT 5

LEARNING TO SAY "NO"

> "JUST SAY NO" is easy to say.
>
> Saying "NO" is difficult.
>
> Find someone who will listen

If your office has an ombudsman, a friendly supervisor or a colleague that you trust, it may be helpful to share your concerns with a sympathetic ear. If you are a contract interpreter, perhaps someone at the interpreter agency is sympathetic. Trust your professional training and your gut instincts.

Saying "no" is hard. Yet often it is the right thing to do.

Sometimes, it is the only right thing to do.

UNIT 5

Challenge # 4: Maintain accuracy

Maintaining accuracy is difficult in real life but remains a fundamental ethical requirement supported by the standards.
Relevant NCIHC standards: 1, 2, 20

Examples:

Challenges to maintaining accuracy include:
- Providers often speak in high register.
- Technical terminology that is difficult to master.
- Little time to prepare.
- Unfamiliar regionalisms.
- People who speak quickly.
- Clients who are soft-voiced, inarticulate, drunk, mentally ill, incoherent, etc.
- Community service settings that are chaotic, making it difficult to concentrate

Note: If someone uses three or four terms you do not know in the first few minutes, the assignment is too hard for you. Withdraw and discuss the issue later with supervisors.

SOLUTIONS

UNFAMILIAR TERMS: Develop a special notebook to note down new terms as they arise with their translations. Study them. Purchase specialized dictionaries, phone apps, etc. Locate bilingual glossaries on the Internet or in print. Ask questions on listservs.

HIGH REGISTER: Outside a session, gently educate the provider on the importance of using simple, direct language. Suggest that the provider give steps one at a time. If the problem is common, propose an in-service to discuss.

TERMINOLOGY. Make time to prepare for assignments. Discuss the importance of preparation with supervisors. Research terminology using online resources like Wikipedia and online glossaries. Ask colleagues for guidance.

PROFESSIONAL DEVELOPMENT: Create a small network of local interpreters. Join an association, a listserv or a translators' forum to ask questions about terminology. Attend specialized seminars or community college classes (e.g., medical terminology for health professionals). Subscribe to technical publications in the field.

UNIT 5

Challenge # 5: Respect confidentiality

The client reveals important information to the interpreter and orders or begs the interpreter to keep it secret. How can the interpreter respect confidentiality yet also share this information with the provider?
Relevant NCIHC standards: 7, 9, 16

Examples:

The client has a bond with the interpreter and reveals personal information about (for example):
- A serious health condition like HIV.
- Domestic violence.
- Family relationships (being a stepparent instead of a parent, for example, could affect eligibility for certain benefits).
- Legal problems.
- A crime that the client has committed.
- Not being the actual client named.
- Finances, e.g., the client makes too much money to be eligible for the service but lies about this to the provider and tells you the truth in private.

SOLUTIONS

If the problem of a client revealing private information is a common one, examine whether you are spending too much time with the client and fostering a relationship of dependence. Always try to promote client autonomy.

<u>During</u> a session: Simply interpret what is said. As needed, remind the client why you must do so. <u>Outside</u> a session: Urge the client to share the information with the provider. Share only urgent information with the client team.

Try to avoid being left alone with the client if is possible. If not, state prior to being alone with the client that anything of substance shared with you will be interpreted later for providers who work with that client.

Consider having a workplace policy on this issue so that you can cite the workplace policy in your introduction and remind the client about it if the client asks you not to share information with the provider. Be aware of relevant state laws regarding confidentiality and your mandate to report abuse.

UNIT 5

Challenge # 6: Promote autonomy

Providers expect the interpreter to perform work that conflicts with the goal of promoting client autonomy and self sufficiency. Clients may share this expectation.
Relevant NCIHC standards: 13, 16, 16, 18, 24, 26

Examples:

This is a particularly important challenge because it is very common for clients to "latch onto" the interpreter and become dependent on you. You are then expected to assist the client (outside the interpreted session) with:
- Correspondence.
- Making phone calls.
- Reducing hospital bills.
- Finding money for school events such as field trips.
- Looking for resources.
- Finding donations of food, clothing and furniture.
- Dealing with gas-and-electric turn-offs or eviction notices.

SOLUTIONS

Is the problem institutional? The whole agency may need training. You could bring this problem to the attention of the person in training or someone in human resources who coordinates staff training.

Inform the client you are not qualified to provide the extra services and refer the client to local cultural/ethnic organizations and community services that promote self-sufficiency.

If you are a bilingual employee, help your organization develop a referral list of literacy and tutoring groups, human services, job training, Head Start, English classes, certificate programs and other services that enhance autonomy.

If the client becomes insistent, cite workplace policy or have a supervisor call the client. The supervisor can explain your role while you interpret for the supervisor. Keep everything clear so that the client knows what you are permitted to do outside the session and boundaries are clear.

UNIT 5

Challenge # 7 Avoid burnout

An employer may expect the interpreter to interpret for hours at a stretch, perhaps for several different providers without a break. Exhaustion impedes accuracy. In addition, there may be no time to perform the interpreter's primary job, or travel from one session to another.
Relevant NCIHC standards: 1, 23, 24

Examples:

- A prenatal clinic lasts several hours without a break.
- A heavy day of walk-ins causes back-to-back assignments.
- No planning is made to allow the adjunct interpreter time to finish his or her real job after being asked to interpret.
- The provider has no understanding of the concentration required to interpret accurately and the need for you to take breaks.
- The provider lacks awareness about long-term interpreter stress and burnout.
- The interpreter experiences secondary trauma when interpreting for refugees, survivors of torture and war trauma, sexual assault or domestic violence, or other painful cases.

DANGER SIGN: The interpreter has thought about resigning due to stress, pressure or overwork.

SOLUTIONS

| The job description should allocate a realistic percentage of time to interpreting. Educate the provider on the need to have sessions scheduled ahead with appropriate breaks. Discuss secondary trauma and strategies to prevent it. | Sit down with a supervisor to discuss specific problems, including problems with colleagues who may be upset about the extra work you cause them when you interpret. Mention stress caused by deadlines. | LEP client appointments should be scheduled *2-3 times longer* than for English speakers. If this problem causes stress, seek an ombudsman or human resource specialist who can educate the workplace. |

If at all possible, as part of written policies on the appropriate use of interpreters, specify the time needed for breaks (e.g., every 2 hours for consecutive, every half-hour for simultaneous). Disseminate this document among frontline staff who schedule interpreters and among providers who work with interpreters.

UNIT 5

Challenge # 8: Support professional ethics and standards

The interpreter sees untrained interpreters who do not adhere to ethics and standards and providers who do not respect written interpreter policies and procedures.
Relevant NCIHC standards: all

Examples:

Some interpreters you know may:
- Give advice.
- Accept gifts.
- Socialize with clients outside the workplace.
- Interpret inaccurately.
- Summarize, omit, or engage in side conversations.
- Fail to mediate appropriately or with skill.

Providers may:
- Insist that "other interpreters do what I ask—why don't you?"
- Ask interpreters to summarize or give advice.
- Refuse to ask for interpreters when they are needed.
- Make formal complaints about interpreters who abide by professional ethics.

SOLUTIONS

If you witness ethical violations and you are a member of a professional association, it may be an ethical obligation to report the incident. It may also be a workplace requirement. Treat ethical violations as critical incidents and notify a supervisor.

If one provider is doing an excellent job working with interpreters, perhaps that provider could educate "difficult" providers on how to work with an interpreter. People often accept information more easily from their peers than from the interpreter.

If a problem is caused by lack of training, you could strongly recommend interpreter training. But if interpreters lack language proficiency, they should not interpret, and you should make this clear to supervisors.

If interpreting quality is impaired because ethics or standards are not followed, such incidents should also be reported. The client's well being and equal access to services is at stake. Stress liability and risk management. Make photocopies of interpreter ethics documents.

UNIT 5

Challenge # 9: Maintain objectivity and neutrality.

Interpreters are biased because they are human.
Relevant NCIHC standards: 9, 10 14, 15

Examples:

Despite your best efforts to remain neutral:
- Some providers are so biased and abrupt that the interpreter strongly dislikes working with them.
- Some clients have strong body odors, use coarse language or exhibit behavior that may alienate you.
- You may resent professionals who are condescending or who treat interpreters poorly.
- Some interpreters have a strong bias against clients with less education than the interpreter.

SOLUTIONS

Staff at many agencies are now diverse, and interpreter agencies are diverse by definition. Holding cultural competence discussions could help everyone in the organization open their eyes about other cultural groups and expose assumptions that you and your colleagues may not be aware of.

Cultural competence and cultural diversity training helps everyone, including the interpreter, to recognize personal bias that has an impact on your performance. You can also read books and articles on this subject, and consult cultural competence checklists to learn more about yourself.

One of the most powerful tools to assess one's personal bias about different groups (based on color, gender, disabilities, age and other criteria) is a famous Harvard program called Project Implicit at www.implicit.harvard.edu. Take the tests online and receive confidential results at once.

If your gut seizes during a session because of something a client or provider did or said, after the session try to write down why you may have felt negative emotions. Examine what you wrote. Assess how attitudes of bias might affect your performance and how you may feel differently about people from certain social groups.

UNIT 5

Challenge #10 True dual role

The interpreter is asked to provide a service and interpret at the same time.
Relevant NCIHC Standards: 16, 17, 18

Examples:

- Home visits. Often, interpreters are expected to act as assistants to the provider conducting the home visit.
- Dual case management. Because the bilingual employee speaks the client's language, she is sometimes a case manager and sometimes an interpreter—at the same time.
- Refugee resettlement. Roles are very blurred for caseworkers, who often interpret while assisting clients.
- Parent-teacher liaisons. School employees often provide services while interpreting.
- Crisis intervention. An interpreter may also be a rape survivor advocate, a counselor for a runaway, a substance abuse/addictions counselor at a homeless shelter, etc.

Note that because bilingual employees are often hired to provide bilingual services and also interpret, supervisors are generally unaware that it is seen as a problem or a conflict by interpreting experts to do both jobs at the same time.

SOLUTIONS

If you feel that these requests are undermining the client's best interests and/or the integrity of the encounter, make every effort to end this type of activity because it may constitute discrimination.

Consult with other interpreters and associations, and conduct Internet and library research and see what information exists on this problem and possible solutions that fit your own workplace and situation.

Assess and monitor the situation. Clarify the problems you have performing both roles at once, then write up a list of your concerns and analyze them. Discuss this list with your colleagues, revise it, then bring it to a supervisor.

Ask for a written job description clarifying your tasks and roles and then discuss your concerns with a supervisor. Explain why performing both roles at once is not feasible (lack of concentration, conflict of interest, inaccuracy, etc).

UNIT 5

Challenge # 11 Advocacy and prejudice

Advocacy is not only risky but intimidating. The interpreter may feel uncomfortable taking action against a colleague, a supervisor or even interpreter. Yet it is not rare to find providers who make derogatory remarks about LEP clients in their presence.
Relevant NCIHC standards: 14, 15, 31, 32.

> **Examples:**
>
> Colleagues may…
> - Make insulting remarks about culture or LEP clients in the workplace.
> - Make derogatory remarks about a client during the session.
> - Offer a different level of service to native speakers.
> - Ignore cultural mediation offered by the interpreter.

SOLUTIONS

> Try to discuss the situation with the colleague respectfully, for example: "When you say X to clients, I feel upset because [describe the impact], and I'm concerned they feel that way too. Were you aware you might be causing these feelings?"

> If the colleague is not approachable or sympathetic, report such incidents promptly. Cultural competence training is obviously needed in that workplace. Consider speaking to the person who oversees staff training.

> *If appropriate,* educate clients about their rights to file complaints, either within the institution or a local office of human rights. Many clients are unwilling to file complaints but most are not aware of their rights.

> If the derogatory remarks are intentional, interpret exactly what is said. If the problem is affecting your ability to interpret or to respect the colleague, take prompt action. If reporting has no effect (or other attempts such as lunch-time talks), try to bring in ethnic speakers to share their experiences of discrimination and cultural misunderstandings.

UNIT 5

BUT REMEMBER...

> Sometimes casual conversations with a colleague
> Can do more to change workplace culture and practice
> than formal policies or education.

Use every opportunity to share your valuable knowledge, experience and expertise, in a warm and positive way, with colleagues and supervisors.

UNIT 5

Professional Development

OBJECTIVE 5.2 (b) Relate ethics and standards to professional development for interpreters..

Training, of course, is not enough: every interpreter is ultimately responsible for continuing his or her education after training. Professional development is an ethical requirement, a standard of practice and a necessity in the field.

This is true even if you are an adjunct interpreter. As stated in Unit 1, one important question that often arises is whether it is practical to expect bilingual staff and volunteers to perform according to the same standards as contract ("professional") interpreters.

The answer is yes: interpreting is interpreting. And interpreters are interpreters. To the extent humanly possible, all community interpreters should strive to support professional ethics and standards, including professional development. That said, in real life there may be significant differences between adjunct, volunteer and contract interpreters to consider. See the next page for examples.

When it comes to professional development, however, adjunct interpreters and volunteers, like contract interpreters, should seek every opportunity possible to continue their interpreter education.

UNIT 5

Bilingual Staff Vs. Contract Interpreters

Differences Between Bilingual Staff/Volunteers and Contract Interpreters	
Contract Interpreters	**Adjunct Interpreters/Volunteers**
Walk away at the end of a session.	Cannot walk away: they are part of the organization.
Report to an outside agency or are self-employed.	Report to supervisors internally.
Are expected to interpret.	Are expected to do many things to support clients in addition to interpreting.
May find it easier to say "no" to requests that are inappropriate.	Often find it hard to say "no" to supervisors, administrators, colleagues and friends.
Usually take pride in their profession.	Often do not often consider themselves to be "professional interpreters."
Try to set clear boundaries.	May find it difficult to set boundaries.
Do not case manage clients.	May case manage clients.
Do not usually provide a service in the target language.	Often provide services in the target language.
Can insist that providers not leave them alone with clients.	Are routinely left alone with clients.
Are not typically supposed to drive or accompany clients.	May drive or accompany clients or make phone calls for them.
Do not offer direct services to clients.	May offer direct services to clients and also interpret for the same clients.
Are not supposed to perform personal services for clients.	Routinely read correspondence, make phone calls, have bills reduced or perform other personal services for clients that are not part of the employee's job description.
Are not supposed to accept gifts.	May have an agency policy that allows small gifts
Do not usually get personally involved with clients.	May socialize with clients, get involved in their family situations (e.g., domestic violence), give their home phone number, etc.
Are sometimes but not usually afraid of losing work if they adhere to professional ethics and standards.	Fear they may lose their job if they say "no" to a boss, even if the request violates interpreter ethics or standards.

These differences between bilingual employees who interpret and contract interpreters do not affect the need for professional development. However, they may affect the kind of professional development that interpreters engage in and the opportunities available. Broadly speaking, bilingual employees who interpret have greater difficulties with boundaries than contract interpreters. Any professional development experience that allows them to increase their knowledge and understanding of ethics, standards and role boundaries will be especially beneficial for adjunct interpreters.

All interpreters need additional work to develop their skills, particularly in sight translation, simultaneous mode, note-taking, message conversion and memory skills.

UNIT 5

The Building Blocks of Professional Development

Conferences
The four most significant annual U.S. conferences in the field for community interpreters are those offered by ATA (fall), IMIA (fall), NCIHC (spring: technically this is an annual meeting, not a conference) and CHIA (spring). Interpreters who perform legal interpreting should also consider the NAJIT conference (spring).

In addition, there are a growing number of conferences hosted by regional and state interpreter associations. Attending conferences is one of the single most important ways that an interpreter can further his or her professional development.

Maintaining Your Languages
Read books, magazines, and Internet articles in both languages. Listen to television, radio and podcasts. Join language clubs. Play word games online. Never assume that your native language is secure: it erodes over time, like any other language.

Study Buddies
Find a study partner and meet once a week to practice interpreting, test each other on terminology, discuss opportunities for professional development and give each other feedback on performance.

Dictionaries, Training Manuals, Interpreter Newsletters and Other Publications
Look at the resource section of this manual for ideas about books and dictionaries to purchase to further your professional development. Subscribe to the newsletters and e-newsletters of any interpreter associations and the community interpreting newsletter of Cross-Cultural Communications (sign up at www.cultureandlanguage.net).

Practice materials
Purchase DVDs and other resources to practice, such as those offered by Acebo (Interpreter's Rx) and the University of Arizona (Interpretapes).

In-Services
Attend or set up in-services at work, at community interpreter services or in any other venue. It is ideal to get a group of interpreters together about once a month to bring in a speaker, discuss issues you have experienced in the field, socialize with other interpreters and ask each other questions about how to handle difficult situations.

Listservs

Join every interpreter listserv you can find, especially those of NCIHC, IMIA and NAJIT.

UNIT 5

Professional Associations

> Professional association: A group of individuals who work together to promote the ethics, standards, work conditions, dignity and autonomy of a profession.

One of the best ways to continue one's professional development is by joining a professional association. The largest and oldest international association of interpreters is the International Association of Conference Interpreters, AIIC (Association internationale des interprètes de conférence). Today there are many interpreter associations around the world and in the U.S.

\multicolumn{3}{c}{**PROFESSIONAL ASSOCIATIONS in the U.S.**}		
\multicolumn{3}{c}{**Examples**}		
Name	**Type of Interpreting**	**Details**
ATA (American Translators Association) www.atanet.org	General	A national body with a code of ethics. ATA certifies translators but not interpreters and has a national registry of member interpreters.
NAJIT (National Association of Judiciary Interpreters) www.najit.org	Legal/court	A strong national body with about 1200 members. Certifies interpreters and has a national code of ethics. Hosts meetings, publications, strong advocacy, continuing education seminars, presentations at conferences, etc.
IMIA (International Medical Interpreters Association) www.imiaweb.org	Medical/health care	An active body that has published some of the most influential standards of practice in the field of medical interpreting and is working on certification. Holds the largest annual conference in any area of community interpreting.
CHIA (California Healthcare Interpreting Association) www.chiaonline.org	Medical/health care	Another active state body that has published influential standards of practice and organizes many activities and an annual conference for interpreters.
SOMI (Society of Medical Interpreters) www.sominet.org	Medical/health care	Regional body (primarily northwest of U.S.).
ATA regional chapters	General	These local chapters, unlike ATA, often put "interpreters" in their name.
AATIA (Austin Area Int. and Translators Assoc), CCIO (Community and Court Interpreters of the Ohio Valley), etc.	Varies by association	There are a number of local or regional associations in the U.S. that are not affiliated with ATA. Very few (if any besides CCIO) address community interpreting in their title or official documents.

Note: The National Council on Interpreting in Health Care is not a professional association. It is a multidisciplinary organization that promotes quality interpreting as a means to support equal access to health care for LEP individuals.

UNIT 5

Why Join a Professional Association?

> **WHAT PROFESSIONAL INTERPRETER ASSOCIATIONS DO**
>
> - Promote professional, quality interpreting.
> - Host listservs.
> - Publish newsletters and other publications.
> - Hold conferences.
> - Offer workshops and seminars.
> - Educate the public about the profession.
> - Defend the interests of the profession.
> - Arbitrate between interpreters and clients.
> - Advocate for, support, and sometimes offer, training and certification.
> - Offer professional resources and networking opportunities.
> - Create a directory/database of members for employers.
> - Investigate wrongdoing by members.

Associations host conferences and listervs, publish guides, newsletters or glossaries, and conduct other activities that promote the profession and the success of its members. Joining a professional association shows that you take that profession seriously.

Why should community interpreters join a professional association?

Ethics and Standards

- Professional associations develop ethics and standards of practice.
- They also support ethics and standards by providing resources.
- Because community interpreting is in its infancy as a profession, it is particularly important to join and support professional associations.

Professional solidarity and development

- To join a professional association is to support colleagues in the profession and to receive support from them.
- Interpreters, including bilingual staff and volunteers, may feel "alone," as if no one understands them. Members of a professional association often understand each other.
- Associations may offer updates and newsletters, networking, advocacy, conferences and continuing education seminars.

Support

- If an interpreter is attacked or fired, the association may be able to provide arbitration and/or legal support.
- For self care, members can share stories with each other on listservs (removing identifying details) or at seminars and may give each other advice.

UNIT 5

Interpreter Safety and Well Being

Professional development takes many forms that we don't always consider. One example is learning how to care for oneself after a difficult session or series of encounters.

Safety

At all times try to protect your safety and health as follows:
- Take universal precautions in health care, including washing hands, wearing appropriate clothing and obeying all institutional requirements.
- Take a break after two hours of consecutive interpreting (try for 10 minutes of down time per hour of interpreting if possible) and after every half-hour of simultaneous (work in a team so that you are interpreting only half the time).
- Exercise self care after traumatic or long sessions.
- Debrief with the provider after any difficult session.
- Withdraw if a situation grows dangerous (e.g., if a client show abusive or violent behavior). Inform the provider why you are leaving.
- Refuse to tolerate verbal abuse from either clients or providers.
- In an emergency, call 911.

Secondary trauma (vicarious retraumatization)

Interpreters from war-torn countries, devastated regions or refugee camps face many challenges when they interpret for clients who discuss traumas that mirror the interpreter's experience. Interpreting in those cases can bring painful feelings to the surface, a phenomenon known as "retriggering." Such interpreters should continually monitor themselves and withdraw if they observe signs of trauma emerging when they interpret. Refugee interpreters may wish to decline sessions for survivors of torture and trauma.

Well being

Self care for interpreters can include time off work, going for a walk, extra time with loved ones, exercise, meditation, reading, prayer, and debriefing with a provider or outside counseling. Each interpreter knows the special behaviors that feel soothing and relaxing, and such activities are particularly helpful after a stressful encounter. Ask yourself…
- What makes me relax?
- What relaxes me quickly after a hard day?
- What special kindness can I show myself after a difficult session?

Always have a series of strategies prepared in advance in case you have a difficult day. **Interpreters do important work. Let's take good care of ourselves!**

UNIT 5

Self Care

Self care can take many forms.

Relaxing with a loved one or engaging in a favorite social activity are examples of self care.
The activity does not have to be expensive
(or calorie-laden), but…

*After a stressful day interpreting,
remember to take care of yourself.*

UNIT 5

REVIEW

UNIT 5 REVIEW EXERCISES

NCIHC Standards of Practice

Standards of Practice

1. How many standards of practice are there in the NCIHC National Standards of Practice?
_____

2. What year were the standards published?
_____

3. List the three NCIHC standards of practice that you find most important. Give one example of each taken from real life (do not use the example quoted in the standard).
_____
_____
_____
_____
_____
_____
_____

4. Why are standards of practice often grouped under headings taken from codes of ethics?
_____
_____
_____
_____

5. There are six NCIHC standards for accuracy, yet only two for confidentiality. Why do you think that is the case?
_____
_____
_____
_____

6. Why are there more standards than ethical principles in the NCIHC documents?
_____
_____
_____

7. Match the following standards to the appropriate ethical principles by drawing a line. (Note: One ethical principle can either pertain to more than one standard or have no standard connected to it at all.)

1. Advise parties that everything will be interpreted.	Impartiality
2. The interpreter promotes direct communication.	Confidentiality.
3. The interpreter limits activity to interpreting.	Professionalism.
4. The interpreter maintains transparency.	Accuracy
5. The interpreter is accountable for performance.	Professional development
6. The interpreter discloses potential conflicts of interest.	Cultural awareness
7. The interpreter speaks out to protect from harm.	Respect
8. The interpreter protects written information.	Advocacy
9. The interpreter discloses skill limitations.	Role boundaries
10. The interpreter seeks feedback to improve performance.	

UNIT 5

Strategies for Promoting and Practicing Standards

1. If you are asked to perform sight translation of a long and complex legal document filled with unfamiliar terms, you should:
   (a) Ask for extra time to prepare.
   (b) Politely decline the request.
   (c) Read the text carefully, ask the provider questions about it, and then consult a l legal dictionary.
   (d) Ask the provider to explain or summarize the text so that you can interpret what the provider says.

2. If an adjunct interpreter is routinely asked to perform so much interpreting that not enough time is left for this bilingual employee's regular job, the interpreter should:
   (a) Make sure that a specific limit on interpreting hours per week is written into the job description.
   (b) Sit down with a supervisor to discuss strategies to allocate time.
   (c) Recommend having formal policies and procedures in place to guide the process of requesting interpreters.
   (d) Any or all of the above.

3. If a provider keeps using third person, the interpreter can:
   (a) Briefly remind the provider what was said during introductions about speaking directly to the client.
   (b) Interrupt the session to mediate and explain the value of using first person (e.g., it is faster, more accurate, more direct, promotes a strong client-provider relationship, helps to establish trust between provider and client and puts less strain on the interpreter's memory).
   (c) Avoiding eye contact, use a subtle gesture or wave of the hand to redirect the provider's attention to the client.
   (d) Any or all of the above.

4. If the provider keeps speaking in a high register, the interpreter should:
   (a) Use simple language, to be sure the client understands.
   (b) Have a detailed discussion with the provider about register during the session.
   (c) Mediate to suggest to the provider that what is being interpreted may not be clear and suggesting the provider change register (not the interpreter).
   (d) Do not discuss register with the provider; simply interpret, then lodge a complaint about the problem with a supervisor after the session.

5. To promote client autonomy and avoid having the client grow dependent on interpreters:

    (a) Develop a list of referral agencies (if the agency agrees) and refer the client to these agencies for assistance, as needed.

    (b) Never do for a client anything that the client can do for himself.

    (c) Sit down with a supervisor to discuss how often clients come to find you after a session and ask you for extra services.

    (d) Any or all of the above.

Challenges with Standards

1. If you arrive at a session and realize you know that client, what steps should you follow?

_____
_____
_____
_____

2. If a provider keeps using third person, what strategies could you try out to change her behavior? (Try not to switch to first person—get the provider to switch to first person.)

_____
_____
_____
_____

3. Give examples of ways that interpreters can show respect.

_____
_____
_____
_____

4. If a client comes to you after the session asking for help (for example, getting a subsidized apartment or preventing a gas or electric cut-off), what could you do?

_____
_____
_____
_____

UNIT 5

Bilingual Staff vs. Contract Interpreters

List some of the differences between contract and adjunct interpreters.

Contract and Adjunct Interpreters	
Contract Interpreters	Adjunct Interpreters (Bilingual Staff/Dual Role)

Professional Associations

Write true or false between each statement.

1. The American Translators Association certifies interpreters. _____

2. The National Council on Interpreting in Health Care is an important medical interpreter association. _____

3. It is a good idea for community interpreters to join a professional association of interpreters. _____

4. Professional interpreting associations support quality interpreting. _____

5. Professional interpreter associations often provide continuing education for interpreters. _____

6. The International Medical Interpreters Association has published influential standards of practice. _____
Professional Development

UNIT 5

Out of the following list, circle the six strategies for professional development that are most realistic and relevant for your own work:

1. Attend conferences, seminars or in-services for interpreters.

2. Join a professional association or a group (like NCIHC) that supports interpreters.

3. Purchase dictionaries and other reference works.

4. Search the Internet for bilingual glossaries of specialized terminology (e.g., for Special Education, Social Security, subsidized housing, oncology, etc.) and study them.

5. Create or find a local network of interpreters.

6. Seek additional training or workshops.

7. Carry a special notepad (e.g., spiral bound) to note down new terms and create your own specialized glossaries.

8. Read books, magazines and articles in your weaker language, in print and/or on the Internet.

9. Find an interpreter partner to practice with once a week.

10. Listen to radio, television, YouTube and podcast programs in your weaker language.

11. Find television shows about your area of interpreting, if possible, e.g., medical or court programs, and note any new terminology.

12. Find word games and games for memory skills on the Internet.

13. While watching television or listening to the radio or Internet broadcasts, try to interpret what is said simultaneously. Try to do this for programs in both or all of your working languages.

14. Purchase self-study resources from organizations that offer them (see the Resources section of this manual for suggestions).

THE COMMUNITY INTERPRETER

"INTERPRETER'S HIGH"

Community interpreting is a wonderful profession for people who want to make a difference.

Good luck!

RESOURCES

RESOURCES

SAMPLE CODES OF ETHICS

1. **MEDICAL/HEALTH CARE INTEPRETING**

NATIONAL COUNCIL ON INTERPRETING IN HEALTH CARE:
A Code of Ethics for Health Care Interpreters, 2004
Only the **basic principles** are below because this code is discussed at length in Unit 1 of this manual. For a full commentary on this code, go to www.ncihc.org. Also refer to Unit 1 of this manual, where these principles are discussed in detail.

1. **Confidentiality**
2. **Accuracy and Completeness**
3. **Impartiality**
4. **Professional Boundaries**
5. **Cultural Awareness**
6. **Respect**
7. **Advocacy**
8. **Professional Development**
9. **Professionalism**

For the IMIA codes of ethics, go to www.imiaweb.org. For the CHIA code of ethics

2. **COMMUNITY INTERPRETING**

COMMUNITY AND COURT INTERPRETERS OF OHIO
Community Interpreter's Code of Ethics

Only excerpts are included below. For the complete document, go to www.ccio.org/CCIO-CodeofEthics-Community.htm.

PRINCIPLES

A. Accuracy and Completeness
The interpreter must interpret exactly what is said without omitting, adding, or altering anything said or written. It includes accuracy of style or register of speech, non-distortion of the meaning of the source language even if it appears incoherent, non-responsive, or offensive. The interpreter advises all parties that everything they say will be interpreted.

B. Confidentiality
The interpreter must understand and uphold the patient-doctor and attorney-client privileges. He/she must respect the confidentiality of the communication… unless required by law.

RESOURCES

C. Impartiality

The interpreter does not advocate, mediate or speak on behalf of either party, or otherwise interfere with the right of individuals to make their own decisions. The interpreter informs all parties of his/her obligation to remain impartial, and demonstrates respect for all parties. The interpreter maintains a non-judgmental attitude about the contents of the discourse to be interpreted. The interpreter shall refrain from conduct that may give the appearance of a conflict of interest.

D. Cultural Bridging

Under certain conditions, the interpreter may provide explanation of cultural beliefs and/or practices:
a. that the explanation is necessary for accurate understanding of the communication;
b. the parties are unable to explain in their own words;
c. all parties consent to this intervention.
The interpreter alerts the parties to potential misunderstandings based upon stereotyping and/or different cultural expectations without contributing stereotypes or personal opinions.

E. Proficiency

By accepting an assignment, the interpreter implies the capacity to perform accurately in the given setting, to interpret efficiently and understand the dialect(s) spoken. The interpreter should decline an assignment that requires knowledge or skills beyond their competence or involves an unfamiliar dialect. Interpreters are responsible for accurately representing their certifications, training, and pertinent experience. Interpreters should strive continually to improve their skills and knowledge through formal and informal continuing education, and to obtain available accreditation and/or certification.

F. Professionalism

Interpreters ensure that their role and obligations are understood by all parties. Interpreters perform their duties as unobtrusively as possible. Interpreters do not promote personal interests while on assignment and shall not receive gifts or secondary remuneration above and beyond their set fees. Interpreters are punctual, prepared, and dress in appropriate manner; they do not bring children or other guests to assignments. Interpreters bring to the attention of an appropriate person any circumstance or condition that impedes full compliance with any principle in this document, including interpreter fatigue, inability to hear, or inadequate knowledge of specialized terminology. Interpreters must decline assignments under conditions that make such compliance patently impossible.

3. COURT AND LEGAL INTERPRETING

NATIONAL ASSOCIATION OF JUDICIARY INTERPRETERS AND TRANSLATORS (NAJIT)

Code of Ethics and Professional Responsibilities

For the complete document, go to www.najit.org (or http://www.najit.org/about/NAJITCodeofEthicsFINAL.pdf).

RESOURCES

Canon 1. Accuracy

Source language speech should be faithfully rendered into the target language by conserving all the elements of the original message while accommodating the syntactic and semantic patterns of the target language. The rendition should sound natural in the target language, and there should be no distortion of the original message through addition or omission, explanation or paraphrasing. All hedges, false starts and repetitions should be conveyed; also, English words mixed into the other language should be retained, as should culturally bound terms which have no direct equivalent in English, or which may have more than one meaning. The register, style and tone of the source language should be conserved.

Guessing should be avoided. Court interpreters who do not hear or understand what a speaker has said should seek clarification. Interpreter errors should be corrected for the record as soon as possible.

Canon 2. Impartiality and Conflicts of Interest

Court interpreters and translators are to remain impartial and neutral in proceedings where they serve, and must maintain the appearance of impartiality and neutrality, avoiding unnecessary contact with the parties.

Court interpreters and translators shall abstain from comment on cases in which they serve. Any real or potential conflict of interest shall be immediately disclosed to the Court and all parties as soon as the interpreter or translator becomes aware of such conflict of interest.

Canon 3. Confidentiality

Privileged or confidential information acquired in the course of interpreting or preparing a translation shall not be disclosed by the interpreter or translator without authorization.

Canon 4. Limitations of Practice

Court interpreters and translators shall limit their participation in those matters in which they serve to interpreting and translating, and shall avoid giving advice to the parties or otherwise engaging in activities that can be construed as the practice of law.

Canon 5. Protocol and Demeanor

Court interpreters shall conduct themselves in a manner consistent with the standards and protocol of the court, and shall perform their duties as unobtrusively as possible. Court interpreters are to use the same grammatical person as the speaker. When it becomes necessary to assume a primary role in the communication, they must make it clear that they are speaking for themselves.

Canon 6. Maintenance and Improvement of Skills and Knowledge

Court interpreters and translators shall strive to maintain and improve their interpreting and translation skills and knowledge.

Canon 7. Accurate Representation of Credentials

Court interpreters and translators shall accurately represent their certifications, accreditations, training and pertinent experience.

Canon 8. Impediments to Compliance

Court interpreters and translators shall bring to the Court's attention any circumstance or condition that impedes full compliance with any Canon of this Code, including interpreter fatigue, inability to hear, or inadequate knowledge of specialized terminology, and must decline assignments under conditions that make such compliance patently impossible.

4. GENERAL INTERPRETING

AUSTRALIAN INSTITUTE OF INTERPRETERS AND TRANSLATORS

Code of Ethics

For the full Code of Ethics and Code of Practice go to:
www.ausit.org (or http://www.ausit.org/eng/showpage.php3?id=650).

AUSIT Code of Ethics
for Interpreters & Translators

GENERAL PRINCIPLES

1. PROFESSIONAL CONDUCT
Interpreters and translators shall at all times act in accordance with the standards of conduct and decorum appropriate to the aims of AUSIT, the national professional association of interpreting and translation practitioners.

2. CONFIDENTIALITY
Interpreters and translators shall not disclose information acquired during the course of their assignments.

3. COMPETENCE
Interpreters and translators shall undertake only work which they are competent to perform in the language areas for which they are "accredited" or "recognised" by NAATI.

4. IMPARTIALITY
Interpreters and translators shall observe impartiality in all professional contracts.

5. ACCURACY
Interpreters and translators shall take all reasonable care to be accurate.

RESOURCES

6. EMPLOYMENT
Interpreters and translators shall be responsible for the quality of their work, whether as freelance practitioners or employed practitioners of interpreting and translation agencies and other employers.

7. PROFESSIONAL DEVELOPMENT
Interpreters and translators shall continue to develop their professional knowledge and skills.

8. PROFESSIONAL SOLIDARITY
Interpreters and translators shall respect and support their fellow professionals.

5. CONFERENCE INTERPRETING

AIIC: ASSOCIATION INTERNATIONALE DES INTERPRETES DE CONFERENCE **(International Association of Conference Interpreters)**

Code of Professional Ethics

For the complete document, go to www.aiic.net (or http://www.aiic.net/ViewPage.cfm/article24.htm).

I - PURPOSE AND SCOPE

Article 1
a. This Code of Professional Ethics (hereinafter called the "Code") lays down the standards of integrity, professionalism and confidentiality which all members of the Association shall be bound to respect in their work as conference interpreters.
b. Candidates shall also undertake to adhere to the provisions of this Code.
c. The Council, acting in accordance with the Regulation on Disciplinary Procedure, shall impose penalties for any breach of the rules of the profession as defined in this Code.

II - CODE OF HONOUR

Article 2
a. Members of the Association shall be bound by the strictest secrecy, which must be observed towards all persons and with regard to all information disclosed in the course of the practice of the profession at any gathering not open to the public.
b. Members shall refrain from deriving any personal gain whatsoever from confidential information they may have acquired in the exercise of their duties as conference interpreters.

Article 3
a. Members of the Association shall not accept any assignment for which they are not qualified. Acceptance of an assignment shall imply a moral undertaking on the member's part to work with all due professionalism.
b. Any member of the Association recruiting other conference interpreters, be they members of the Association or not, shall give the same undertaking.
c. Members of the Association shall not accept more than one assignment for the same period of time.

RESOURCES

Article 4
- Members of the Association shall not accept any job or situation which might detract from the dignity of the profession.
- They shall refrain from any act which might bring the profession into disrepute.

Article 5
For any professional purpose, members may publicise the fact that they are conference interpreters and members of the Association, either as individuals or as part of any grouping or region to which they belong.

Article 6
- It shall be the duty of members of the Association to afford their colleagues moral assistance and collegiality.
- Members shall refrain from any utterance or action prejudicial to the interests of the Association or its members. Any complaint arising out of the conduct of any other member or any disagreement regarding any decision taken by the Association shall be pursued and settled within the Association itself.
- Any problem pertaining to the profession which arises between two or more members of the Association, including candidates, may be referred to the Council for arbitration.

III - WORKING CONDITIONS

Article 7
With a view to ensuring the best quality interpretation, members of the Association:
- shall endeavour always to secure satisfactory conditions of sound, visibility and comfort, having particular regard to the Professional Standards as adopted by the Association as well as any technical standards drawn up or approved by it;
- shall not, as a general rule, when interpreting simultaneously in a booth, work either alone or without the availability of a colleague to relieve them should the need arise;
- shall try to ensure that teams of conference interpreters are formed in such a way as to avoid the systematic use of relay;
- shall not agree to undertake either simultaneous interpretation without a booth or whispered interpretation unless the circumstances are exceptional and the quality of interpretation work is not thereby impaired;
- shall require a direct view of the speaker and the conference room. They will thus refuse to accept the use of television monitors instead of this direct view, except in the case of videoconferences;
- shall require that working documents and texts to be read out at the conference be sent to them in advance;
- shall request a briefing session whenever appropriate;
- shall not perform any other duties except that of conference interpreter at conferences for which they have been taken on as interpreters.

RESOURCES

Article 8
Members of the Association shall neither accept nor, a fortiori, offer for themselves or for other conference interpreters recruited through them, be they members of the Association or not, any working conditions contrary to those laid down in this Code or in the Professional Standards.

Version 1994

6. SIGN LANGUAGE INTERPRETING

REGISTRY OF INTERPRETERS FOR THE DEAF (RID) AND NATIONAL ASSOCIATION OF THE DEAF (NAD)

National Code of Ethics (Draft, July 2003)

Summarized and abridged by the authors. For the complete document, including the commentary, go to www.rid.org (or http://www.rid.org/UserFiles/File/NAD_RID_ETHICS.pdf).

1. CONFIDENTIALITY
Interpreters bear a unique responsibility […] because of their role as language and cultural mediators, bridging the communication divide. Maintaining confidentiality is essential to protect all those involved in interpreted exchanges.

2. PROFESSIONAL COMPETENCE AND INTEGRITY
2.1 Interpreters maintain high standards of professional competence and integrity.
2.4 Interpreters should be willing to give back to the community by providing pro bono services
2.5 Before accepting assignments, interpreters should determine whether they are qualified.
2.7 Interpreters decline or withdraw from an assignment when they are unable to provide the requisite level of professional services.
2.9 Interpreters render messages faithfully, always conveying the content and spirit of what is being communicated.
2.11 Interpreters remain neutral […] and refrain from providing counsel, advice, or personal opinions.
2.12 Interpreters remain impartial and unbiased.
2.13 Interpreters refrain from engaging in inappropriate sexual contact with, sexually exploiting, or committing any type of harassment of individuals encountered in connection with interpreting.

3. RESPONSIBILITY TO THE PROFESSION
Interpreters recognize that their actions reflect on the interpreting profession as a whole and endeavor to advance the stature of the profession by developing their skills and knowledge.

RESOURCES

4. RESPONSIBILITY TO CONSUMERS
4.1 Interpreters foster communication and cultural understanding.
4.2 Interpreters respect and use the language choice of the consumer.
4.3 Interpreters recognize the right of all consumers to make informed decisions for themselves.
4.4 Interpreters actively strive to understand the diverse cultural backgrounds of consumers and hearing clients.

5. RESPONSIBILITY TO COLLEAGUES
Interpreters treat colleagues with respect, courtesy, fairness, and good faith.

6. SPECIAL CONSIDERATIONS IN VARIOUS SETTINGS:
[The code offers information about ethical considerations for the types of interpreting listed below. Please consult the original document for details.]
A) Educational Setting
B) Healthcare Settings
C) Legal Settings
D) CDI
E) Video Interpreting

7. PROFESSIONAL COMPETENCE AND INTEGRITY
7.1 Interpreters strive to be aware of how their own cultural, racial, religious and ethnic identity values and beliefs may affect the interpreting process and accept assignments accordingly. Interpreters accurately translate the
information at hand, setting aside personal differences of opinion, bias, or belief.

RESOURCES

TERMINOLOGY

Keeping up to date with terminology is a challenge for all interpreters. Here are some helpful resources.

DICTIONARIES AND GLOSSARIES

All community interpreters need a bilingual dictionary or glossary. Some large dictionaries can be kept on site, but each interpreter may wish to have a personal copy.

For bilingual employees or volunteers who interpret in health services but who are not specialized in health care terminology, it is highly recommended that they purchase a glossary in addition to a dictionary. A medical glossary provides a brief, clear definition of the medical term in English, often with a translation (or several translations) of the term in the target language. One series is put out by the Cross-Cultural Health Care Program in Seattle; each glossary costs up to $28 with a $4 shipping charge. There is also one in English only. Currently about 20 languages are available. For details or to order, go to http://www.xculture.org.

How Can I Find the Right Dictionary?

Solicit references from professional interpreters, where possible. Join the NCIHC listserv at www.ncihc.org and post a question online, e.g., how to find an English-Farsi medical dictionary. While the Internet is now an excellent resource for bilingual dictionaries, interpreters may also wish to consult a specialized bookstore such the following:

Intrans Books
P.O. Box 467
24 Hudson Street
Kinderhook, NY 12106
1-800-343-3531
www.intransbooks.com
This is perhaps the best known U.S. bookstore that specializes in resources for interpreters and translators.

REITER'S Bookstore
1990 K St NW
Washington, DC 20006
202-223-3327
www.reiters.com
books@reiters.com
Offers many dictionaries and other resources.

RESOURCES

Tempo Books
4905 Wisconsin Avenue NW
Washington, D.C. 20016-4103
Phone: 202-363-6683
Fax: 202-363-6686
The store's theme is foreign languages. Specialties include language books, tapes, videos, CD-ROMs, dictionaries and translation aids. 6000 + titles for ESL.

Schoenhof's Foreign Books
76 A Mount Auburn Street
Cambridge, MA 02138
Tel.: 617.547.8855
www.schoenhofs.com
E-mail: weborders@schoenhofs.com
Features a number of bilingual medical dictionaries

Language Automation's website offers dozens of glossaries, both general and topic-specific, in many languages, including some of the less common languages, in addition to other resources. For more information, go to http://www.lai.com/lai/glmain.html

Interpreters may also wish to visit a website offered by a Nova Scotia interpreters association on interpreter dictionaries, at http://www.atins.org/english/tools/dictionaries.shtml.

To search the Internet for print dictionaries, try a general site with bilingual dictionaries in many languages and specialties, such as http://www.booksformts.com/booksdicmulti.html or http://www.medword.com/booksdicmulti.html (covering the same dictionaries). Alternately, interpreters can try a user-friendly search engine such as Google and type in (for example)"French-English Medical Dictionary" to see how many titles appear. The searcher will often have to weed through online dictionaries and other sites to reach a practical reference.

Pocket-sized electronic dictionary-translators are also available from several companies in a variety of languages, most costing between $100 and $300 (and up). Vocabulary may be limited to regular dictionary entries rather than specialized terminology. For a sampling of what is available, go to: http://translator.aimhi.com/.

Interpreters can also conduct searches at www.Amazon.com and other online bookstores by plugging in keywords like "German medical" or "Albanian dictionary." However, too many keywords may narrow the search down too far.

RESOURCES

ONLINE DICTIONARIES AND GLOSSARIES

Note: Only general online dictionaries are provided below. For medical, educational or social services glossaries, please see below for the special resource sections for each of these three areas.

MULTILINGUAL SITES

Multilingual
- http://www.freedict.com/ offers links to bidirectional dictionaries in 16 languages.
- www.yourdictionary.com

http://www.lexicool.com/
Lexicool.com's online dictionary search engine currently has links to over 7500 bilingual and multilingual dictionaries and glossaries.
- http://www.drdict.com/: online Chinese-English medical dictionary, recommended by an interpreter.

Glossary of Mental Health Terms for Interpreters and Translators, Queensland Transcultural Mental Health Centre. English, Chinese, Italian, Spanish and Vietnamese
http://catalogue.nla.gov.au/
Searchable Directory of Glossaries and topical Dictionaries
http://www.thefreedictionary.com/
Technical and popular medical terms
http://users.ugent.be/~rvdstich/eugloss/language.html
A website with examples of dictionaries for some other languages is available at:
- **http://culturedmed.binghamton.edu/index.php/dictionaries-a-glossaries**

RUSSIAN: Several medical dictionaries are available online. Simply conduct a search on Amazon, Intrans Books, Powell's books or other online bookstores.
CHINESE: www.esaurus.org/
Bilingual medical dictionaries and glossaries from the People's Republic of China, Taiwan and Hong Kong. The above are only examples of the many resources now available online.

Colloquial and vulgar language

Interpreters often say they cannot interpret the "bad words" because they don't know them. For Spanish interpreters, the following may be a helpful resource:

Glosario de Términos Vulgares e Insultos. Malas Palabras http://www.avizora.com/glosarios/glosarios_i/textos_i/insultos_eufemismos_i_0001.htm

GENERAL ONLINE DICTIONARIES IN SPECIFIC LANGUAGES

The following are only examples of those available today on the Internet. Use with caution: quality varies widely from dictionary to dictionary.
Chinese

RESOURCES

http://zhongwen.com/zi.htm

English
http://www.uiuc.edu/cgi-bin/oed (Oxford English Dictionary)
http://humanities.uchicago.edu/forms_unrest/ROGET.html (Roget's Thesaurus)

Hindi
http://www3.aa.tufs.ac.jp/~kmach/hnd_la-e.htm#wordanalysis (no verbs)
http://www3.aa.tufs.ac.jp/~kmach/hnd_la-e.htm#wordanalysis (verbs)

Japanese
http://www.freedict.com/onldict/jap.html

Khmer
http://www.ximplex.com/khmer/dicts/ek.asp

Korean
http://www.human.toyogakuen-u.ac.jp/~acmuller/cjkdict.htm

Russian
http://www.angelfire.com/vt/kuzy/dictionary.html (links to English-Russian and Russian-English dictionaries)
http://www.freedict.com/onldict/rus.html

Serbian
http://129.97.74.78/cgi-bin/cgiwrap/vkeselj/r2cnik.pl
http://www.grad.math.uwaterloo.ca/%7Evkeselj/#contact

Spanish
http://www.vox.es
http://www.freedict.com/onldict/spa.html

Swahili
http://www.yale.edu/swahili/
http://www.freedict.com/onldict/swa.html

Tagalog
http://www.foreignword.com

Urdu
http://host.bip.net/tracker/dict/index.html/ (English-Urdu only)

Vietnamese
http://www.saigon.com/~vietdict/index.html

RESOURCES

RESOURCES FOR MEDICAL INTERPRETERS

Important U.S. healthcare interpreter associations

National Council on Interpreting in Health Care: www.ncihc.org
International Medical Interpreters Association: www.imia.org
California Healthcare Interpreters Association: www.chiaonline.org
Diversity Rx: www.diversityrx.org
Texas Association of Healthcare Interpreters and Translators: www.tahit.org
Medical Interpreter Network of Georgia: www.mingweb.org
Northwest Translators and Interpreters Society Medical Interpreters SIG: http://www.notisnet.org/notis/SIGS/medsig.htm

MEDICAL DICTIONARIES

The following medical dictionary has been recommended for Spanish by a number interpreters: Onyria Herrera McElroy, Lola L. Grabb, Vincent A. Fulginiti (1996). *Spanish-English English-Spanish Medical Dictionary/Diccionario Médico Español-Inglés, Ingles-Español.* 3rd edition, 2006. Publisher: Lippincott Williams & Wilkins.

For English-Spanish problems in interpreting or translation, and terms easy to misinterpret, consult: Fernande Navarro (2005). *Diccionario Crítico de Dudas Inglés-Español de Medicina*, 2nd ed. McGraw-Hill (available at www.intransbooks.com).

For dental care in English and Spanish, try: *Betty Ladley Finkbeiner et al,* Eds. (2003). *Spanish Terminology for the Dental Team* [with CD-ROM]. C.V. Mosby.

For bilingual medical *print* glossaries that provide brief explanations of medical conditions and terms (these glossaries are available in about 20 languages), and for an interpreter's guide to common medications, go to www.xculture.org.

The remarkable *English-Spanish Glossary of Medical Terms* by Estela McDonough (also available in Portuguese) organizes medical terms by themes. Thus, terminology is arranged according to words for pain; drugs, tests and procedures; diseases; body systems; abbreviations and so forth. This is an invaluable resource for medical interpreters. To order, contact Estela McDonough, Interpreter Services Department, UMass Memorial Medical Center, mcdone01@ummhc.org, 508-856-2792.

Also by Estela McDonough: *The Medical Translation Workbook* teaches medical vocabulary by subject and offers practice exercises. To order, see contact information above.

RESOURCES

For a very comprehensive French medical dictionary:

Djordjevic, Svetolik (2004). *Dictionary of Medicine French-English with English-French Glossary*, 2nd ed. Rockville, MD: Schreiber.

For Russian medical dictionaries:

- (1996). *Collins Russian-English English-Russian dictionary = Anglo-russkii slovar*. Moscow: Fabula.
- Carpovich, E. A. (1960). *Russian-English Biological & Medical Dictionary*. New York: Technical Dictionaries Company.
- Eliseenkov, I. U. B. (1995). *Russko-angliiskii meditsinskii slovar: okolo 50000 terminov*. Moscow.

MEDICAL DICTIONARIES ONLINE

Spanish Medical Dictionaries
MANUAL MERCK DE INFORMACIÓN MÉDICA PARA EL HOGAR
The entire manual is available for free consultation online:
http://www.msd.es/publicaciones/mmerck_hogar/

Merck Manual in English/Spanish –www.onelook.com/?d=all_med&v=&sort=&langdf=spanish
Spanish medical glossaries.
http://www.msc.es/estadEstudios/estadisticas/docs/diccionarioSiglasMedicas.pdf A 105-page volume of medical terms and abbreviations in Spanish.

- **http://www2.niddk.nih.gov/HealthEducation/EnEspanol/default**
- Publications in Spanish on specific illnesses: diabetes, digestive diseases, kidney diseases, urologic diseases.
- The Multilingual Lemma Collection. Medical terms in 11 European languages.

http://users.ugent.be/~rvdstich/eugloss/multi001.html
- **HIV/AIDS medications in Spanish (La Red: Glosario de Medicamentos):
http://www.aidsinfonyc.org/network/lared/glosmed.html**

www.nlm.nih.gov/medlineplus/spanish/anatomy.html
Medline Plus provides information on health and health terms in Spanish.
ENGLISH-SPANISH DICTIONARY OF HEALTH RELATED TERMS
The dictionary can also be downloaded at no cost at:
http://www.hablamosjuntos.org/resources/pdf/engspdict.pdf
Real Academia Española
http://buscon.rae.es/diccionario/drae.htm

RESOURCES

Health information

There are hundreds of websites for health information, and many of them are multilingual. However, one that interpreters swear by for the quality of the information is Medline Plus at www.nlm.nih.gov/medlineplus.

For an explanation of common diagnoses go to www.drkoop.com. It has multimedia and streaming video presentations and as descriptions of diseases in lay terminology. Because the multimedia presentations have sound, interpreters can also hear how the terminology is pronounced in English.

Listservs

To ask other medical interpreters questions about specific terms or about anything related to healthcare interpreting, join the NCIHC listserv or the IMIA listserv. One must become a member of NCIHC or IMIA to join. Many interpreters ask questions related to terminology, and the answers are interesting. To join, go to www.ncihc.org or www.imiaweb.org.

In addition, you may ask questions about medical interpreting, language access and cultural competence on the CLAS-talk listerv, an excellent, extremely active listesrv that is free. For information about how to join it go to http://www.diversityrxconference.org/Your-Voice/CLAS-talk-Listserv/145/.

Finally, some interpreter and translator associations, such as the American Translators Associations (www.atanet.org) and state associations offer listervs to their members for either general and/or healthcare interpreting. A list of such associations across the country is available at www.ncihc.org.

Translation Toolkit and Public Health Glossary

The Massachusetts Health and Human Services *Translation Toolkit* website offers many valuable resources, including translation guidelines and a glossary of public health terms, available in Spanish, French and Portugese, is on a website with many tools for translation. It was developed by the http://www.mass.gov/?pageID=eohhs2terminal&L=6&L0=Home&L1=Provider&L2=Guidelines+and+Resources&L3=Guidelines+for+Services+%26+Planning&L4=Health+Systems+%26+Workforce+Development&L5=Health+Equity&sid=Eeohhs2&b=terminalcontent&f=dph_health_equity_p_translation_materials&csid=Eeohhs2.

NHeLP

The National Health Law Program (NHeLP) is a nonprofit organization that supports access to health care for low-income residents. It has many excellent documents about language access and language services in health care. Their website is www.healthlaw.org. (The page on LEP/language access publications may change but is currently http://www.healthlaw.org/index.php?option=com_content&view=article&id=118&Itemid=187.)

RESOURCES

This website should be checked regularly as NHeLP continues to publish *many valuable documents* relevant to the field of healthcare interpreting and language access. Examples of documents available at the NHeLP site include:

- The High Costs of Language Barriers in Medical Malpractice (2010)
- Language Services Resource Guide for Pharmacists (2010)
- What's in a Word: A Guide to Understanding Interpreting and Translation in Health Care (2010)
- Health Care Interpreters: Are They Mandatory Reporters of Child Abuse? (Updated 2009)
- Summary of State Law Requirements Addressing Language Needs in Health Care (March '08)
- Language Services Resource Guide for Health Care Providers (Oct. '06)
- Language Access in Health Care Statement of Principles: Explanatory Guide (Oct. '06)
- Providing Language Services in Small Health Care Provider Settings: Examples from the Field (April '05)

CLAS STANDARDS

Federal standards for Culturally and Linguistically Appropriate Services (CLAS Standards) were developed by the Office of Minority Health of the U.S. Department of Health and Human Services. CLAS Standards were created for organizations that offer health services.

This is a historic document: the first set of national standards to guide service delivery to immigrants, refugees and other diverse populations speaking many languages. *Currently these standards are being redeveloped and updated.*

The impact of these standards has extended well beyond health services. Although the 14 standards target health services, they are a critical resource for other community services. Four standards target language access; others target cultural barriers, cultural competence and institutional access.

Ideally, administrators should read and apply these voluntary standards. For more information, including the final report, go to: http://minorityhealth.hhs.gov/assets/pdf/checked/finalreport.pdf.

MEDICAL TERMINOLOGY

TEST YOUR KNOWLEDGE OF MEDICAL affixes and roots. For quizzes and self-assessment tests on medical terminology affixes, go to:

English Center Medical Terminology: http://ec.hku.hk/mt/, which offers quizzes and other activities for medical terminology

Medical Training Resources (medtrng.com): For sample tests on overall knowledge of medical terminology, human physiology and related topics, go to http://www.medtrng.com/quia.htm

MICNEL: http://users.utu.fi/micnel/medical/, a website with many links to activities and self-assessment resources for medical terminology.

RESOURCES

RESOURCES FOR SOCIAL AND HUMAN SERVICES INTERPRETERS

For general research and information on social and human services, online encyclopedias such as www.wikipedia.com are a valuable source of information in more than 200 languages.

GLOSSARIES

Nancy Geshke (1998). *Essential Spanish for Social Services.* Living Language, Comes with cassettes and covers common situations such as filling out an assessment, providing counseling, explaining HIV and STD prevention and testing, establishing eligibility for government programs, dealing with addiction and investigating cases of sexual abuse or domestic violence. The 384 phrasebook covers more than 2,500 Spanish words and phrases organized by topic.

Helena El Masri (varying dates), *Glossary for Public Service Interpreters.* West Sussex UK: DPSI Online in several languages.
This glossary contains has over 10,800 words in English and has been translated into Albanian, Arabic, Farsi, Italian, Kurdish, Polish, Portuguese, Russian, Somali and Tamil.
In England, community interpreting is called public service interpreting, and while some of the terminology is different, a great deal of it is similar to the U.S. This glossary was designed for students who are working to earn their Diploma in Public Service Interpreting. The glossary covers medical, legal, housing, business, technology and general terminology. The glossaries are available in downloadable PDF format and some are available as a printed book. To view samples or to order the glossaries, go to http://www.dpsionline.co.uk/glossary.html

Gebredo, Jarvis Gebredo (1999). *Spanish Phrasebook for Medical and Social Services Professionals.* This appears to be more a bilingual dictionary than a phrasebook.

For non-native Spanish speakers:
Kelz, R. K. (1999). *Conversational Spanish for health professionals: Essential expressions, questions, and directions for medical personnel to facilitate conversation with Spanish-speaking patients and coworkers.* Albany, NY and London: Delmar Publishers and International Thomson Publishing. (Out of print but it may be available through online book services.)

Melton, Myelita (2002). *Survival Spanish for Social Services.* SpeakEasy Communications, Inc. Comes with audio CD.

ONLINE DICTIONARIES/GLOSSARIES ON SPECIFIC SUBJECTS

Social and human services glossaries

For glossaries of commonly used terms in human and social services, in Chinese, Russian, Spanish and Vietnamese put out by the San Francisco Department of Human Services, go to: http://languagedoc.sfhsa.org/

http://www.fns.usda.gov/fsp/outreach/Translations/French/pc-french.pdf
Food

English-Spanish food glossary:
http://www.lingolex.com/spanishfood/foodglossary.htm

Nutritional assistance (food stamps)

For informational materials available in many languages about Supplemental Nutrition Assistance Program (Food Stamp Program), go to: http://www.fns.usda.gov/snap/outreach/translations.htm

Social Security (Spanish only)

This glossary was put out by the U.S. Social Security Administration. http://www.socialsecurity.gov/espanol/glossintro.html

RESOURCES FOR EDUCATIONAL INTERPRETERS

INTERPRETING

Barbara Thuro (2009 Revised Edition). *A Bilingual Dictionary of School Terminology*. English-Spanish. $19.95

Ammie Enterprises (www.ammieenterprises.com) offers several valuable resources for interpreters in public school settings. They include:

> *School Terminology Handbook*
> *A Bilingual Dictionary of School Terminology*
> *School Letters in English and Spanish*
> *Reporting to Parents in English & Spanish*
> *Spanish for the School Nurse's Office*
> *School Office Spanish*

EDUCATION GLOSSARIES

For bilingual glossaries of Department of Education Terminology in several languages (Arabic, Bengali, Chinese, Haitian Creole, Korean, Russian, Spanish and Urdu), go to the website of New York City Schools:
http://schools.nyc.gov/Offices/Translation/TipsandResources/Default.htm

Terms in English (Education): http://www.schoolwisepress.com/smart/dict/dict.html

LD glossary on line   http://www.ldonline.org/glossary
Mental Health Term: http://smhp.psych.ucla.edu/conted/gloss.htm#glossary

RESOURCES

Special Education   http://www.texasprojectfirst.org/GlossaryA.html

http://www.disabilityrights.org/glossary.htm

http://www.familiestogetherinc.org/glossaryofterms.html
http://www.lsnjlaw.org/english/schoolandlearning/children/index.cfm
http://www.lsnjlaw.org/english/schoolandlearning/children/iep/index.cfm

Autism   http://www.autism-resources.com/autismfaq-glos.html

Glossary of Arlington County Public Schools (VA)
http://www.apsva.us/1540108291924563/blank/browse.asp?a=383&BMDRN=2000&BCOB=0&c=54309

Glossary of Education Terms (VA)
http://www.doe.virginia.gov/glossaries/glossary.pdf

IES (Institute of Education Sciences)
http://ies.ed.gov/ncee/wwc/help/glossary/#gd

Internet users' Spanish glossary. Rafael González Clavo
http://www.ati.es/novatica/glosario/glosario_internet.html

Los Angeles Unified School District glossary
http://www.translationsunit.com/Forms/Glossary/search.lasso

Salt Lake City School District glossary
http://www.slc.k12.ut.us/depts/trans/pdf/glossary.pdf

IATE (Interactive terminology for Europe)
http://iate.europa.eu/iatediff/switchLang.do?success=mainPage&lang=es

Special Education (Spanish). National Dissemination Center for Children with Disabilities.
http://www.nichcy.org/spanish/publicaciones/Pages/temasAZ.aspx

Spanish language resources for education
http://www.tgslc.org/spanish/glossary/index.cfm
http://www.tgslc.org/spanish/index.cfm

EUDISED European Education Thesaurus
http://www.freethesaurus.info/redined/en/index.php?tema=1416

CALIBER-NET. Open and distance learning glossary, Europe
http://www.caliber-net.odl.org/htdocs/outcomes/glossary/indexS.html

RESOURCES

Spanish-English education glossary
  http://www.translationlinks.com/pdf/EducationGlossary.pdf

BILINGUAL EDUCATION SITES AND PROGRAMS

Educación Especial NICHCY http://www.nichcy.org/Pages/Home.aspx
  http://www.nichcy.org/spanish/Pages/default.aspx

CADRE. The National Center on Dispute Resolution in Special Education
  http://www.directionservice.org/cadre/
  http://www.directionservice.org/cadre/index_espanol.cfm

ECLKC. Headstart. http://eclkc.ohs.acf.hhs.gov/hslc
  http://eclkc.ohs.acf.hhs.gov/hslc/espanol

Bright Future http://www.brightfutures.org/georgetown.html
  http://www.brightfutures.org/spanish/index.html

National Parent and Teacher Association (NPTA) http://pta.org/
  http://www.pta.org/spanish/index.asp
  http://www.pta.org/4037.asp

Bachillerato Internacional
  http://www.ibo.org/es/programmes/documents/schools_guide_pyp_es.pdf
  http://www.ibo.org/es/programmes/documents/basis_pyp_es.pdf

Two-Way Immersión. Center for Applied Linguistic. http://www.cal.org/twi/
Rubrics (Arlingotn,VA) http://www.cal.org/twi/Rubrics/index.html

CAL Center for Applied Linguistics (inglés) http://www.cal.org/

Child welfare http://www.childwelfare.gov/glossary/terms_english_spanish_t-z.cfm#W

Although the following publication targets educational interpreters for the deaf, they may also interest spoken interpreters in education:

http://www.rid.org/publications/overview/index.cfm
"Educational Interpreting: A Collection of Articles From VIEWS"
© 2000 RID Publications
For interpreters, parents, school administrators, and teachers. Includes 30 articles covering a wide range of educational interpreting topics. Also includes RID's Standard Practice Paper on Educational Interpreting and the Code of Ethics. *$19.95*

RESOURCES

Individuals with Disabilities Education Act
http://idea.ed.gov/explore/home

Council for Exceptional Children
www.cec.sped.org

IDEA Practices Law and Regulations
The 2004 reauthorization of Individuals with Disabilities Education Improvement Act http://www.p12.nysed.gov/specialed/idea/
http://idea.ed.gov/explore/home
Family and Advocates Partnership for Education
FAPE aims to inform and educate families and advocates about the Individuals with Disabilities Education Act of 1997, the 2004 reauthorization and promising practices. Go to www.fape.org.

RESOURCES FOR LEGAL INTERPRETERS

RESOURCES FOR SELF-STUDY

While most self-study resources target court interpreting rather than non-courtroom legal interpreting, the terminology (and interpreting) practice they provide will still be of immense benefit to legal interpreters. It will also enhance their confidence and professionalism and help prepare for the certification test, if that is a goal of the interpreter.

Multilingual resources

ACEBO puts out many products for legal interpreters. *The Interpreter's Edge* by Holly Mikkelson is a famous resource for legal interpreters available in nine languages (Spanish, Cantonese, Mandarin, Korean, Vietnamese, Polish, Russian, Japanese, Portuguese), as well as a language-generic version. It consists of a book and a series of CDS or cassettes for practicing consecutive, simultaneous and sight translation modes. The book includes a bilingual legal glossary. However, this program also provides excellent practice for building legal terminology. While the focus is on court interpreting, it will be useful for any legal interpreters.

The Interpreter's Edge, Spanish, 3rd edition, $80
The Interpreter's Edge, Generic Edition (all languages) $65
The Interpreter's Edge, Generic Edition *with CD sets in any of the other
   languages:* $105
The Interpreter's Companion, Fourth Edition $28.00
The Interpreter's Companion on CD-ROM $28.00
Edge 21: An Interpreter's Edge for the 21st Century (Spanish only):
   Edge 21: Consecutive Interpreting $70.00
   Edge 21: Simultaneous Interpreting $80.00
   Edge 21: Sight Translation $65.00

There are additional self-study products available, particularly for Spanish interpreters. The cost varies according to the product. For more information, go to www.acebo.com

RESOURCES

LingvoSoft FlashCards 2008 offers a software program for English-Spanish and also for many other languages. Created as a vocabulary building activity for language learners, it includes not only legal terminology but business, computer, medical, and three different levels of general vocabulary. Cost is $39.95 plus shipping. For more information, go to www.lingvosoft.com/Windows-Language-Learning-Software-items/

Spanish resources

The NCSC Court Interpreter Practice Examination Kit – Spanish

The kit includes an instruction Manual, CD with audio files containing the practice exam and a passing performance on the examination, and hard copies of the test scripts. The kits cost $39.95 each. For more information go to http://www.ncsconline.org/D_Research/CIPEK.html

Interpretapes

Produced by the University of Arizona Agnes Haury Institute for Court Interpretation, are three sets of CDs designed to help aspiring court and legal interpreters enhance their interpreting skills. The only equipment necessary to successfully use INTERPRETAPES is a CD player with headphones and an additional recording unit. Each of the three sets of Interpretapes costs $99, including shipping and handling.

Federal Court Certification Practice Exam (Oral and Written)

The website for the NCSC Consortium on certification offers information about the Federal Court Interpreter Certification Exam (FCICE) as well as a Sample Written Examination for court interpreters and information about online practice oral testing. The practice test is available along with answer key as part of the Examine Handbook. This full-length practice examination for both the Written and Oral Examinations may help the interpreter concentrate on areas where additional study and practice is needed. There is no charge for obtaining the handbook online. The practice test is identical in structure to the FCICE. The Examinee Handbook also has suggestions for preparing for both the Written Examination and the Oral Examination, including reference materials. For information about the federal court certification program go to http://www.ncsconline.org/D_RESEARCH/Consort-interp/fcice_exam/index.htm.
For information about the examinee handbook, go to http://www.ncsconline.org/D_RESEARCH/Consort-interp/fcice_exam/handbook.htm

The handbook itself, including the practice exam, is available at http://www.ncsconline.org/D_Research/Consort-interp/fcice_exam/FCICE-ExamineeHandbookOnline.pdf

Online programs

Online training in legal interpreting is increasingly available, e.g., through Bromberg & Associates and delaMora Interpreting and some community colleges.

RESOURCES

DICTIONARIES AND GLOSSARIES (print resources)

Spanish/English Dictionaries for judiciary interpreters

Butterworths Legal Publishers English/Spanish Legal Dictionary. Diccionario Jurídico Ingles/Español by Guillermo Cabanellas de las Cuevas and Eleanor C. Hoague (2 vol. set)

Bilingual Dictionary of Criminal Justice Terms (English/Spanish) By Virginia Benmaman, Norma C. Connolly, Scott Robert Loos Gould Publications.

Bilingual Dictionary of Immigration Terms Norma C. Connolly Gould Publications Phone (407) 695-9500 ISBN 0-87526-541-3

Bilingual *Dictionary of Domestic Relations and Juvenile Terms* Norma C. Connolly Gould Publications Phone (407) 695-9500 ISBN 0-87526-540-5

Barron's Spanish Idioms ISBN 0-8120-9027-6. Simon and Schuster's International Dictionary, Eng./Span., Span./Eng., Simon and Schuster, Inc., Prentice Hall, NY

Guillermo Cabanellas de las Cuevas and Eleanor C. Hoague (1998), *Dictionario Juridico Espanol-Ingles.* Editorial Heliasta

Terminos Juridicos Ingles-Espanol Spanish-English (1995, 688 pp.)

Bilingual Dictionary of Criminal Justice Terms (English-Spanish)

The following general and specialized dictionaries in various languages other than English and Spanish can be looked up on the Internet to order online or through a bookseller.

Arabic
Al Mawrid (1998) English-Arabic/Arabic-English dictionary)
Al Mawrid (2002): A Modern English-Arabic Dictionary
Arabic-English Faruqi's Law Dictionary (also available in English-Arabic)

Chinese
Chinese-English Dictionary (1991), 1401pp.
English-Chinese Dictionary (1991) 1769pp.
Chinese-English New Practical Dictionary (1987) 1418pp.
Chinese-English (Mandarin) Dictionary (1967), 660 pp.
English-Chinese Glossary of American Criminal Law (1989) 246 pp.
Glossary of Selected Legal Terms English-Cantonese: Office of the Administrator of the Courts, State of Washington. Distributed by ACEBO, P.O. Box 7485, CA 93962

French
Dictionnaire Encyclopedique, 2 vols (1994), 2124 pp.
Le Nouveau Petit Robert: Dictionnaire De La Langue Française (2002)
Harper Collins Robert French Unabridged Dictionary (2002, 6th ed) 2142 pp

RESOURCES

English-French Lexicon of Legal Terms S:\RTS\Interpretation\Interp-consortium\Web\Web site redesign\Web 4 Essential Dictionaries.doc

Haitian Creole

Haitian Creole-English-French Dictionary
Deslan Rincher & Associates
22-11 Church Ave
Brooklyn, NY 11226
(718) 693-0461

Haitian Creole-English-French Dictionary (1981)
Bloomington Indiana-Creole Institute
Haitiana Publications
170-08 Hillside Ave.
Jamaica, NY 11432
(718) 523-0135

Haitian Creole-English Dictionary
Targetej, Dunwoody Press
A legal bilingual dictionary

Italian

*Italian Encyclopedia Universal Dictionary (*1860 pp)
Italian-English English-Italian Dictionary (Sansoni)
English-Italian Law Dictionary (1994)
Italian-English Law Dictionary (1996)

Korean

Korean-English Dictionary (1994) 2182 pp., Publisher**:** Minjungseorim
English-Korean Dictionary (1994) 2687 pp., publisher: Minjung
English-Korean Glossary (www.acebo.com)

Polish

The Great Polish/English Dictionary (1992) 2 Volume set, 1728 pp
The Great English/Polish Dictionary (1992, 1404 pp)
Format: Hardcover; 1404 pp.
Polish/English Dictionary of Legal Terms
English/Polish Dictionary of Legal and Economic Terms (1991) 724 pp.

Portuguese

Portuguese Dictionary-Novo
Pequeno Dicionário Enciclopédico Koogan Larousse
Editoria Larousse do Brasil, Rio de Janeiro
Imported Books. P.O. Box 4414 Dallas Texas
(214) 941-6497
Dictionary Portuguese-English, 2 volumes, 1328 pp
English-Portuguese Dictionary, 1151 pp.
Legal bilingual dictionaries:
Dicionário Jurídico, 3rd edition *(1987)* a legal bilingual dictionary
Maria Chaves de Mello. Rio de Janeiro: Barristers's Editors

RESOURCES

Noronha's Legal Dictionary (1993)
Durval de Noronha Goyos, Jr.
Sao Paulo: Editora Observador Legal, 1993

Russian

Russian Encyclopedic Dictionary (1632 pp)
English-Russian Dictionary (1988, 2 Volumes, 2108 pp)
Russian-English Translator's Dictionary (1991, 735 pp)
Russian-English Legal Dictionary
English-Russian Dictionary of American Criminal Law
       Available from Greenwood Publishing Group
       P.O. Box 5007, Westport, CT 06881-5007

Vietnamese

Vietnamese-English/English-Vietnamese Dictionary (1992) 826 pp.
A legal bilingual dictionary: *English-Vietnamese Glossary* (www.acebo.com)

LEGAL GLOSSARIES

Print legal glossaries in five Asian languages—Cantonese, Korean, Vietnamese, Khmer, and Laotian—are available from a well-known company called Acebo. Each glossary contains translations of approximately 450 of the most widely used English legal terms. These glossaries were developed by certified, working court interpreters under the direction of the Washington State Office of the Administrator for the Courts and the State Justice Institute of Alexandria, Virginia. Glossaries are loose leaf and three-hole drilled for insertion into your own binder. The cost is $5 each plus shipping. For more information, go to http://acebo.com/asian.htm

ONLINE LEGAL DICTIONARIES AND GLOSSARIES

ENGLISH

English Legal Glossary. National Consortium of State Courts, 49 pp. http://www.ncsconline.org/wc/publications/Res_CtInte_EnglishLegalGlossaryPub.pdf

Glossary of Selected Terms. For juvenile cases. Tennessee Administrative Office of the Courts, 9 pp. http://www.tsc.state.tn.us/geninfo/Publications/Forms/Interpreters/Juvenileglosss.pdf

Street Terms: Drugs and the Drug Trade. Executive Office of the President, Office of Drug Control Policy, 38 pp. http://www.streetdrugs.org/pdf/street_terms.pdf

Immigration: for a glossary of immigration terms by the U.S. Citizenship and Immigration Services, go to www.uscis.gov click on Education & Resources, then Glossary (immigration terms). For another glossary of immigration terms put out by an organization called Immigration Equality, go to: http://www.immigrationequality.org/template.php?pageid=26.

RESOURCES

General legal glossaries:
http://www.nycourthelp.gov/TermsGlossary.html
http://www.nolo.com/glossary.cfm
http://www.nwjustice.org/glossary/index.html

SPANISH

The Language of Justice. A Spanish Glossary for New York City. The Vera Institute. 50 pp. http://www.vera.org/publication_pdf/395_774.pdf

English-Spanish Legal Glossary. Superior Court of California, County of Sacramento. 212 pp. http://www.saccourt.com/geninfo/legal_glossaries/glossaries/English%20Spanish%20Legal%20Glossary%20Rev%200806.pdf

Glossary of Legal (and Related) Terms and Courthouse Signs. English/Spanish. New Jersey Administrative Office of the Courts. 19 pp. http://www.judiciary.state.nj.us/interpreters/glossary2.pdf

Free Glossary/dictionary of English/Spanish Court Terms, 161 pages, compiled by Ernesto Romero: http://www.ernestoromero.net/LS.pdf

Spanish-English Glossary. The United States District Court, Southern District of New York. http://www.sdnyinterpreters.org/glossary.php
In addition to the ability to type in a word in English and ask for the translation into Spanish, there is a drop-down menu called "Categories." Click on subjects like "attorney-client interviews," "legal," "idioms," etc. This glossary was created by SDNY interpreters. It is a work in progress but has many terms. The search box can be set to English or Spanish.

The NCSC Spanish examination practice kit **dictionaries**/test items (these are free): http://www.ncsconline.org/D_Research/CIPEK_Dictionaries.html

CHINESE

Translating Justice: A Traditional Chinese Glossary for New York City. The Vera Institute. 50 pp. http://www.vera.org/publication_pdf/396_775.pdf

HMONG

Hmong Legal Glossary. Wisconsin Court System, 74 pp. http://www.wicourts.gov/services/interpreter/docs/hmongglossary.pdf

FRENCH

Dictionnaire d'l'anglais économique et juridique. http://www.inventerm.com/Resultat.aspx
This resource is put out by Quebec Office de la langue française. The interpreter can perform a search *e.g.*, for "legal" and come up with 976 terms (in March 2008) with a French-French glossary.

ARABIC

English-Arabic Legal Glossary. Superior Court of California, County of Sacramento, 105 pp. http://www.saccourt.com/geninfo/legal_glossaries/glossaries/Arabic_English_Legal_Glossary.pdf

MULTILINGUAL

Multilingual Legal Glossary. Vancouver Community College. http://www.legalglossary.ca/dictionary/

RESOURCES

This is a search-by-term online glossary of 5,000 Canadian legal and court-related terms in English Plain Language. These terms are available in Chinese (Simplified), Chinese (Traditional), Farsi, Punjabi, Russian, Spanish and Vietnamese. For more information about how the glossary works, see http://legalglossary.ca/dictionary/about.asp.

IMPORTANT WEBSITES

National Center for State Courts
This organization offers a wealth of information and publications on legal interpreting from across the country. It also gives information on which states are now part of the consortium of courts that certifies interpreters in several languages and offers them orientation and training.
http://www.ncsconline.org/

National Association for Judiciary Interpreters and Translators
This professional association supports legal interpreters across the country and provides a wealth of resources, including a code of ethics, a very active listserv, a quarterly newsletter called *Proteus*, glossaries, manuals, and other publications. NAJIT also offers workshops and seminars for training and continuing education and sponsors presentations at national meetings of other interpreters and translators associations and related professions.
www.najit.org

Cornell Legal Information Institute
One of the first Legal Research sites on the Internet, Cornell Law School's Legal Information Institute has an extremely large collection of law-related resources and links. The site includes links to case law, statutes and regulations at both the federal and state levels.
www.law.cornell.com

FINDLAW
Findlaw provides an impressive collection of case law and boasts free access to US Supreme Court decisions dating back to 1893. The site's news page tracks recent legal news on a wide array of topics (http://legalnews.findlaw.com/). Findlaw's Health Law topic page http://www.findlaw.com/01topics/19health/index.html) holds dozens of links to useful health law resources on the Internet.
www.findlaw.com

"Access to Justice: Protection Orders and Limited English Proficiency."
This free NCSC DVD is a training tool designed both for court staff who may have to assist petitioners with limited English proficiency and as a resource for domestic violence advocates who interpret for clients. To receive a free copy, write to cgreen@ncsc.dni.us.

Hieros Gamos
According to this website, "Hieros Gamos" means the harmonization of seeming opposites. The "opposites" that this website seeks to harmonize are electronic and written information. To do this, the creators of this website have amassed an index of over 100,000 web pages dealing with law and government, which can be accessed via either keyword search or browsing by topic.

RESOURCES

www.hg.org

The Internet Law Library
This site was discontinued on May 28, 1999. Originally developed by the US House of Representatives in 1994, it included the US Code, other federal laws, state and territorial laws, as well as treaties and international law. The US Code was transferred to the Office of the Law Revision Counsel (http://uscode.house.gov/), while the rest of the collection was made available to other sites.
http//law.house.gov

Law Library Resource Exchange
This site is updated on the 1st and 15th of every month with articles of interest to legal researchers. This site is an excellent resource for those trying to conduct legal research on the Internet.
www.llrx.com

The Virtual Chase
This site was created by a law librarian with extensive experience in online research. The site contains links to hundreds of legal research resources on the Internet. The site's Annotated Guide to Resources for Legal Professionals is particularly useful.
www.virtrualchase.com

The Health Law Resource
The focus of the website is on provider transactions and legislation affecting health care businesses. Topic pages on this website include privacy, Medicare/Medicaid, and fraud & abuse.
www.netreach.net

PROFESSIONAL CONCERNS IN COMMUNITY INTERPRETING

Certification

- For an excellent overview of the field of interpreter certification, see Kelly, Nataly (2007) Interpreter *certification* programs in the U.S.: Where are we headed? *The ATA Chronicle* 36 (1): 31-39.

- For an in-depth monograph on the subject of healthcare interpreter certification, consult Roat, Cynthia (2006) *Certification of Health Care Interpreters in the United States: A Primer, a Status Report and Consideration for National Certification.* Menlo Park, CA: The California Endowment.

For information about the two national medical interpreter certification programs, go to www.healthcareinterpretercertification.org and www.certifiedmedicalinterpreter.org.

RESOURCES

For information about certification for court interpreters, go to http://www.ncsconline.org/D_Research/CourtInterp/ClCourtConsort.html.

Language Proficiency Testing

See Unit 1 of this manual for an overview of language proficiency testing for interpreters. For an online Foreign Language Assessment Directory (FLAD) put out by the Center for Applied Linguistics (CAL) go to http://www.cal.org/CALWebDB/FLAD/. The information that follows may be of special importance and interest to those working in the field of education:

> The Foreign Language Assessment Directory (FLAD) is a free, searchable database with information on more than 200 assessments in over 90 languages other than English. FLAD contains information about assessments currently used in elementary, middle, secondary, and post-secondary school programs around the United States.
>
> Please note, this resource contains information about various assessments. It does not contain actual assessments or sample assessments. This information was provided by test developers or administrators. It does not necessarily reflect the views of CAL staff members and the quality of these tests has not been evaluated by CAL.
>
> *Understanding Assessment: A Guide for Foreign Language Educators*
> CAL has developed an online tutorial to serve as a companion resource to the FLAD. This tutorial introduces key concepts in language testing to help with selecting tests and using test results appropriately and efficiently. A list of assessment resources and a glossary of assessment terms are also included in the tutorial.

LANGUAGE ACCESS LAWS

TITLE VI of the CIVIL RIGHTS ACT

General information about Title VI
Go to the federal website for Title VI at www.lep.gov, which offers many links and resources.

Department of Health and Human Services (HHS)
For general information on language access in health and human services, go to http://www.hhs.gov/ocr/civilrights/resources/specialtopics/hospitalcommunication/eclep.html

RESOURCES

Department of Education

For general information about language access in education, go to http://www.ed.gov/about/offices/list/ocr/docs/tviassgn.html

Department of Justice (DOJ)

For general information about language access in legal settings and law enforcement, go to http://www.justice.gov/crt/about/cor/13166.php. For a copy of the DOJ policy guidance on Title VI of June 18, 2002, go to http://www.justice.gov/crt/about/cor/lep/DOJFinLEPFRJun182002.php.

For other policy guidance statements, go to http://www.lep.gov (or http://www.lep.gov/guidance/guidance_index.html).

STATE AND LOCAL LANGUAGE ACCESS LAWS

ALL STATES

For an overview of state language access laws that affect health care, see Jane Perkins and Mara Youdelman (2008) *Summary of State Law Requirements Addressing Language Needs in Health Care* (March 2008 update). Washington, DC: National Health Law Program. Go to: http://www.healthlaw.org/library/item.174993

EXAMPLES OF STATE LAWS

A number of states have passed general language access laws. Here are just three examples.

MARYLAND

Maryland's LEP law, passed in 2002, is similar to Title VI. However, it applies to agencies, programs and services that receive state (as opposed to Federal) funding.

For the law itself, go to http://www.peoples-law.org/node/966. **For helpful background information, go to** http://www.peoples-law.org/multilingual/english/MD%20translationlaw.htm

MINNESOTA

Minnesota Human Rights Fact Sheets are Translated in Hmong, Spanish, and Somali and available at http://www.humanrights.state.mn.us/yourrights/factsheets.html A 1998 state law required the development of an LEP plan: for information from the state Department of Human Services (DHS) on these developments, go to http://www.dhs.state.mn.us/main/idcplg?IdcService=GET_DYNAMIC_CONVERSION&RevisionSelectionMethod=LatestReleased&dDocName=id_016631

HAWAII

Hawaii's language access law passed in 2006. For more information, go to http://hawaii.gov/labor/

RESOURCES

ola/ola-links/what-the-law-says

A few states have also passed laws about the certification of interpreters in health and human services (Washington) or medical interpreting (e.g., Oregon and Indiana). Only Washington state has fully implemented its law. For information on Oregon's law, go to http://www.oregon.gov/OHA/omhs/intrprtr/laws.shtml
http://apps.leg.wa.gov/documents/laws/wsr/2000/07/00-06-014.htm. For information on Washington's law, go to http://www.leg.wa.gov/wac/index.cfm?fuseaction=Section&Section=388-03-050.

LOCAL LANGUAGE LAWS

An increasing number of cities and municipalities have enacted language access legislation. Here are just a few examples of local initiatives across the country.

Monterey Park, California. December 17, 2003, the Monterey Park City Council voted to adopt a historic formal policy and action plan aimed at assisting residents that speak little or no English. The plan addresses interpreting, hiring bilingual staff and translation. For more information, contact Jerry Schwartz (626) 307-1385 or JSchwartz@MontereyPark.ca.gov or go to http://www.nhelp.org/pubs/nlaap/MontereyParkAdminPolicy.doc.

Oakland, California. In 2001, Oakland passed an "Equal Access to Services Ordinance" reinforcing some of the provisions of Title VI. For background information, go to http://www.asianweek.com/2001_04_27/bay4_oaklandpolygot.html

New York City passed a law on December 15, 2003 that requires offering free language assistance at municipal agencies to LEP individuals. For more information go to http://www.nyc.gov/html/imm/downloads/pdf/language_access_law.pdf

Philadelphia. On September 29, 2001, the mayor passed an executive order mandating that the city assess its compliance with federal language access legislation. For background information, go to http://www.philly.com/mld/inquirer/news/local/8074129.htm?1c.

Washington, D.C. On April 21, 2004, the District passed a language access law very similar to Maryland's. For more information, call Ken Saunders (OHR) at 202-727-4559 or go to http://comm-org.utoledo.edu/pipermail/announce/2004-April/000468.html.

VIDEOS

If cultural competence trainings are not available at the interpreter's workplace, or funding is too scarce for them, bilingual staff and volunteers might wish to consider sharing videos in the workplace during in-services and staff meetings or at brown-bag lunches. Videos often make a helpful impact and generate valuable discussion that can open the eyes of other staff members to the importance of interpreting and of using only professionally trained, qualified interpreters.

RESOURCES

Videos on Interpreting

Communicating Effectively Through an Interpreter, 1998
    Produced by the Cross-Cultural Health Care Program, a nonprofit agency in Seattle specializing in cultural and linguistic competence.
    Although it is now somewhat dated in certain respects, this 22-minute VHS tape/DVD remains a highly effective tool for educating interpreters and/or one's workplace. It includes three segments on interpreting sessions that show (more clearly than any other film reviewed by the authors) the differences between trained and untrained interpreters. This tape can also help to generate discussion with a quiet group.
    Cost: $150.
    Ordering information: Go to www.xculture.org or call 206-860-0329.

Mental Health Interpreting: A Mentored Curriculum, 1997
Produced by Dr. Robert Pollard, a psychiatrist, and the University of Rochester Medical Center. This 32-minute video shows 11 vignettes on interpreting in mental health. It is accompanied by a small nine-chapter text guide. *A warning: certain vignettes appear to contradict some of the standards of practice laid down in this manual. Sometimes the word "translation" is used to refer to interpreting. Any excerpts from this tape should be carefully considered.*
Cost: $48.00 for both video and text.
Ordering information: Call 585- 275-3544 or send an email to Robert_Pollard@urmc.rochester.edu

The Healthcare Interpreter's Tools for Successful Communication in the Triadic Encounter
    Produced by Cross Cultural Communication Systems. This series of 3 VHS tapes (20, 40 and 25 minutes respectively) constitutes an interpreter training video series. The modeling of an interpreter introduction on Volume 1 one may be helpful. Although the triangle position is employed here (a position this manual does not endorse), most interpreting practices displayed in the video are current.
Volume 1: Interpreter Training Video
Volume 2: Interpreting for Sensitive Topics
Volume 3: Clinical Insight in Medical Interpretation
    Cost: $65 per video or 3 for $150.000
    Ordering information: Go to www.cccsorg.com (http://www.embracingculture.com/products.php).

Videos on Cultural Issues

Most of the following videos address health care.

Working Together to End Racial and Ethnic Disparities: One Physician at a Time, 2005
    Produced by the American Medical Association (AMA).
    The vignettes on this CD-ROM are brief, and most are powerful. Voices of authentic patients and real doctors are represented. Although most vignettes do not however portray foreign-

RESOURCES

born patients, they can contribute to the cultural competence and cultural sensitivity of interpreters and staff.
Cost: AMA members: $10; non-AMA members: $15
Ordering information: Visit www.ama-assn.org/go/healthdisparities or call the AMA at 800-621-8335, Item #OP325305.

Worlds Apart, 2003
Produced by Fanlight Productions, a distributor of videos and films on social issues, this suite of four vignettes is well known among clinicians who train on cultural diversity issues. This series of four episodes totaling 49 minutes appears realistic and tackles complex issues. The facilitator's guide is excellent.
Cost: $398 (for DVD)
Ordering information: Call 800-937-4113; email orders@fanlight.com or go to www.fanlight.com (http://fanlight.com/catalog/films/912_wa.php).
*Other interesting films from this producer include **Community Voices** and **Hold Your Breath.***

Kaiser Permanente, Clinical Cultural Competency Series, 2003:
The Multicultural Health Series (two-video set totaling c. 90 minutes)
Cultural Issues in the Clinical Setting: A and B (one video of 70 minutes)
Produced by The Kaiser Permanente/California Endowment Clinical Cultural Competency
About 160 minutes, this series offers dramatic vignettes of about 8 to 14 minutes each. Each tells a little story on cultural subjects in health care, some of them with LEP patients. The first series, Cultural Issues in the Clinical Setting, Parts A & B: deals with obstetrical themes, such as Hmong birth practices; gender and acculturation in Iranian immigrants; a Latina diabetic in labor; and a circumcised Somali woman in labor. The second is a set of two tapes (or DVD): the Multicultural Health Series, Part I and Part II that addresses various cultures and ethnicities.
Cost: $50 per DVD, including a facilitator's guide on CD-ROM.
Ordering information: To order, send request and payment to:
The order form is available at *erc.msh.org/provider/OrderCulCom.DOC*

Using Names as Tools for Communication. Volume 1 of "Meeting the Challenge of Delivering Culturally Competent Services."
Produced by Cross Cultural Communication Systems (CCCS)
This 18 minute VHS or DVD addresses the cultural issue of how to address clients and patients by name. What's in a name? What does a name mean for LEP and foreign-born clients? How should their names be used?
Cost: $75.00
Ordering information: www.cccsorg.com (http://www.embracingculture.com/products.php)

A Family Physician's Practical Guide to Culturally Competent Care
This nine-hour free, CME accredited (9 credits) e-learning program sponsored by the HHS Office of Minority Health contains many individual vignettes that are very useful. One can take obtain the DVD even if one is not a physician. This production is based on the Culturally and Linguistically Appropriate (CLAS) Standards and supports them.

RESOURCES

Cost: Free.
Ordering information: https://cccm.thinkculturalhealth.org

Patient Diversity: Beyond the Vital Signs, 2002
Produced by CRM. Geri-Ann Galanti authored the leader's guide.
This 18 minute film includes five interesting vignettes set in a hospital. The vignettes are entertaining and helpful. The guide includes exercises and role plays for 2-4 hours of training on cultural diversity in health care. Patients include a Mexican who is stereotyped by a nurse for being too "expressive" of his pain (which is quite real); a Cambodian boy covered in welts caused by a traditional healing remedy; and a Chinese patient who refuses hospital food for cultural reasons. Unfortunately, the vignettes are interrupted by each other, so the complete 18-minute video must be played.
Cost: $595 for video or DVD (free trial viewing available online)
Ordering information: Phone: 1-800-421-0833 URL: www.crmlearning.com

The Letter
This one-hour video looks at what happens to a small, predominantly white town in Maine when an influx of Somali refugees arrives. The mayor writes the Somali community a public letter, asking them to bring no more relatives and friends to the town. His letter has an electrifying impact that reverberates across the town and nation. Fascinating and provocative, this documentary humanizes everyone presented. A wise and compassionate story, it is told entirely in the voices of the residents.
Cost: $19.99 for home use DVD and $300 for Institutional use.
To order, go to: http://www.arabfilm.com/item/300/

WORD GAMES

Merriam-Webster provides a free online dictionary, thesaurus, audio pronunciations, Word of the Day, word games, and other English language resources.
http://www.m-w.com/game/

Vocabulary University participants learn English vocabulary in context (grades 5-12) with free word puzzles. Thematic word games and creative activities. www.vocabulary.com/ -

Learn about word origins and etymology, Tough and educational word game
www.etymologic.com/ -

Free on-line interactive word games, boggle, anagrams, puzzles, crosswords, cryptograms, cryptoquotes, jumble. Play and solve word games. Word plays.
www.wordplays.com/

Vocabulary University® recommended word-related web sites. ... CROSSWORD, wants your thoughts and suggestions for additional super word links. ...
www.vocabulary.com/VUogoodlinks.html

RESOURCES

Internet Park is the most interesting and friendly place to play word games live on the Internet. One game, Ready Mix is very popular and addictive. ...
www.internet-park.com/

A word a day with Wordsmith.Org, the home of A.Word.A.Day, Internet Anagram Server, wordserver,
www.wordsmith.org

Previous Cryptograms (P). Hangman (P) Solve the phrase by guessing each word Previous Hangman Games (P).
www.dictionary.reference.com/fun/

BIBLIOGRAPHY

Aguirre, B., Barthelemy, R., David, B., Fequiere, A., and Fitzpatrick, J. (1997). Translating/Interpreting for the Schools: A Burgeoning Field in Jerome-O'Keefe (ed.) *Proceedings of the 38th Annual conference of the American Translators Association*. Alexandria, VA: American Translators Association.

Ahmad, Munir (2007). Interpreting communities: Lawyering across language differences. *UCLA Law Review*, 54:999-1086.

Angelelli, Claudia (2004-a). *Medical Interpreting and Cross Cultural Communication.* Cambridge, UK/ New York, NY: Cambridge University Press.

Angelelli, Claudia V. (2004-b). *Revisiting the Interpreter's Role*. Amsterdam/Philadelphia: John Benjamins.

Bancroft, Marjory (2004) *Standards of Practice for Interpreters: An Environmental Scan.* Santa Rosa, CA: National Council on Interpreting in Health Care.

Bancroft, Marjory (2005). *The Interpreter's World Tour: An Environmental Scan of Standards of Practice for Interpreters.* Menlo Park, CA: California Endowment.

Bancroft, Marjory (2005) *Lifting Victims Through Service and Collaboration: Cultural Competence in Victim Services, A Manual for Trainers.* Columbus, OH: OCJS.

Bancroft, Marjory (2009a). Community Interpreting: A Historic Moment for a Timeless Profession. *ATA Chronicle* (American Translators Association). 35(7):20-23.

Bancroft, Marjory (2009b). Community Interpreting: The Growth of a New Profession in Janet Bonet, Ed. *Voices and Visions: Celebrating a World of Difference Through Language and Art.* Omaha, NE: p. 17.

Beltran Avery, Maria-Paz (2001). *The Role of the Health Care Interpreter: An Evolving Dialogue*. The National Council on Interpreting in Health Care Working Paper Series. Washington, DC: NCIHC, www.ncihc.org.

RESOURCES

Bot, H. (2005). *Dialogue interpreting in mental health care*. Amsterdam/New York: Rodopi.

California Healthcare Interpreting Association (2000). *California Standards for Healthcare Interpreters*. Sacramento, CA: CHIA, **www.chiaonline.org/**

De Jongh, E.M. (1992). *An Introduction to Court Interpreting: Theory and Practice.* Lanham, MD: University Press of America.

Carr, Sylvana, Roda Roberts, Aideen Dufour, and Dini Steyn. *The Critical Link*. Papers from the 1st, 2nd, 3rd and 4th International Conferences on Interpreting in Legal, Health, and Social Service Settings, Geneva Park. Amsterdam, Philadelphia: John Benjamins Publishing.

Downing, B. T. and Tillary, K. H. (1992). *Professional Training for Community Interpreters: A Report on Models of Interpreter Training and the Value of Training.* Minneapolis: Center for Urban and Regional Affairs, University of Minnesota.

Dubslaff, F. and Martinsen, B. (2003). ICommunity interpreting in Denmark: Results of a Survey. In Brunette, L., Bastin, G., Hemlins, I. and Clarke, H. (Eds.). *The critical link 3: interpreters in the community*. Amsterdam / Philadelphia, PA: John Benjamins Publishing Co. (pp. 113-125).

Erasmus, Mabel (2000). Community interpreting in South Africa. Current trends and future prospects. In Roberts, R., Carr, S. E., Dufour, A. & Abraham, D. (Eds). *The critical link 2: interpreters in the community*. Philadelphia, PA / Amsterdam: John Benjamins Publishing Co. (pp. 91-206).

Foer, Joshua (2011a), Secrets of a Mind Gamer. *New York Times Magazine,* February 15, 2011.

Foer, Joshua (2011b), *Moonwalking with Einstein: The Art and Science of Remembering Everything*. New York, NY: Penguin Press, 2011.

Framer, Isabel, Bancroft, Marjory, Feuerle, Lois and Bruggeman, Jean (2009). *The Language of Justice: Interpreting for Legal Services.* Washington, DC: Ayuda.

Fulcher, Glenn and Davidson, Fred (2007). *Language Testing and Assessment: An Advanced Resource Book.* (Routledge Applied Linguistics). New York, NY: Routledge.

Gerver, David & Sinaiko, H. Wallace, Eds. (1978). *Language Interpretation and Communication*. New York & London: Plenum Press.

Gilbert, J. (Ed) (2003). *Principles and Recommended Standards for Cultural Competence Trainings of Health Care Professionals*. Los Angeles, CA: California Endowment.

Gonzalez, Roseann Duenas, Vasquez, Victoria F., and Mikkelson, Holly (1991). *Fundamentals of Court Interpretation: Theory, Policy and Practice.* Durham, NC: Carolina Academic Press.

RESOURCES

Grant, Alexis (2011). The 50 Best Careers of 2011. *US News and World Report,* December 6, 2010. http://money.usnews.com/money/careers/articles/2010/12/06/the-50-best-careers-of-2011.html

Gutzler, Anna and Kuta, Lou (2003). *An Overview of the United States Health Care System and Its Workforce.* National Center for Health Workforce Analysis.

Hale, Sandra Beatriz (2007). *Community Interpreting.* New York, NY: Palgrave Macmillan.

Hale, Sandra (2008-a). Controversies over the role of the court interpreter. In Valero-Garcés, C. & Martin, A. (Eds.). *Crossing borders in community interpreting.* Amsterdam/Philadelphia: John Benjamins, pp. 99-121.

Hale, Sandra (2008-b). Working with interpreters effectively in the courtroom. Paper presented at the AIJA conference: "The use of interpreters in courts and tribunals". 12-14 March 2008, Freemantle, WA.

Harris, Brian (2010). Earliest depiction of an interpreter. Blog posting, July 5, 2010. http://unprofessionaltranslation.blogspot.com/2010/07/earliest-depiction-of-interpreter.html

Healthcare Interpretation Network (2009). *National Standards Guide for Community Interpreting Services.* HIN: Toronto. http://www.multi-languages.com/materials/National_Standard_Guide_for_Community_Interpreting_Services.pdf

International Medical Interpreters Association/Massachusetts Medical Interpreters Association/Education Development Center (1995). *Medical Interpreting Standards of Practice.* Boston, MA: IMIA.

Isham, William P. (1985). The Role of Message Analysis in Interpretation. In McIntire (Ed). *Interpreting: The Art of Cross-cultural Mediation,* Proceedings of the 1985 RID Convention. Silver Spring, MD: RID Publications. Pp. 113-122.

Jacobsen, Bente (2009). The community interpreter: A question of role. *Hermes, Journal of Language and Communication Studies* 49:155-166.

Kelly, Nataly (2007). Interpreter Certification Programs in the United States: Where Are We Headed? *ATA Chronicle*, January 2007. (Republished in Irish *Translators and Interpreters Association Bulletin*, April 2007).

Kelly, Nataly (2008). *Telephone Interpreting: A Comprehensive Guide to the Profession.* Victoria, BC: Trafford.

Kelly, Nataly and Stewart, Robert G. (2010). The Top 35 Language Service Providers. Four-page excerpt from *Language Services Market 2010.* Lowell, MA: Common Sense Advisory.

Kelly, Nataly and Bancroft, Marjory (2007). The Critical Role of Healthcare Interpreting: Views from the Literature, Promising Practices and Lessons Learned in the United States. In Leon Epstein, Ed,

RESOURCES

Culturally Appropriate Health Care by Culturally Competent Health Professionals. Caesaria, Israel: Israel National Institute for Health Policy and Health Services Research, pp. 85-100.

Kelly, Nataly, Willett, Kevin and Bancroft, Marjory (2006) "Bridging the Cultural Divide: Cultural Competence in Public Safety. *ENP Magazine*, 24(4):62-70 (May 2006).

Kreps, G.L. & Kunimonto, E.N. (1994). *Effective Communication in Multicultural Health.* Thousand Oaks, CA: Sage Publications.

Massachusetts Medical Interpreters Association and Educational Development Center, Inc. (1995). *Medical Interpreting Standards of Practice.* Boston, MA: Massachusetts Medical Interpreters Association (now the International Medical Interpreters Association).

McKay, Corinne (2006). *How to Succeed as a Freelance Translator.* 2 Rat Press.

Metzger, Melanie (1999). *Deconstructing the Myth of Neutrality.* Washington, DC: Gallaudet University Press.

Mikkelson, Holly (1991). *The Interpreter's Companion.* Spreckels, CA: Acebo Press.

Mikkelson, Holly (1992-a). *The Interpreter's Edge.* Spreckels, CA: Acebo Press.

Mikkelson, Holly (1992-b). *The Interpreter's Rx: Practical Exercises in Medical Interpreting.* (Includes instructor's/self-study notes, and audio practice tapes.) Spreckels, CA: ACEBO.

Mikkelson, Holly (2001). Interpreting is Interpreting--Or Is It? www.acebo.com.

Mikkelson, Holly (1996). Community Interpreting: An Emerging Profession. *International Journal of Research and Practice in Interpreting*, 1(1), available at www.acebo.com.

Mikkelson, Holly (2008). Evolving views of the court interpreter's role. Between Scylla and Chrybdis. In Valero-Garcés, Carmen/Martin, Ann (eds.), *Crossing Borders in Community Interpreting: Definitions and dilemmas.* Amsterdam/Philadelphia: John Benjamins, 81-97.

Morris, Ruth (1995) 'The Moral Dilemmas of Court Interpreting', in Mona Baker (ed) The Translator. Studies in Intercultural Communication 1(1), Manchester: St. Jerome Publishing, 25-46.

Morris, Ruth (2010), Images of the court interpreter: professional identity, role definition and self-image. *Translation and Interpreting Studies* 5(1): 20-40(21).

National Council on Interpreting in Health Care (2003). *Guide to Interpreter Positioning in Health Care Settings.* Washington, DC: NCIHC. www.ncihc.org.

National Council on Interpreting in Health Care (2004). *A National Code of Ethics for Interpreters in*

RESOURCES

Health Care. Washington, DC: NCIHC. www.ncihc.org.

National Council on Interpreting in Health Care (2005). *National Standards of Practice for Interpreters in Health Care.* Washington, DC: NCIHC. www.ncihc.org.

National Health Law Program (2005). *HIPAA and Language Services in Health Care.* Washington, DC: NHeLP. Available at www.nhelp.org.

Niska, Helge. *Community Interpreting in Sweden.* Stockholm: Stockholm University, 1998.

Pedersen, P. (1985). *Handbook of Cross-Cultural Counseling and Therapy.* Westport, CT: Greenwood Press.

Pedersen, P., Draguns, J., Lonner, W., & Trimble, J. (1981). *Counseling across Cultures.* Revised and expanded edition. Honolulu: University Press of Hawaii.

Pedersen, P., & Marsella, A. (1982). The Ethical Crisis for Cross-Cultural Counseling and Therapy. *Professional Psychology*, 13, 492—500.

Pedersen, PB. (1978). Four Dimensions of Cross-Cultural Skill in Counselor Training. *Personnel and Guidance Journal*, 56(8), 480—484.

Pöchhacker, Franz (2004). Critical linking up: Kinship and convergence in interpreting studies. In Wadensjö, Cecilia, Dmitrova, Birgitta Englund and Nillson, Anna-Lena, Eds., *The Critical Link 4: Professionalization of Interpreting in the Community*. Philadelphia, PA: John Benjamins.

Rheingold, Howard (2000), *They Have a Word for It: A Light-Hearted Lexicon of Untranslatable Words and Phrases*. St. Paul, MN: Consortium Books.

Roat, Cynthia (2006). *Certification of Health Care Interpreters in the United States: A Primer, a Status Report and Consideration for National Certification.* Menlo Park, CA: The California Endowment.

Roberts, Roda. "Community Interpreting Today and Tomorrow," in Peter Krawutschke, ed. *Proceedings of the 35th Annual Conference of the American Translators Association.* Medford, NJ.

Romanek, Elizabeth (1991). *Contemporary Communication Skills That Work.* Chicago, IL: Contemporary Books.

Rozan, Jean-François (1956/2005). *Note-taking in Consecutive Interpreting.* Cracow: Tertium.

Sofer, Morry (2009). *The Translator's Handbook*, 7th ed. Rockville, MD: Schreiber Publishing.

Steyn, Dini & Wilks, Georgina. *Curriculum: Community Interpreter Skills Training Program.* Calgary, Alberta: Alberta Vocational Centre.

RESOURCES

Udvari, Stephen S. (1978). *Communicating with Others*. Austin, TX: Steck-Vaughn.
Weir, Cyril (2005). *Language Testing and Validation: An Evidence-based Approach*. New York, NY: Palgrave MacMillan.

Valero-Garcés, Carmen (2005.) Emotional and Psychological Effects on Interpreters in Public services: A Critical Factor to Keep in Mind. *Translation Journal,* 9(3). http://translationjournal.net/journal//33ips.htm

Weir, C. (2005). *Language Testing and Validation: An Evidence-based Approach.* New York, NY: Palgrave-Macmillan.

Zimányi, Krisztina (2009). On impartiality and neutrality: A diagrammatic tool as a visual aid. *Interpreting & Translation* (1(2):55-70.